The Shape

Understanding Toronto's Sprawl

It is impossible to understand major North American cities without considering the seemingly never-ending sprawl of their surrounding suburbs. In *The Shape of the Suburbs*, activist, urban affairs columnist, and former Toronto mayor John Sewell examines the relationship between government decision making and the extension of infrastructure such as water, sewage, and highway systems to show how the suburbs have spread, and how they have in turn shaped the city from which they emerged.

Drawing on an intimate knowledge of city politics and a wealth of information gathered from municipal archives and other sources, Sewell describes the major social and political forces that allowed for the rapid development of the suburbs. Meanwhile he considers responses by planners over the years, ranging from proposals to curb suburban sprawl dating as far back as the 1960s, to the recently adopted plan for the Greater Toronto Area. Combining insightful commentary with critical debate, Sewell demonstrates the ways in which suburban political, economic, and cultural influences have impacted the older, central city, culminating in the forced Megacity amalgamation of 1998. Rich in narrative and visual detail, *The Shape of the Suburbs* is a lively and challenging look at municipal planning and development.

JOHN SEWELL, a former city councillor and mayor of Toronto, has been a columnist for the *Globe and Mail*, *NOW Magazine*, and *Eye Weekly*, and was the founder of Citizens for Local Democracy.

JOHN SEWELL

THE SHAPE OF THE SUBURBS
Understanding Toronto's Sprawl

UNIVERSITY OF TORONTO PRESS
Toronto Buffalo London

© University of Toronto Press Incorporated 2009
Toronto Buffalo London
www.utppublishing.com
Printed in Canada

ISBN 978-0-8020-9884-9 (cloth)
ISBN 978-0-8020-9587-9 (paper)

Printed on acid-free paper

Library and Archives Canada Cataloguing in Publication

Sewell, John, 1940–
The shape of the suburbs : understanding Toronto's sprawl /
John Sewell.

Includes bibliographical references and index.
ISBN 978-0-8020-9884-9 (bound)   ISBN 978-0-8020-9587-9 (pbk.)

1. City planning – Ontario – Toronto Suburban Area – History.
2. Toronto Suburban Area (Ont.) – History.
3. Suburbs – Ontario – Toronto – History.   I. Title.

HT169.C22T5956 2009   307.1'21609713541   C2008-907217-0

University of Toronto Press acknowledges the financial assistance to its
publishing program of the Canada Council for the Arts and the Ontario
Arts Council.

University of Toronto Press acknowledges the financial support for its
publishing activities of the Government of Canada through the Book
Publishing Industry Development Program (BPIDP).

To Liz

Contents

Preface

In the spring of 2005 I was approached by Terry Fowler, a professor of urban politics and planning whom I have known since the late 1960s. Terry administered the Kitty Lundy Memorial Fund, which sponsored annual lectures on urban issues at Atkinson College, York University, and he wondered if I would be the presenter that November. He thought maybe I could base the lectures on the material in my book from 1993, *The Shape of the City: Toronto Struggles with Modern Planning,* which deals with planning and development issues.

It seemed like a good thing to do, but then I had second thoughts. Most of my life has been spent worrying about these issues within the City of Toronto and its immediate environs. That's what I did as a member of Toronto City Council throughout the 1970s and as mayor of Toronto between 1979 and 1980. My 1993 book had conveyed most of the things that I had learned about city decisions on planning in the twentieth century, and I had given many speeches and lectures on these issues. Repeating it once more seemed stale. Terry and I chatted about alternatives and agreed I would do the four lectures on the planning and development of the areas just outside Metro's boundaries, the so-called 905 area. (Metro Toronto's area code for telephones is 416; the surrounding area, 905.)

This would involve considerable new research, but there was a small amount of money attached to the lectures that would support this work, and I dove in without a strategy about how the lectures would be structured. Quite quickly it made sense to begin by talking about infrastructure issues such as roads, water and sewage, then move onto governmental bodies.

The lectures proceeded in November 2005 with a moderate amount of new information, and a whole bunch of theories about what I thought might have happened. As Terry noted in his introduction to the event, 'These lectures will focus on growth outside of Metro Toronto and how the framework was laid for it to happen. It will also draw some conclusions about the impact of that growth, and the quality of city that has emerged.' I didn't skimp on the conclusions.

Yet there was enough that was new to attract others. I was asked by friend and architect Kim Storey if I would present the material at a special series of lectures sponsored by the Toronto Society of Architects in February 2006. Kim noted that the lectures had been first presented in late afternoon at York University, a difficult time to attract a large audience. She thought that if the TSA events were held in the evening downtown at the Gladstone Hotel – a new and influential cultural hub – more people would be likely to attend. A modest sum accompanied the TSA lectures, and that permitted me to pursue more research.

The TSA lectures were very popular, attracting more than 500 people for the first one. I presented the material with illustrations, as a slide show, which gave a popular flavour to the evenings, although the format considerably downplayed the scholarly aspects to the work and the detailed sourcing. The success convinced me to do more research and shape the material into a book. Financial assistance from Alan Broadbent, and then from the Neptis Foundation, gave me the ability to complete a manuscript.

During its various phases, my work took me to a number of different venues. I explored material in the (always helpful and surprising) Urban Affairs Library of the Toronto Public Library, then rummaged through the archives of the Region of Peel, uncovered historical material in the Town of Richmond Hill and in the Region of York. The Ontario Archives proved a useful venue, and I was kindly given access to the provincial Legislative Library. Once again I was amazed at how helpful librarians and archivists are to writers such as me, and I thank them.

I also began to recognize the large gaps in the historical record. The records for the Ministry of Highways in the critical period of the 1930s seem to have disappeared. No useful or comprehensive history of the men and women who developed the land in the 905 area has yet been undertaken – one must make do with anecdotal bits and pieces. As I sorted through papers in various archives, I felt I was tilling virgin ground, and wondered if I had found all there was to find. I hope others will come forward to correct and enlarge the record.

It would be difficult to call me a dispassionate author, even though I attempt to let the evidence speak for itself without being contaminated by what I consider to be fair conclusions. During my fourteen years on Toronto City Council I often attempted to use my position to influence events outside of Metro Toronto. For example I helped get City Council to undertake a study that strongly opposed the Pickering Airport (which has yet to be built) and I often spoke and wrote about the wrong-headedness of low-density suburban growth. In the early 1990s I chaired the Commission on Planning and Development, a provincially established royal commission. Its report, which we called *New Planning for Ontario*, attempted a significant intervention in suburban planning. I have worked with many groups in the 905 area to oppose the kind of growth and development that has occurred. I was one of the leaders of Citizens for Local Democracy, the group which helped focus opposition to the forced amalgamation of the municipalities within Metro. I wrote a weekly column about city politics from the early 1990s until the manuscript was in its final drafts, and my columns often engaged in issues that related to the 905 area.

So my passion is well established, and it undoubtedly led to my interest in determining as best as I could some of the reasons for what has happened over the last seventy years. I have tried to integrate my role into the story in an unobstrusive third-person manner, restricting any emotional tone, which undoubtedly accompanied my intervention at the time. My objective was to try to convey the story in a dispassionate manner. I have generally not contrasted the events in Toronto with events in other cities, mainly because my energy was consumed trying to learn the Toronto story, and as is obvious in chapter 3 where I discuss planning for the future, there isn't nearly as much scholarly information about the details of growth and development on city edges as there should be. Generally, I shied away from the comparisons between cities on things like population change – something on which there seems to be quite a bit of data – since I didn't think those comparisons added much to the story I wanted to tell. I struggled over the use of imperial or metric measurements. For much of the period under consideration, imperial units – acres and miles – were common usage, and then in the 1980s metric units – hectares and kilometres – came into use in Canada. In the United States, imperial units remain the standard. In the end, I decided to generally use imperial measures for the whole of the text, although in the last few chapters metric equivalents are found in footnotes.

I wish to thank John Bousfield for the wonderful lunches we had together as he told me his stories of the development of the 905, and for those who provided advice, in some cases reading and commenting on portions of the manuscript, including Don Stevenson, Lionel Feldman, Jim Cameron, and Steve Munro. Their advice and perspectives were most appreciated. I wish to thank my copy editor, Beth McAuley, for sharpening the text and significantly improving the footnotes.

I am delighted to dedicate this book to my marvellous wife, Liz Rykert, who has been so supportive during the past decade while I have scratched away on this opus.

1

Introduction: Intimations of Growth

To some, the period following the Second World War promised nothing more for Toronto's outskirts than the continuation of a bucolic dream. The countryside would change in
only limited ways, the farms would become more productive,
and the burden on rivers and streams would mostly come from
weekend city folk looking for a place to picnic.

This was the picture painted in 1950 by the provincial Department of Planning and Development in its *Don Valley Conservation Report*.[1] The opening photo in this 300-page opus shows a
sylvan scene with the caption: 'The natural beauty of the upper
Don Valley with its shade trees and cool streams should be protected for all time.' A photo centred on the Yonge and Sheppard intersection notes that 'farms, small holdings, horti-
culture, suburban housing and artificial drainage are easily
identified,' as they are.

One map documents the many small settlement areas north
of Toronto's city limits a mile north of Lawrence Avenue: the
communities of Lansing and Willowdale on Yonge Street near
Sheppard Avenue; Northmount, a half mile farther north; New-
tonbrook, south of what is now Steeles Avenue; the settlement
of Thornhill at Highway 7, and several miles farther north,
Richmond Hill. Another map shows population distribution,
one dot representing 100 people. As expected, the population
was clustered around Yonge Street, but it was sparse – several
hundred in Thornhill, not quite two thousand in the Richmond Hill area. Another map charted existing woodlands, with
one tree representing sixty-five acres of woodland. In North
York, to judge from this map, there were more than 2,000 acres
of woodland in among the farms (see fig. 1.1).

The rural nature of Toronto's outskirts was also reflected in
the report's recommendations advocating better farm practic-
es, improved farm ponds, better soil conservation, more assistance for farmers, and the protection of wild life, including a
study to 'determine the state and trend of meadow mouse population.' The report recommends that the Don Valley forest be
formally established; that the range of speckled trout be studied
and determined; foot bridges be built and paths improved; that
3,000 acres just north of the town of Maple, at the northern

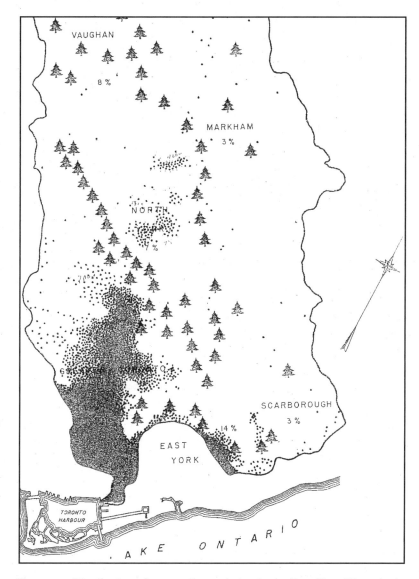

Figure 1.1 Distribution of trees and population in the Don River Watershed, 1949. One dot represents 100 people; one tree represents 65 acres of woodland, showing the dominant rural quality of the environs of Toronto immediately following the Second World War.
Source: Province of Ontario, Department of Planning and Development, *Don Valley Conservation Report*, 1950.

reaches of the watershed, be zoned for forestry; and that the City of Toronto and the Borough of East York enhance sewage disposal techniques so as to improve the water quality in the lower reaches of the Don River.

This report set the pattern for provincial approaches to Toronto's fringes for the next five decades (see fig. 1.2). It focused on important problems and made useful recommendations to address those problems, but it included no mechanisms to ensure implementation and it totally overlooked underlying forces that would render its proposals irrelevant. The Don Valley and the proposed Don Valley forest should have been protected rather than being swallowed up by sprawl. Water quality should have been maintained so that streams could continue to swarm with trout. Farms should have been protected to help serve the city. All of these things could have occurred even while growth was encouraged in and around existing settlements if the report had been comprehensive and had acknowledged and reasonably addressed the pressures the area was facing.

The underlying currents that would shape the future around Toronto were perfectly clear, but they were not broached in this report. The end of the Second World War promised much change for the city, not the least of which was a giant stream of immigrants from Europe bringing their ambitions, cultures, and skills along with their demand for consumer goods and places to live. Immigrants began arriving as quickly as the war ended, and by the early 1960s almost three million immigrants had come to Canada, about one-quarter of whom settled in the Toronto area.[2] Some newcomers may have expected the streets to be paved with gold, but as Vince Pietropaolo notes, quoting one new immigrant, 'When they got here they learned three things: first, that the streets were not paved with gold; second, that the streets were not paved at all; and third, that "we were expected to pave them."'[3]

Others in the provincial government were not so short-sighted, but were preparing for the coming change – witness the Department of Highway's plans for the superhighways described in chapter 2. These new roads were laid out before the Second

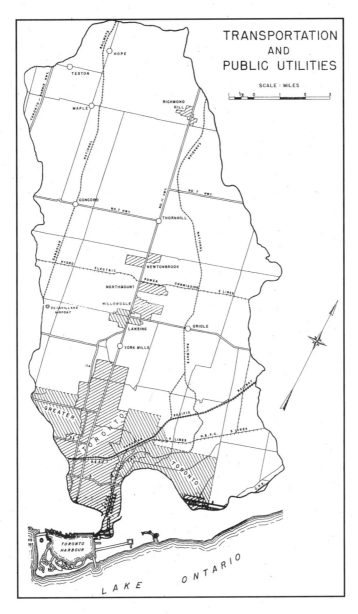

Figure 1.2 Transportation, public utilities, and settlement areas in the Don River Watershed, 1949.
Source: Province of Ontario, Department of Planning and Development, *Don Valley Conservation Report*, 1950.

World War and awaited the end of the war when resources would be freed up for their construction. The City of Toronto itself was fuelled with ambition. With its strong and growing financial sector, it had become the leading economic centre in the country. Manufacturing, which had boomed during the war years, continued to expand, and investors looked at opportunities to meet both the pent-up and new demands. Investors such as industrialist E.P. Taylor branched out into new areas of financial investment, namely, land development and housing, and planners such as Eugene Faludi and Macklin Hancock created comprehensively planned communities embodying new values in new forms.

All the signs were that Toronto would grow quickly, and it did. The area of settlement pushed beyond city boundaries and by the mid-1950s it had spilled into the Townships of North York, Etobicoke, and Scarborough, Toronto's new partners in the Metro federation which was established in 1953. Growth accelerated in the 1960s and burst beyond Metro's boundaries into the surrounding fringes (see fig. 1.3). The new development forms were at low densities and they sprawled over the countryside. The population of the Toronto area increased from about one million at mid-century to some five million people fifty years later. Contrary to the recommendations of the Conservation Report, the Don Valley became mostly a transportation corridor and the Don Valley forest was cut down for suburban tracts. The intimations of growth had been met with a failure of imagination. There was a great gulf between planning and development, one that never disappeared.

The avalanche of suburban growth around Toronto relied on a steady supply of new water service, sewers, and roads to continue its relentless pace. Government decision-makers were there to assist, and enabled growth in the fringes at considerable cost and without a serious plan. Innovations were made in regional governance structures and regional plans, and these innovations set Toronto apart from most other urban areas in North America, even if these new mechanisms did not always shape good decisions. At key points in the process officials argued that growth at all costs was not a good choice, but they

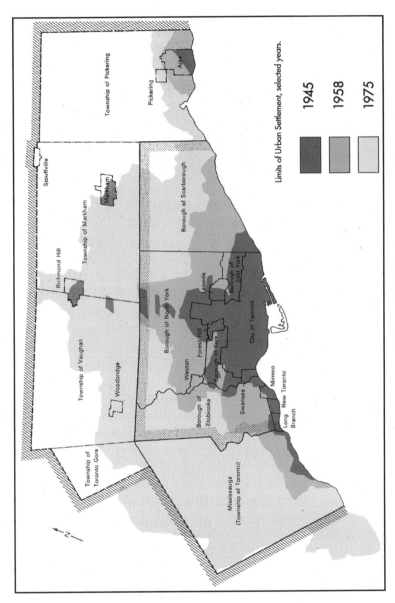

Figure 1.3 General boundaries of urban settlement in the Toronto area, 1945, 1958, 1975.
Source: Compilation by author from Metro Planning Department documents.

were often brushed aside. Significant public funds were devoted to fuelling suburban growth, but the regional innovations often gave a context for decisions. It meant that Toronto grew at an alarming rate, but in ways that made city administrators from other jurisdictions envious, even if Toronto officials lamented the lost opportunities.

The stories of growth in other North American cities after the Second World War are similar to those in Toronto. They differ in degree, timing, and detail, but all share a history of growth that spread outwards as developers constructed new houses on large lots at low densities in the fringes. The automobile became the popular means of transportation in the new suburbs, and retail was focused on shopping centres. The demand for suburban houses seemed insatiable for the last half of the twentieth century. Suburbia was certainly not without its critics,[4] but by the end of the century the sprawl had become so ubiquitous that some academics sang the joys of suburbia, or at least made the point that the criticism was largely misplaced.[5] They argued that sprawl was the new normal, and that its economic success, given the millions of suburban homes that had been built and purchased, proved that it generally met and fulfilled public expectations.

What the recent praise for suburbia reveals is that the sprawl that occurred in the Toronto area was significantly different from the sprawl around other cities. If density is the appropriate measure (and there are many reasons to believe it is), Toronto's sprawl is twice as dense – or half as sprawling – as development around comparable American cities.[6] The similarities of these cities and an accounting for these differences provide the themes for this book, which tells the story of suburban growth around Toronto and its attempts to plan it during the 1950s into the 1990s. Providing a reasonable rationale for why Toronto grew the way it did might point future development in a more positive direction.

What is remarkable about the Toronto story is that unlike most other large cities in North America, it begins with a strong central planning tradition, as recounted in chapter 3. The plans seem remarkably prescient, yet they often were ignored in both the vortex of growth and in the interplay of departmental interests. As described in chapter 4, the superhighway system seemed to have a life of its own and was divorced from concerns about the long-term effects on land use. The good intentions about supplying transit and commuting systems, recounted in chapter 5, dissipated as the extraordinary public cost of providing these services to low-density communities revealed itself. Everything was compounded by the pressure from developers and local governments to provide water and sewage services for new subdivisions, and, as set out in chapter 6, the provincial government forgot the very good lessons it should have learned from Metro Toronto, namely, that when it comes to hard services, municipalities should be required to pay their own way. That lesson may have been the most powerful planning tool available to the province, but it apparently had few champions.

When it came to reforming local government in the late 1960s, interesting options were advanced but were quickly trampled by narrow local interests, as noted in chapter 7. The province missed the chance of using local government structures – as had occurred in Metro Toronto – as a way to shape land use and social policy. Instead, the province allowed itself to become captive to the forces for growth, as detailed in chapter 8, and quite quickly the new values of the low-density subdivisions became dominant, as outlined in chapter 9. Those new values contrasted significantly from the political values within Metro Toronto and apparently were so threatened by these older values that the provincial government responded by destroying Metro in an extraordinary series of events, recounted in chapter 10. The growth that once was seen as a way forward for the Toronto area had become a monster that pushed aside some of the important innovations that had fuelled Toronto's rise. Chapter 11 recounts the attempts of the provincial government to then pull back from the brink, building on the planning strengths of the past. The hope that was apparent fifty years earlier was no longer present, but there were still signs and fragments of the framework left by earlier decisions. It is those signs and fragments that lead one to conclude, as noted above, that Toronto is not the same as other cities, and seems to hold more promise.

2

Toronto in Mid-Century

Toronto in mid-century was a prosperous city that experienced almost a decade of stagnation during the Depression of the 1930s, followed by tightly leashed growth in the first half of the 1940s as resources were ploughed into the war effort. There was significant pent-up energy for growth, and it manifested itself in the next decade. The private sector organized itself to profit from that growth, and the public sector made sure it was an enabler. A new regional structure for local government was put in place in the Toronto area, one that was designed to respond to growth pressures and to the provision of the necessary infrastructure. It was a period of significant optimism.

At the end of the Second World War, the Toronto urban area was dense and compact. It consisted of three urbanized municipalities: the City of Toronto, with a population of almost 700,000; the Borough of East York, abutting the north-east corner of Toronto with 100,000; and the Township of York, abutting the north-west corner of Toronto with a further 100,000.[1] This urban area comprised less than fifty square miles, so the density was a healthy 20,000 persons per square mile.

Surrounding this compact city was farmland and small farm settlements. In North York Township to the north there was a grand total of 10,500 houses, with a population of under 40,000. The Township of Scarborough to the east had a population of 35,000, and to the west, Etobicoke was home to about 30,000, most of whom lived in the settlements of Long Branch, New Toronto, and Mimico, along the lake.[2] These communities were later to be incorporated, with others, into the Metro Toronto Federation, the area of which contained a total population in 1949 of about 1.1 million.

The urbanized area was compact enough to be considered an efficient urban form where services paid their own way. The example of transit shows the efficiencies of the urban form and the growth that occurred. Private transit had been operating profitably in the city since 1891, although when those private operators refused to extend lines beyond the city boundaries, the city formed its own company, the Toronto Civic Railway, in 1911, to provide service along Danforth Avenue, Gerrard, Lans-

downe, St Clair Avenue, and Bloor Street West.[3] Public disen-
chantment with the private service led to pressure for a public
transit service, and after Toronto electors had authorized the
city to purchase the private transit operations, the Toronto
Transit Commission was established by provincial legislation in
1920 to run them as a public service. The Toronto Civic Railway,
already city owned, was folded into the new TTC, along with the
Toronto and York Radial Railways, then owned by Ontario Hydro. The TTC improved service and rebuilt track lines, and by
1929 ridership had climbed to 200 million a year. It was a successful service, paid for by its riders without public subsidy.
Even after the transit ridership drop caused by the Depression,
the TTC continued to see a strong future. In 1942, Toronto
considered its first serious suggestion for subways, one running
north up Bay Street from Union Station, then slicing over to
Yonge Street and north to St Clair Avenue; another running
east–west along Adelaide Street from the Don River to Bathurst
Street and beyond.[4] But the Second World War was not the
time to devote scarce resources to transit, even though ridership burgeoned with higher employment rates as the war economy boomed and a shortage of consumer goods meant fewer
cars were available to buy.

By 1946, the TTC had 310 million riders a year and was accu-
mulating a reasonable financial surplus to be put to some future
transit use.[5] That year saw the proposal for a Yonge Street subway from Union Station north to Eglinton Avenue, and another
subway along Queen Street, from Logan Avenue in the east to
Shaw Street in the west. Toronto voters were asked their opinion
on the Yonge Street subway that year, and they approved it by a
ratio of nine to one.[6] The ground breaking for the Yonge Street
subway occurred in September 1949. Half of the funding came
from the surplus that the TTC had generated during the war;
the remainder came from debentures issued by the TTC.

What is most amazing to a reader in the early twenty-first century is the financial aspect of this story. Transit was not incur-
ring a deficit. The fares paid by riders was more than enough to
pay all operating costs, and in some years produced a surplus
which was then put towards a new rapid transit line. The fact

that transit paid its own way indicated that the compact and dense urban form was exceedingly efficient, even though few buildings were higher than four or five floors, save for those in the very centre of the city's financial district. As the city spread, and as communities with much lower densities were constructed, efficiencies were lost, and (as we shall see in chapter 5) transit began to incur an operating deficit which quickly climbed into the hundreds of millions of dollars a year. But at mid-century, transit's success was a result of an efficient urban form.

The three Toronto urbanized municipalities were well served by water and sewage services, the cost of which was entirely borne by local taxpayers through both property taxes and user fees. Provincial subsidies were not required (or available) for these services. Provincial subsidies for the construction of roads began in 1927 and changed over time. County roads and suburban roads (which were under the jurisdiction of suburban road commissions) received a subsidy equal to 40 per cent of the cost of construction and 20 per cent for maintenance; these were generally raised in 1947 to 50 per cent for both construction and maintenance, although the city was obligated to top-up the provincial subsidy by paying 25 per cent of the cost of suburban road construction. Cities received a 50 per cent subsidy for both road construction and maintenance, although that was reduced in 1949 to one-third of the cost of both.[7] The City of Toronto received no subsidy preference from the province; in fact, the share required of Toronto was often larger than that from other municipalities. The *Highway Improvement Act* required the City of Toronto, as the generator and attractor of traffic, to contribute to suburban roads. In 1936, for instance, the city paid $80,000 to the County of York, about half the cost of suburban roads that year around Toronto. Legislation was amended so the city's share of such roads decreased, but in 1948 Toronto Mayor Hiram MacCallum noted that Toronto still paid 25 per cent of the cost of suburban roads, the province picking up 50 per cent, and the county picking up the remaining 25 per cent.[8] The efficient form of the developed city meant that it could pay its own way and more.

This is not to say there were no concerns about the ability of the roads to carry all the traffic that wanted to use them: traffic congestion downtown was a major bone of contention. The area south of Dundas Street, between Simcoe and Victoria Streets, was jokingly referred to as 'suffering acres.' Commuter traffic destined for this area was extremely heavy yet the amount of available parking was very limited. The situation was so bad, some suggested, that by 1958, the 'suffering acres' would be 'agonizing acres' (See fig 4.10 in chapter 4.) City decision-makers proposed two solutions: a subway under Yonge Street and a new downtown expressway. Transportation planner Norman Wilson reported to Toronto city staff in 1946 on an elevated roadway on Spadina Avenue running as far north as St Clair, and the next year he proposed it should link up with a new superhighway to the north.[9] This was the first sign that a Spadina expressway was on offer, as it would be for almost twenty-five years. As early as 1939, Wilson also proposed that a serious road be constructed in the Don Valley. He wrote to Tracy leMay, Toronto's chief planner, saying, 'Some day the Don Valley will be utilized for a great major boulevard system to the north and northeast. The only relevant question is where the money is to come from.'[10] The result was the construction of two roads over the next few decades, one on each side of the Don River, the Bayview Extension (one of the few examples of a road being extended southerly in Toronto) and the Don Valley Parkway.

The growth pressures in Toronto following the Second World War were substantial, and since the existing form was already dense and compact, that growth sought out land just outside the built-up area, such as in Scarborough, North York, or Etobicoke. However, that growth required water and sewage services these farming communities were unable to provide. The Toronto and York Planning Board, with responsibilities for the city and a broad area around the city, noted that these municipalities had been unable or unwilling to attract the non-residential development needed to produce substantial property tax dollars to pay for these services (residential properties alone did not generate enough tax revenue),[11] and it recommended that the municipalities amalgamate into one body. The pres-

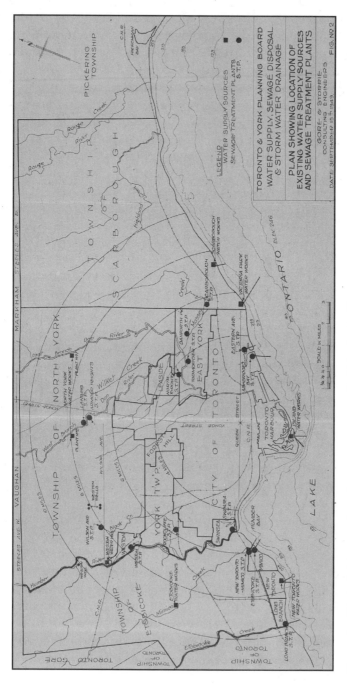

Figure 2.1 Map of water supply and sewage treatment facilities in the Toronto area, 1949.

Source: Gore & Storrie report, 1949. Reprinted from Richard White, *Urban Infrastructure and Urban Growth in the Toronto Region, 1950s to the 1990s*, figure 1. Used with permission of the Neptis Foundation.

sure to take that course of action was increased when the engineering firm Gore & Storrie reported in 1949 to the Toronto and York Planning Board on water and sewage needs (see fig. 2.1). The City of Toronto was well served by large sewage treatment plants in the east (Ashbridges Bay) and in the west (Humber River). East York had two small plants on the east branch of the Don River, in Todmorden Park and Danforth Park; and the Town of York had the Weston and Rockcliffe Sewage Treatment Plants. The problem was what lay beyond those borders.

The Gore & Storrie report estimated that the population in the areas immediately surrounding Toronto, York, and East York would increase by 1970 to about 550,000 people. It noted, using North York Township as an example, that severe servicing problems already existed. Of the 10,500 houses in North York, only 2,400 were connected to the two sewage treatment plants on the west branch of the Don River (one serving Lansing, the other Armour Heights, near the present-day corner of Yonge Street and Sheppard Avenue); 6,000 homes had septic tanks, and 2,100 relied on outhouses.[12] Small sewage treatment plants on streams and rivers were called 'package plants,' and they were the preferred mode of servicing. Scarborough had a package plant on Massey Creek, just east of Victoria Park Avenue and north of Danforth Avenue, built to serve the GECO plant on Eglinton Avenue east, which manufactured bombs and ammunition during the Second World War. In Etobicoke there were two sewage treatment plants on the lake, one serving New Toronto–Mimico, the other Long Branch.

Water services were equally limited. Weston, the settlement on the far north-west edge of the urban area, was served by four communal wells. Etobicoke and North York Townships both had wells supplying water in the middle of their political jurisdictions. Scarborough made do with two small water supply plants on the lake, both just east of Toronto's boundary. General water quality in the main rivers was poor, heavily polluted with sewage. As the Gore & Storrie report noted, 'The cost of cleaning up the lower reaches of the Humber and Don Rivers to make same safe for bathing would be prohibitive.' Instead of addressing this problem directly, the report suggested turning a blind eye and building swimming pools.[13] So commenced the framework for public policy about water in Toronto.

Thus, there were three clear problems with regards to infrastructure in these rapidly expanding communities. One was the need for a vastly expanded system to provide water and sewage services to the growing area. A second was the need to create a comprehensive system from the hodgepodge of disconnected facilities. The third was to take a holistic approach that worked with, rather than against, natural processes. The Gore & Storrie report addressed the first two questions. It made recommendations to extend water and sewage supply within the immediate areas of the Townships of North York, Scarborough, and Etobicoke. Regarding the need for a comprehensive system, it stated, 'The sooner a unified control is established over the whole area, the more efficient and economical will be the results in the end.' Specifically, it recommended what it called a 'Metro Area Authority' to cover all thirteen municipalities which made up the Toronto urban area and its immediate hinterlands in the late 1940s.[14] 'This is the only satisfactory and efficient way to secure a unified control,' the report noted.[15] In his study on urban infrastructure, Richard White concludes that this report was a powerful incentive for the creation of a federation of municipalities a few years later (see fig. 2.2).[16] The third issue – working with natural systems rather than against them – did not find its way onto the agenda, and it has not had much luck doing so since then. Building pools, rather than cleaning the nest, seemed the preferred approach.

The governance questions would be solved, according to Toronto's political leaders, by the city simply amalgamating the surrounding municipalities. In 1949, the Toronto and York Planning Board recommended that eight municipalities between the Humber River and the city's eastern boundary with Scarborough be amalgamated. The next year, Toronto City Council applied to amalgamate the twelve surrounding municipalities with a population of 350,000, creating a city of more than one million residents and still leaving considerable room for growth within the proposed new city limits. This kind of application required approval of the Ontario Municipal

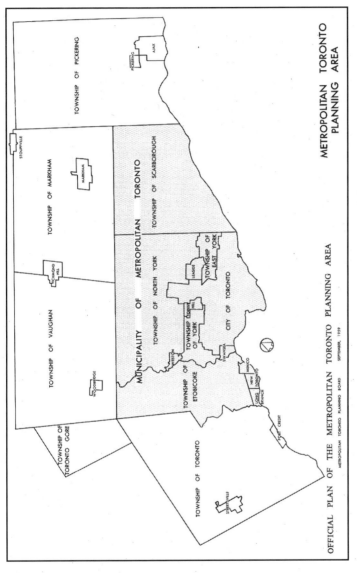

Figure 2.2 Map showing boundaries of Metropolitan Toronto, the Metro Planning area, and municipal boundaries, 1953 to 1971.

Source: Metro Official Plan, 1969. Reprinted from Richard White, *The Growth Plan for the Greater Golden Horseshoe in Historical Perspective*, 13. Used with permission of the Neptis Foundation.

Board (OMB), originally established by the province in the last few years of the nineteenth century to review municipal borrowing requests to determine if they were reasonable, but since expanded to be a general watchdog on municipal decisions about governing structures, finances, and planning. The Board operated as a quasi-independent administrative tribunal, which meant it could provide a relatively full airing of any issue before it, providing a forum for those with opinions both for and against. Most of those municipalities the city wished to gobble up said they were opposed – the County of York; the Towns of Leaside, New Toronto and Weston; the Villages of Forest Hill, Long Branch, and Swansea; the Townships of Etobicoke, York, North York, and Scarborough; and the Borough of East York. The Town of Mimico began by wanting to implement a regional government responsible for major services, but eventually agreed to support Toronto's amalgamation bid.[17]

Lorne Cumming, chair of the Ontario Municipal Board, headed the panel which dealt with the application. Cumming had been a lawyer in Windsor, then city solicitor of Windsor, before being appointed chair of the Board in the late 1940s. The way he dealt with this important application established him as something of a wizard about municipal issues, and he was later appointed Deputy Minister of Municipal Affairs in Ontario. Cumming concluded, in words that resonate fifty years later, that amalgamation would result 'in immediate and prolonged administrative confusion of the most serious kind.'[18] Further, he concluded, 'The process of adjustment would be immensely complicated by sectional differences, ignorance of local conditions and a great number of difficult personnel problems which would prolong the period of adjustment almost indefinitely. In the meantime administrative conditions could easily become chaotic.' Amalgamation would also 'result in a substantial increase of taxation due to the practical necessity of bringing all suburban wage and salary scales and working conditions up to city levels.'[19]

Having rejected amalgamation, Cumming and the Board had to decide what to do. He dismissed the idea that there was a substantial, inherent problem between local and regional governments, stating:

The central question is whether the continued existence of local municipal governments, carrying out necessary and important functions of a local nature, is, after all, completely inconsistent with the concurrent existence of a senior metropolitan government equipped with adequate powers and resources to deal with area-wide problems.[20]

Cumming drew on the long history of municipal government in Ontario reaching back to 1849, when the *Baldwin Act* introduced the ideas of local and county government to the province. He noted: 'A number of fundamentals of the county type of federation which have survived the test of long experience may be recognized in the Board's proposals.'[21] And with that example in mind, he referred to the *British North America Act* at the heart of the Canadian experience and proposed for Toronto a federated structure, concluding:

The Board is convinced that the only way in which services of this type [that is, services accommodating the present and future population] can be provided when and where they are needed is to place them under the jurisdiction of the central authority and to make the combined resources of the entire area available to finance them.[22]

The Board decided on a structure that represented and gave legitimacy to two different (and sometimes competing) values, the regional and the local. This was unusual, to say the least, but as the next fifty years indicated, absolutely critical to the success of the Toronto urban area. It gave reality to the famous dictum from F. Scott Fitzgerald's story *The Crack-Up:* 'The test of a first rate intelligence is the ability to hold two opposing ideas in mind at the same time, and still retain the ability to function.'[23] The structure gave legitimacy to both local and regional points of view, and a forum for expressing, and hopefully resolving, whatever differences were brought to the table. Fifty years later, the idea of finding a structure which embodied two competing ideas would be considered mainstream by the emerging ideas of complexity theory, which gives credence to the importance of complementary pairs. As those theories propose, finding structures which embody complementary pairs provides the best chance that they will appropriately interact. The tension between the pairs is obvious (in fact, many claimed over the years that Metro looked much too messy as debates between the local and the regional erupted), but as Cumming sensed, the genius of the scheme lay in recognizing that both viewpoints were of equal validity, and if one wanted to reflect the complexity of the real world, they should not be separated. Others might have opted for one viewpoint or the other in the name of simplicity or clarity; but the ability of Cumming to find a structure which recognized the importance of both simultaneously was brilliant.[24]

The creation of Metro meant that twelve municipalities were removed from the County of York. The county lost more than 85 per cent of its population and assessment, and was reduced to the status of a rural municipality with a combined population of just 65,000.[25] Cumming considered limiting the size of Metro to the then-developed urban area, but rejected that in favour of the existing outer boundaries of North York, Scarborough, and Etobicoke, 'which are still used chiefly for agricultural purposes but which are in every proper sense a part of the metropolitan area and in the direct path of its continued outward expansion.'[26]

So emerged the idea of two-tiered government for the Toronto area, thirteen municipalities joined together in a regional structure.[27] The Board went on to allocate powers to both tiers, defining the wholesale functions (given to Metro) and retail functions (continued at the local level). Metro was responsible, for example, for filtering water, then selling that water to local municipalities, which piped it to local homes. Local municipalities collected garbage and refuse from homes and businesses, delivering it to transfer stations; Metro then took it to landfill sites. As a wholesaler Metro provided services to the local municipalities; the local municipalities retailed these services to residences and businesses. It has been a powerful model. The OMB also addressed the fact that the Toronto and York Planning Board, which was responsible for the city, the surrounding twelve municipalities, and the County of York had planning powers extending beyond the boundaries of the thirteen municipalities covered by the new regional government. It concluded that such planning must continue, saying: 'It is an unfortunate fact that most rural municipalities fail to recognize the need to control and direct their physical development until irreparable mistakes have been made.'[28] The failure of either the province or the surrounding municipalities to plan in the past decade had been taken up by the City of Toronto, and the Board determined that must continue.

The OMB decision was greeted with favour. The Metro Toronto Federation was established quickly and it was immediately deemed a success, certainly in part because of the leadership of Frederick G. Gardiner, the first chair of Metro. Gardiner, a lawyer, had been reeve of the small suburb of Forest Hill, and he proved to be the strong force needed to ensure services were delivered to the communities surrounding the urban areas of Toronto, York and East York. He earned his nickname 'Big Daddy' fairly. In 1957, Cumming was asked to review his creation, and the changes he suggested in this review were entirely minor in nature.[29]

The success of Metro lay in the fact that the mechanisms needed to provide the services enabling urban growth – water, sewage, and roads – already existed in the developed municipalities, particularly Toronto, and they were made readily available to the growing municipalities, particularly Scarborough, North York, and Etobicoke. Those municipalities could rely on the existing system of decision-making, the high levels of staff expertise, as well as the city's financial strength. It was a perfect match: without access to these higher levels of skills and resources, those growing communities would have had great difficulty processing the many development applications being filed; with access, growth was accommodated in a reasonably efficient manner. Since the instruments of local government continued to exist, and Toronto City Council and other local municipalities retained control of local decisions affecting them, the arrangement met with political support as well.

Figure 2.3 Cartoon by Duncan Macpherson, including Frederick Gardiner,
chair of Metro, and Nathan Phillips, mayor of Toronto.
Copyright: Estate of Duncan Macpherson. Reprinted with permission –
Torstar Syndication Services.

The harbinger of post-war growth was E.P. Taylor's development of Don Mills. Taylor, perhaps Canada's leading industrialist, began in 1947 to purchase farmland north and east of the
developed city, and within a few years had assembled a tract of
2,000 acres. A plan created by the young Macklin Hancock proposed something radical – a new community consisting of four
neighbourhoods, an area for walk-up apartments, a central
shopping mall, and industrial uses at the edges. Hancock proposed a looping, discontinuous street system, considerable
green space, and large lots for single and semi-detached homes.

Figure 2.4 Cartoon by Duncan Macpherson, 'Enter Maharajah of Metrostan.'
Copyright: Estate of Duncan Macpherson. Reprinted with permission –
Torstar Syndication Services.

Since this development was proposed a few years before Metro
had been created, Taylor undertook to build a sewage treatment plant for the Township of North York and to purchase the
bonds North York would need to issue to fund the trunk sewers,
thus relieving the municipality of almost all financial obligations resulting from the development. Taylor also developed
ideas that helped the (then) small construction companies
build the 8,000 new units housing more than 25,000 people.[30]
The demand for new units was high, and Taylor's Don Mills was
so successful that when only a small portion of the development

had been completed he decided to buy even more land – this time, a chunk of farmland three times as large as Don Mills – to the west of Metro. Taylor's success encouraged others to follow his model, and soon all development proposals in the Toronto area were based on the loopy street model, with houses set on large lots, and where some land was designated for shopping plazas and industrial use. With Metro ready to provide servicing structures, the financing for services that Taylor had provided for Don Mills was not needed, and that fuelled even more growth.

The Metro Federation proved the perfect structure for the city's post-war growth. It offered financial stability and entrepreneurship without the need for massive subsidies to make it function well; it responded to the demand for housing and jobs; and it seemed to meet the regional and local political needs of the day without undue stress or rancour. Again, a good example of that success was the transit system. The Yonge Subway, which had been planned, funded, and constructed by the City of Toronto, opened in March 1954 to great success. The TTC became a Metro function, and Metro agreed with the idea of expanding the transit system, confirming that support when Metro Council assumed responsibility in 1964 for the city's debentures issued for the Yonge Subway, assuming about half of its $68 million cost.[31]

The TTC turned its energy to planning the Bloor–Danforth Subway, which was approved in 1958. A Y intersection was planned to allow cars coming from the east and west along Bloor–Danforth to turn down University Avenue to Union Station.[32] Construction began almost immediately on the University Avenue section, and it was operational in February of 1963. The Y was used when the Bloor–Danforth line opened in February 1966, but was abandoned in September of that year because of what TTC management called operational problems.[33] Metro and the TTC funded the capital expenditures of this subway together, Metro paying 55 per cent of the costs, the TTC 45 per cent.[34]

The Bloor–Danforth line, stretching between Woodbine Avenue and Keele Street, was opened in 1966, and the extensions to Warden Avenue in the east and Islington Avenue in the west opened in 1968.[35] The province agreed to its first subway subsidy (about $20 million, or 8 per cent of the total capital cost) with these extensions: it agreed to pay 50 per cent of the cost of roadbed construction.[36]

By 1970, the TTC was carrying 324 million riders a year. With a population in Metro Toronto of not quite 2,000,000, ridership was 160 rides per capita, and the TTC experienced a surplus of $1.9 million.[37] It was a remarkable achievement, showing that transit was very popular with Metro residents – popular enough to not require any operating subsidy since it paid for itself through fares.

Metro continued to grow. By 1971, North York's population had passed the half million point, from less than 100,000 at mid-century. Scarborough and Etobicoke grew more slowly, but by 1971 they had populations of 334,000 and 202,000, respectively.[38] The population of the bigger city had almost doubled since 1950, to more than two million by 1971. Taxable assessment had increased threefold during that period.[39] Metro was a great success, and as development spread towards the limits of its boundaries, developers began looking beyond Metro for new opportunities. But those new opportunities had to be taken in areas where local government did not have the benefits Metro offered, such as the financial capacity to borrow large sums to build the needed infrastructure, and the staff expertise needed to make sophisticated decisions. On the fringes, it was a different ball game.

3

Planning
for the
Future

Toronto set itself apart from other cities on the continent by its attempt to plan its future. In particular, the plans of 1943 and 1959 were remarkable in their ability to think comprehensibly about where the city might be headed. Their influence and success most certainly was a result of the fact that structures were available – first the City of Toronto and its Planning Board; then the Metro Federation – to give them operational opportunities. The ideas in both plans were reflected in the later planning by the provincial government, particularly the Toronto-Centred Region Plan of 1970. That plan proved ineffective mostly because there were no mechanisms available to turn its intentions into reality, and even less political will.

The Toronto City Planning Board was established in mid-1942 as a result of the pressure the Board of Trade put on City Council to establish such an institution. It was an appointed body, not directly responsible to City Council, thereby reflecting the general belief that planning needed to be done at some distance from political decision-making. The Board's first piece of business was to prepare a plan for Toronto. Tracy D. leMay had been the city's planning commissioner since 1930 and was naturally put in charge of this work (see fig. 3.1). LeMay had been appointed City Surveyor in 1910 at age twenty-six, and had become a powerful force in the city bureaucracy. In 1922, planner Norman Wilson called him 'primarily the father of town planning, as it is working out in Ontario.'[1] He was eminently suited to the role of plan maker, since he concerned himself with all of the big city issues – office growth, high-rise buildings, traffic, land speculation, housing, and zoning.

With the help of Eugene Faludi, a planner in private practice, leMay wrote the Master Plan for the City of Toronto and Environs, which was adopted by the Board in 1943. It was a short, unpaginated, sixteen-page booklet with a snappy red cover, and the text was interrupted by only one city map (see fig. 3.2), spreading over the two centre pages,[2] which Faludi had been responsible for preparing. His office was in The Grange, one of the city's oldest structures, located immediately adjacent to the Ontario College of Art, where Faludi looked for a student to

Figure 3.1 Tracy D. leMay, Toronto's influential planner from 1930 to 1954.
Source: City of Toronto Archives, series 372, sub-series 4, item 154.

draw the map. That student was Harold Town, who became a
significant artist in Toronto.[3]

The intention of the plan was stated plainly in its conclusion
as 'a people's plan aimed at meeting the crisis created by the
necessity of building a modern city on the framework of the old
pre-machine age town.' It covered an area three times larger
than the City of Toronto, and contemplated much growth and
construction after the war was over, estimating that the then-
population of about 900,000 in the urban area would jump to
between 1,250,000 and 1,500,00 by 1974, only thirty years hence.
It noted that 'the political boundaries of the City bear no relationship to the social and economic life of its people,' and 'the
Master Plan is therefore an attempt to co-ordinate the physical
development of the Metro Area as one geographic, economic
and social unit.' It conceived a boundary for growth traced in a
circle around the city, nine miles in diameter, from the putative

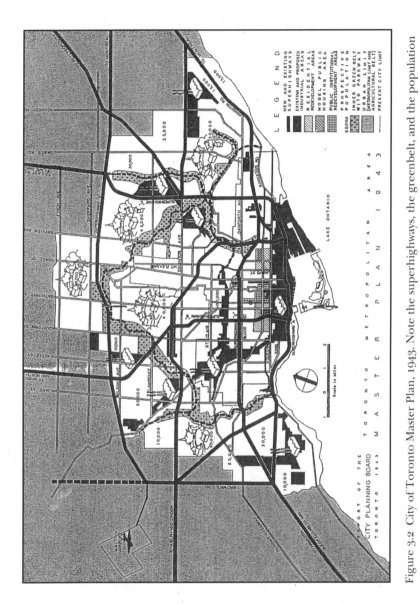

Figure 3.2 City of Toronto Master Plan, 1943. Note the superhighways, the greenbelt, and the population allocations for new communities.

Source: City of Toronto Planning Board, 1943.

city centre at Yonge and Queen Streets. This encompassed 100 square miles, about double the then built-up area in the municipalities of Toronto, East York, and York, and thus was regional in scope. Within that area of growth, the plan called for a necklace of parks in the Don and Humber River valleys.

The plan did little to build on the city's strength: its compact, mixed-use form which was efficient for transit and other servicing, and which apparently produced a relatively civil community where social problems were not overwhelming. Instead, the plan reflected the latest thinking of the day, as expressed by two of the most active and influential planners at the time in Canada, Eugene Faludi and Humphrey Carver. They thought lower densities were better than the existing densities of the city.[4] The plan states that a suitable density for the new areas would be 10,000 people living and working in a square mile. Since the city's residential density was then more than 20,000 residents per square mile, this plan proposed new areas built to be half as dense. Without providing reasons for this change, or showing why the new areas would be better places to live and work, the plan opted for a settlement much more spread out, as though the existing city was too crowded.

The plan included proposals for underground rapid transit – routes along Yonge, Queen, and Bloor Streets, and through the Garrison Creek Valley west of the downtown between Queen Street and St Clair Avenue. It also included a number of expressways, either depressed slightly below grade or elevated, which it called 'superhighways,' and they were labelled A though E. A's route was where the Gardiner Expressway was later built; B ran north along the route of the planned Spadina Expressway; C ran north from Lake Ontario up Coxwell Street in the city's east end; D's route ran where the current Highway 401 is located; and E ran along Bloor Street. Another superhighway, without a letter, ran west along Eglinton, and then headed southeast through Forest Hill and Rosedale to the Don Valley. The plan urged that the superhighway proposed by the province north of the city (later known as Highway 401) proceed past the city boundaries to join with the city's expressways. It proposed to extend Jarvis Street north of Bloor, and to push

Spadina Avenue north through the escarpment by Casa Loma. Apparently leMay thought these proposals would help alleviate traffic problems, an issue he had been struggling unsuccessfully to resolve over the past fifteen years. No rationale was provided for these roadways, perhaps because it was thought that none was needed.

The plan designated land for industry, mostly along railway tracks, as well as in the southern portion of the downtown. Residential redevelopment areas were located on either side of the downtown, where the urban renewal projects of both Alexandra Park and Regent Park were later established. On the edges of the planning area, new neighbourhoods were indicated with population targets matching the density figures referred to earlier.

The plan was formally endorsed by City Council in 1944, but with an important proviso: 'it being understood that the said approval shall not be construed as committing the city to proceed with the plan or any particular part thereof without the approval of council, which is hereby expressly reserved.'[5] The politicians had pulled their punches, agreeing to the plan as long as it did not constitute a firm decision.[6] After the Ontario government passed the *Planning Act* in 1946, a significant strengthening of the 1937 *Planning and Development Act,* Toronto City Council had its planners prepare the required 'official plan,' but it was a workaday affair concerned with local infrastructure, and did not address the larger questions of the 1943 Master Plan or regional issues beyond the city's boundaries.

But it is important to note the significance of the 1943 Master Plan. Only two other regional plans had been prepared in North America in the previous fifty years: Daniel Burnham's 1909 plan for Chicago and the Regional Plan Association's plan for New York in 1929, the 'two great monuments of American planning in the early twentieth century.'[7] Both were privately funded, unlike the Toronto plan, which was developed with public funding under the auspices of the independent Planning Board. But both those plans seemed to hit a dead end, as regional planning in America faced 'a period of prolonged crisis'[8] not least because the suburbs rejected interaction with the city centre.[9] Neighbourhood plans were created in some American cities, particularly to accomplish urban renewal, and in both San Francisco and Philadelphia regional studies were commenced in the 1930s, but they quickly petered out for lack of support.[10]

Thus, the very existence of the 1943 Master Plan was unusual, and showed Toronto's interest in regional land use planning. In retrospect, it is also fair to say that the plan informed decisions made in the following years. Densities of new developments generally reflected those proposed, and many elements of the transportation proposals were built. Of course, the pressures of growth, wealth, and cars had their own agendas. As Richard Harris notes about growth in this era:

People needed homes and wanted space; new transportation technologies brought cheaper suburban land within the reach of many; rising incomes made it feasible for governments to mandate (and enforce) building standards for health and safety. Land subdividers, developers, builders, and lenders were happy to oblige. What else is there to say? It is true that these trends were bound to shape the suburbs. It is also true that suburbs were, and are, artificial constructions.[11]

The next plan for the city came after the creation of the Metro Federation in 1953. Tracy leMay was appointed Metro's first planning director in 1953, but he died within a year. That did not stop the initiative since the need for a plan was apparent. Murray Jones, a graduate of the planning program at McGill University was hired to head the Metro planning department. He brought in as senior staff Len Gertler, also a McGill graduate, who had been struggling with regional planning in Alberta, and Eli Comay, an American who had received planning training at Harvard, and then worked in both London and Chicago before arriving in Toronto in 1953. Gertler summed up the planning challenge: 'The prevailing pressures pushed upwards in the centre and outwards on the periphery. Suburban development seemed to have an irresistible, almost organic energy.'[12]

Appointed as Jones' deputy was Hans Blumenfeld, most recently a senior planner in Philadelphia, a man with internation-

al experience and an international reputation. In his auto-
biography, Blumenfeld addressed directly the question 'whether it makes sense to attempt long-range comprehensive plans,
sometimes called "official" or "master" plans.' He began with the
realization that such plans always start with assumptions about
the aspirations of a community, technology and what it can accomplish, and the will to actually implement the resulting plan.
'We know,' he continued wisely,

that all three assumptions are quite unrealistic – particularly the third
one. And yet we must make the attempt, because without such a 'guiding image' of the future, it is impossible to anticipate the effects of any
present decision concerning one particular element on all other elements. The plan presents a possible and a desirable balance between
all elements – population, work, services, etc. If any one element de-
velops differently than has been assumed, the plan serves as a frame of
reference to indicate what adjustments have to be made in other elements. The plan is not a static blueprint, but a dynamic guide.[13]

As befitting these individuals, the 1959 Official Plan was serious and professional, several hundred pages in length, with
three or four dozen supporting maps. The Metro Federation
covered an area of 240 square miles, but the Metro Planning
Board held responsibility for planning a much larger area, to-
talling 720 square miles. Less than half of the Metro area had
been developed by the mid-1950s, and there were only small settlements beyond Metro's boundaries. Metro planners were being asked to plan for these quickly growing jurisdictions, since
those municipalities did not have substantial planning mechanisms of their own. The plan intended to cover the period up
until 1980, when it expected the population of the whole area
would reach 2.8 million, almost doubling the 1958 population.
It assumed that the bulk of the population, 2.3 million persons,
would be resident within Metro's boundaries, and 500,000
would live in what it called the fringes, beyond Metro's boundaries. The planners noted that the population of the Toronto
area had increased about 55,000 a year for the previous ten
years, and they assumed it would increase by about that much a
year until 1980. Of the increase, 800,000 was projected to be by

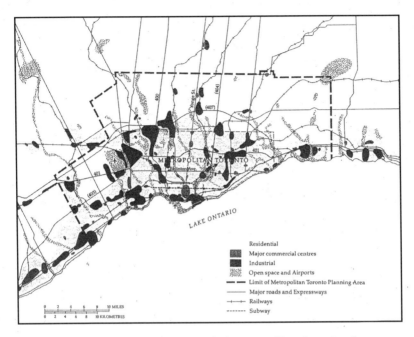

Figure 3.3 Metro Toronto draft Official Plan, 1959. Note how the plan attempts to limit development to a small area north of Steeles Avenue. Source: Metro Toronto Planning Department. Reprinted from Richard White, *The Growth Plan for the Greater Golden Horseshoe in Historical Perspective*, 16. Used with permission of the Neptis Foundation.

immigration; 450,000 was 'natural,' that is, a result of more births than deaths.[14]

The plan (see fig. 3.3) began by reviewing the different patterns which the area of urban settlement might take – a main city surrounded by satellite communities; a star-shaped city; a ribbon or linear city. It concluded by recommending a compromise called 'the Toronto scheme,' an 'urban ribbon which [was] to be developed to the maximum possible extent' with an undeveloped rural area to the north.[15] It noted that, while the urban settlement area will merge with the Town of Richmond Hill to the north, Woodbridge and Markham would remain satellite communities 'not merging with the compact urban area.'[16] It also noted that developers were assembling land west of the Credit River, but once developed, that land 'will not be a completely isolated satellite town but will be contiguous with the urban ribbon at the western end of the planning area.'[17]

This attempt to contain urban spread by creating a ribbon- or linear-shaped city is clearly seen in the visual presentation of the plan. One reason advanced by the planners for containment was the difficulty of providing services in the fringes, both because of their distance from Lake Ontario and because of the limited ability of municipal structures in the fringes to create good services. The plan stated

that in these municipalities [in the fringes] the state of development and the limitation of [municipal] financial resources make their application most difficult. As already noted, [services] can be successfully applied only if development is kept to areas not too distant from Lake Ontario ... In areas distant from the lake, a limited amount of development can be supplied with water from local surface and sub-surface sources.[18]

The plan was careful to define the densities expected to be achieved by 1980. This was measured in both residents per square mile and employment per square mile. The City of Toronto's density was planned to be 19,500 residents per square mile, not much different than it was in the 1950s. The density of what was referred to as the 'inner suburbs' – the settled municipalities of Leaside, East York, Forest Hill, Borough of York, Weston, Swansea, Mimico, New Toronto, and Long Branch – was also very similar to that of the mid-1950s, 14,600. The densities of the 'outer suburbs' – Etobicoke, North York, and Scarborough – was planned to be 7,000 residents per square mile by 1980, although planners thought that some land, about twenty-six square miles within Metro, would remain to be developed after 1980.[19] This meant the residential density in the Metro area averaged out at 9,500 residents per square mile.[20] In the areas beyond Metro's boundaries, but still within the Planning Board's jurisdiction – the fringes – the density was very low, 1,000 residents per square mile, partially because planners

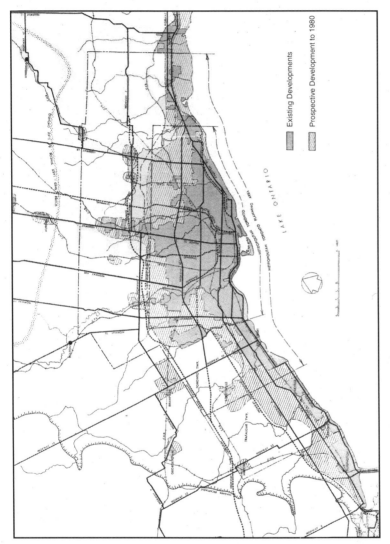

Figure 3.4 Existing development limits in 1959; and prospective development to 1980. Again, note attempt to contain development to the north of Steeles Avenue; also note height of land and edge of Lake Ontario watershed, just south of Aurora.

Source: Metro Toronto draft Official Plan, 1959.

thought that not all of the fringes would be developed by 1980. The plan assumed that 360 of the 478 square miles available in the fringes for development would be developed,[21] but that wasn't the whole story: generally, the planners were calling for lower densities in the fringes than in the outer suburbs. On a person-per-acre basis in 1980, densities were allocated as follows: Toronto fifty-seven; inner suburbs, thirty-five plus or minus; outer suburbs, twenty to twenty-two; the fringes, fourteen.[22]

This allocation of densities, sharply descending from the city centre, was reflected in employment densities, which were planned to be 8,000 jobs per square mile in Toronto and the inner suburbs; 2,320 in the outer suburbs; and 360 in the fringes, although in the area now known as Mississauga, employment densities were estimated to be 850.[23] The visual presentation of the plan makes it clear that the planners were fair in distributing industrial areas throughout the settled areas (some thought far too much land had been so designated)[24] and there were reasonable allocations for office areas, although in both cases they generally assumed lower densities as one moved away from the city centre.

The plan called for a system of expressways to be constructed, of which only the Spadina, the Crosstown, and the Scarborough expressways did not get built. Blumenfeld had proposed much of this system, arguing, 'Urban freeways should always form a closed system, with every freeway ending in another freeway, never in a city street.'[25] A number of subway lines were proposed: extending the Yonge Subway north from Eglinton to Sheppard; the Bloor–Danforth line; Queen Street, and the University/Spadina line, which Blumenfeld proposed should join with the Bloor line so cars could move effortlessly from one line to another.[26] The plan was silent on the desired modal split expected between private transportation and transit. Certainly, with the lower densities planned outside of the central area, transit would have a difficult time providing reasonably cost-effective service. The plan strongly advocated the construction of affordable housing throughout the area, and set strong goals for parkland and land designated for public schools.

The plan showed much concern about services in the fringes.

Noting that unlike fringe municipalities, Metro had the financial capability to build the servicing systems it needed for development, the planners warned: 'It is not possible at this time to
define a definitive sewerage plan for the Toronto Township
area [later to become Mississauga] as is the case for the Metro
Toronto area.'[27] Regarding the Markham/Vaughan area, the
planners expressed concerns about both water and sewage, the
latter because of the impact a poor sewage system would have
downstream, that is, within Metro itself. 'The provision of adequate sewage treatment facilities [north of Metro] is obviously
of vital concern to urban areas lying to the south on the respec-
tive watercourses, especially as the valleys of these watercourses
are the basis of the Metro Parks system.'[28] That area also had
water supply problems, the planners warned, 'It cannot be anticipated that this requirement [for water] could be met from
groundwater sources,'[29] and they suggested there should be a
temporary extension of Metro's services into this area.

The plan was finalized in 1959 and presented to, but never
formally adopted by, Metro Council. The reasons it was not
adopted are disputed. Some argued that adoption of a plan at
the Metro level 'would have necessitated the amendment of the
Official Plans of the local municipalities' to conform with the
Metro plan, and that would be 'resisted by most local politicians.' Some felt that, if confirmed, the plan would represent a
loss of power for local governments within Metro. Metro chair
Fred Gardiner commented, 'It [adoption of the plan] would
have only stirred up trouble. It would have been a lot of fuss for
minimal gain to the metropolitan operation. We were getting
things accomplished for the metropolitan area without having
to set it all down in a plan.'[30] Thus, the plan never had serious
legal status, although one suspects that if an attempt had been
made to force the issue, the plan would have been watered
down, as seems to be the fate of most official plans adopted by
municipal councils in the Toronto area, allowing many developments to proceed in spite of their inability to fit within the
constraints of the plan. Perhaps this was a reasonable status for
this document, since it became a touchstone for staff decisions
of a regional nature particularly in regard to hard services, yet it

allowed local decisions to flourish even if the context was less formal than some might have wished.

There was no regional planning document in North America similar to the Metro plan, on either a formal or informal basis. One reason, surely, was the extent to which urban areas in the United States were jurisdictionally fragmented.[31] In Toronto, the Metro Planning Board possessed planning responsibilities for areas far beyond those immediately facing development pressures, and there was no comparable body in the U.S. Another reason must have been the British influence. The London County Council had been created at the turn of the century, and had gained some reputation for the cause of regional decision-making. As the Second World War drew to a close, the Reith report urged regional planning for all areas in the United Kingdom with a population of 60,000 or more, and that was embodied in the *New Towns Act*, passed in 1946.[32] A number of Brits with extensive British planning experience were employed by the City of Toronto, including Dennis Barker, Walter Manthorpe, and Matthew Lawson, and surely they must have influenced the situation. A third explanation may simply have been the Canadian values that favoured planning as a way of making decisions. Lemon sets out contrasting American/Canadian values, including 'excess/restraint, exclusion/inclusion, polarization/compromise, anti-government/pro-government, populist/elitist, corporate/small scale, consumer/citizen,' and proposes that the 'United States tends more to the former while Canada leans more to the latter.'[33] In any case, Toronto established a prominent place for itself as a jurisdiction that took regional planning very seriously.

The next planning initiative for the Toronto area was led by provincial staff in the Department of Municipal Affairs. Their concern was the transportation infrastructure around Toronto and how it seemed too limited to cope with the quickly increasing demand. The study began in 1962 as the Metro Toronto and Region Transportation Study (usually referred to as MTARTS), and by 1964 it had come to the conclusion that roads wouldn't solve the problem but that a commuter rail system was needed. (That story is told in chapter 5.) After two

more years of study, in 1967 MTARTS issued a report titled
Choices for a Growing Region. It projected that the Toronto area
population would climb from 2.8 million in 1964 (a figure
which the Metro Plan just eight years earlier had suggested
would not be reached until 1980) to more than 6 million by the
millennium. The necessity of a regional plan was clear to
MTARTS: 'The urgency for a regional plan cannot be stressed
enough,'[34] it stated in desperation. Four different options were
proposed for growth in the Toronto area. Two were serious,
and two were as-much-as-admitted long shots for discussion
only. Both serious options included a commuter rail system
along the north shore of Lake Ontario from Hamilton to Oshawa (implemented a year earlier as the GO Transit commuter
system), and a green parkway belt just over a mile in width, located five miles north of Lake Ontario. These simple proposals
would help constrain development in a way that would make
transportation efficient. Fearing that the province might not
adopt a plan for Toronto, MTARTS proposed that, in the event
that there was no plan, then 'a special agency with a provincial-
municipal base for the express purpose of large scale regional
planning' should be established, using the City of Paris as its
model.[35]

In 1970, the plan MTARTS had so desired was released, the
Toronto-Centred Region Plan (see figs. 3.5 and 3.6).[36] It bore
many similarities to the Metro Official Plan of 1959, almost la-
menting that this earlier document had not been formally
adopted and rigorously implemented. It began with a warning:
'Within the commuting area surrounding Metropolitan Toronto, quantities of land are being removed prematurely from agricultural and recreational use, both for low density residential
purposes and for speculation.'[37] Unfortunately, the plan did not
directly address these problems. One objective of the plan was
'to develop a transportation pattern to provide the best possible
service for all parts of the region.'[38] This would be done by creating a linear succession of settlements along the lake, bounded
by a parkway to the north, and with limited development north
of the parkway. As the plan pointed out, 'The linear arrangement [of the TCR Plan] would generate sufficient traffic to

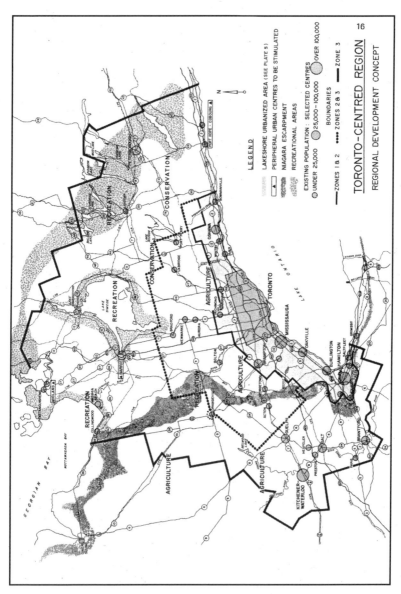

Figure 3.5 Toronto-Centred Region Plan, conceptual. Development would be limited to the inner Zone 1, with the peripheral area (Zone 2) retained for agricultural purposes.
Source: TCR Plan, Province of Ontario, 1970.

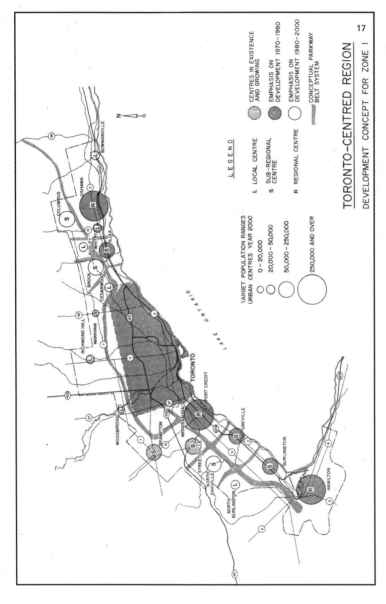

Figure 3.6 Toronto-Centred Region Plan showing limits of development for the Toronto area. Note the proposal to create a parkway belt to contain development, 1970.
Source: TCR Plan, Province of Ontario, 1970.

make workable a highly sophisticated transit system, compared with the less desirable, somewhat unbalanced, automobile-oriented traffic system normally accompanying trends.'[39] The plan went further, 'Unstructured sprawl, where it exists, can create costly road and service systems, and reduce the choice of transportation means, thereby decreasing efficiency.'[40]

The plan proposed to constrain growth to the north of Toronto, particularly the growth that was beginning to creep up the Yonge Street corridor, by designating the land here as rural and recreational in what was referred to as Zone 2. Growth instead would be encouraged to the east and west of the urban area along the lake as a kind of ribbon of development contemplated in the 1959 Metro Plan. Within Zone 1, the area allocated for growth, there would be a parkway belt ensuring that the second-tier growth in the Mississauga/Malton and North Pickering areas was separate and distinct from the growth in Toronto itself. In the west, Hamilton would be an anchor, and certainly an independent community. Oshawa would serve the same function to the east.

The Toronto-Centred Region Plan was lauded as a very intelligent, if somewhat tardy, response to the burgeoning suburbanization of Toronto. The plan noted that too many problems had already surfaced: 'Some problems of extensive urbanization are those of pollution, bad housing, traffic congestion, lack of recreation, unsuitable urban design, poor access to and from the hinterland and sheer lack of space.'[41] There was some concern that by simply trying to direct where growth might occur, the plan had not come to grips with the more important issue of the nature of growth. One group of critics noted: 'The intention of the TCR is not to discourage growth, but to structure it; however, there is good reason to believe that it will also promote it, not because anyone has decided that growth is particularly good, but simply because that is the way it has always been. It is a hard habit to break.'[42]

But the TCR did not respond well to the local concerns within a regional context, and that proved its undoing. Unlike the Metro federation into which the Metro plan was launched, there was no viable structure into which the regional and local viewpoints could both be considered with care and attention, and the plan was seen as little more than provincial meddling. It was attacked unmercifully by local politicians vying for development and by the powerful development industry, as just an uninformed attempt to control growth. That partnership of developers and local politicians was powerful enough to render the TRC Plan impotent, and push it aside almost immediately. The plan lost impetus within a few months of being announced, and provincial politicians made no attempt to ensure its goals in respect to development controls were met. An update was issued a few years later under the title Central Ontario Lakeshore Urban Complex, and it showed all of the missed opportunities, including new services and the penchant for new highway construction contrary to TCR objectives.[43] Provincial politicians renounced planning in favour of bringing services to wherever development was bursting out. The provincial plan, if one could call it that, was to keep up with the development industry, not to lead it.

Tentative steps were taken to secure parts of the parkway belt advocated in the Toronto-Centred Region Plan, but implementation was upset by a development industry which found ways to get development approvals for key parcels they owned, located within the proposed parkway belt. Since much of the land in the Belt was owned by Ontario Hydro, it has largely survived not as a park but as a service corridor for, among other things, Highway 407.

The Toronto-Centred Region Plan was the last attempt of the provincial government to do regional planning in the Toronto area in the twentieth century. The TCR Plan was the 'guiding image' for the greater Toronto area, the image Blumenfeld had urged to set elements in context and provide a sense of balance, but it was not the image decision-makers wished to be guided by. Instead, the hard services came first, and it was on that infrastructure that development decisions were then made. Yet it would be foolish to conclude that the plans were of no effect. The three plans generally pointed in the same direction, urging a ribbon pattern for the city and orderly development around a compact centre.[44]

Growth could not occur without transportation modes and routes, whether for car or transit, or without water and sewage works. It is to a history of that infrastructure in the developing areas within Metro and quickly beyond, in the fringe, that we now turn – roads, public transit, sewage and water works. Once the patterns of these elements of infrastructure were set, the structure of regional government was then determined by the provincial government, perhaps in the hope that these new regional/local governments would be able to exist as a forum for structuring the regional/local planning context which had so successfully played out within Metro. In retrospect, the cart was before the horse, and the hard decisions came before the vision. The next few decades resulted in a confusion of priorities.

4

Building a
Superhighway
System

P erhaps the most powerful planning tools that exist are the roads, but roads are usually planned and controlled by engineers, not by land-use planners, and they often subvert what the planners had hoped for. In the Toronto area, the construction of the superhighway system was a major influence on the pace, size, and scope of urban growth, beginning with the innovative Queen Elizabeth Way in the 1930s. Sadly, few records remain of the thinking behind the first of the 400 series of highways, yet once they were completed, their very existence proved the most powerful justifications for even more superhighways.

The harbinger of significant growth in southern Ontario was most certainly the provincial Department of Highways. Perhaps the intentions of the department were unknown to the writers of the *Don Valley Conservation Report* in 1950, but twenty years before that, the department had big plans, of which the first was a large new road to the west, which would gain fame as the Queen Elizabeth Way.

In 1931, the Department of Highways planned to build a new and significant road from Queen Street in Toronto west to Hamilton. It would replace Middle Road, appropriately named, as it was located between Lakeshore Road and Dundas Street, which is also Highway 5 west of Toronto. (The name survives as an arterial roadway in Oakville, known as Upper Middle Road.) This new highway was to consist of four lanes, each ten feet wide, two in each direction. Since it ran along the existing Middle Road, driveways and connecting roads would remain in place for some years, until access was restricted to engineered entrances and exits (see fig. 4.1). Work began in 1934 with the building of a bridge over the Credit River, but since the Depression was in full swing, construction faced considerable financial restraint. Nonetheless, the department saw this as a turning point and proudly noted in that year's annual report that this was the 'development of the Middle Road as a superhighway.'[1]

Thomas B. McQuesten was appointed Minister of Highways in 1934, when the Hepburn government assumed power at Queen's Park, and the nature of the new Middle Road changed. McQuesten had a deep interest in large park infrastructure design. He had been raised in Hamilton in the 1880s

Figure 4.1 Middle Road, west of Oakville, an example of the 'dual highway
construction.' This photo, from the Department of Highways 1937 Annual
Report, shows that the 'old way of doing things' – that is grafting this road
onto an existing right of way with driveways intersecting – did not limit access.

and 1890s, and after attending university in Toronto, he re-
turned to Hamilton in 1909 to practise law. He was elected al-
derman on the Hamilton City Council in 1913, and quickly
showed an interest in parks and public works. In the 1920s he
was a member of the Hamilton Parks Board of Management,
and was strongly committed to the construction, during the
1920s, of the Royal Botanical Gardens. He was heavily involved
in planning the north-west entrance into Hamilton, using architect John Lyle and planner Humphrey Carver to design the
famous entranceway marked by magnificent stone pylons and
plantings.[2] He was an active member of the Liberal Party, was
elected to the legislature in 1934, and as Minister of Highways
he had a new outlet for his interest in a grand landscaped setting for roads (see fig. 4.2). He thought the new Middle Road

Figure 4.2 Thomas B. McQuesten, the innovative
Minister of Highways in the 1930s.
Source: Whitehern Historic House and Garden,
Hamilton, Ontario.

could incorporate some aspects of a well-designed park, and
suggested that a grass median should be inserted between the
lanes running in different directions.

New ideas were coming to the design of roadways. A parkway
system was being developed around New York, with roads set on
their own right of way, some with controlled access. They were
also well landscaped with grassy areas, shrubs, and larger plantings. Bridges were attractive, and sometimes picturesque. Most
of these roads were two lanes (one in each direction) but some

were 'dual carriageways,' that is, two lanes in each direction, and in a few cases there was a grassy sward between the lanes. Hutchison River Parkway, Saw Mill River Parkway, and Cross County Parkway, all on the edges of New York City, were examples of these new kinds of roadways.[3] In 1932 in Germany, the first autobahn was built as a four-lane roadway between Cologne and Bonn.

McQuesten was clearly aware of this new thinking, and to ensure that Ontario incorporated the latest trends into the new Middle Road, he 'asked staff to study Hitler's new Autobahn [in Germany] and the latest advances in highway construction in the United States.'[4] Ontario staff made the visit and did the research, and the province quickly leapt to the forefront of new expressway design. The right of way for the new road was widened to accommodate a grassy sward dividing the four lanes, and the road gained the appellation of 'dual highway.' One ministry engineer, A.A. Smith, thought traffic would soon be traveling at sixty or seventy miles an hour – twice the speed limit in the province – and that roads would have to be designed with lower gradient changes, fewer curves, and no grade railway crossings.[5] The department's annual report for 1936 noted: 'The year saw the beginning of dual highways, namely a double road surface with a centre boulevard,' and work on the new Middle Road continued between Toronto and Burlington.[6] (See fig. 4.3 for a view of the Burlington underpass.)

The idea of the new superhighway was clearly a matter of great pride for the highway engineers. They noted the following year: 'In the development of the modern "Divided Highway," Ontario is making a start. This new type of highway not only gives a means of rapid transit over long distances, but provides this with a degree of safety not possible in any other type of Highway heretofore developed.'[7] That same year saw the completion of the first cloverleaf in Canada, on the new Middle Road near Port Credit, and it was opened to traffic.[8] This was just eight years after the first cloverleaf in North America had been opened near Woodbridge, New Jersey. The new Middle Road was also the first concrete road in Canada.[9] Ontario was clearly on the cutting edge. The first large dual highway to

Figure 4.3 'Semi-clover leaf' near Burlington on the new Middle Road, 1936.
In the top of the photo one can see the railway grade separation.
Source: Department of Highways Annual Report, 1936.

open in the United States was the Pennsylvania Turnpike in
1940 – dual highways did not become a regular feature of American highway building until after the Second World War.

McQuesten pushed staff further: divided highways were
thought appropriate for other parts of the province, and construction work soon began there. A new kind of powerful sodi-
um lighting was used as an experiment on the new Middle
Road. Then McQuesten suggested the new Middle Road be extended beyond Hamilton to Niagara Falls, where the road
would run along Lake Ontario rather than west of it, along the
top of the escarpment where roads had been built in the past.
The problem had been the lay of the land: many creeks flowed
from the escarpment toward the lake. Given the power of the
larger body of water which was subject to storms blown by east
winds, the streams became ponds or 'drowned mouths' at the
edge of the lake. To minimize the expense of lengthy bridges
over these bodies of water, original roads had been established
well to the west of these water bodies, and towns sprang up
there rather than along the lake. A government now willing to
invest in the many bridges needed to create a road way close to

the lake had no trouble finding available land there (see fig. 4.4).

In keeping with the new thinking that so enamoured McQuesten, the new highway was to be set in a park and be seen as a work of art, rather than simply another road. Humphrey Carver did the landscape planning west of Highway 27 to Bronte Creek.[10] Bridges would be aesthetic statements; sculpture would be placed along the roadway; trees and other plantings would decorate the verges. In 1937, McQuesten instructed the Niagara Parks Commission (a body for which he was also responsible as minister) to plant 20,000 trees and 47,000 shrubs along the highway. Henley Bridge near St Catharines was designed by Canada's premier sculptors, Florence Wyle and Frances Loring, as a Viking ship, and it can be seen there today as one travels on the highway (see fig. 4.5). A tall, powerful pillar with lions at its base, also designed by Loring, was placed in the median near the Humber River (see fig. 4.6), although it was moved into a nearby park when the roadway was expanded.

By 1938 the new thinking had taken hold. The department's annual report noted, 'In keeping with modern highway development, emphasis was placed on roadside embellishment, sodding and planting on boulevards and slopes adding much to the beautification of the highways.'[11] Another change was in the planning for these superhighways. Staff noted, 'The right-of-way for these [superhighways] was from 150 to 200 feet in width and about 80 per cent of this right-of-way did not follow or develop existing roads, but was an entirely new right-of-way across private property.'[12]

These were major changes. The transportation planners had learned that it made more sense to locate these superhighways in open fields rather than trying expand existing highways, as had occurred with the first sections of the new Middle Road. It was difficult to limit access on existing roads and restricted access was needed for these new ones. The road planners also realized that simply doubling the traditional one-chain width of a normal road right of way (66 feet) to two chains, or 132 feet, was not enough. Providing the amenities required for the dual highway required a right of way of at least 300 feet.[13]

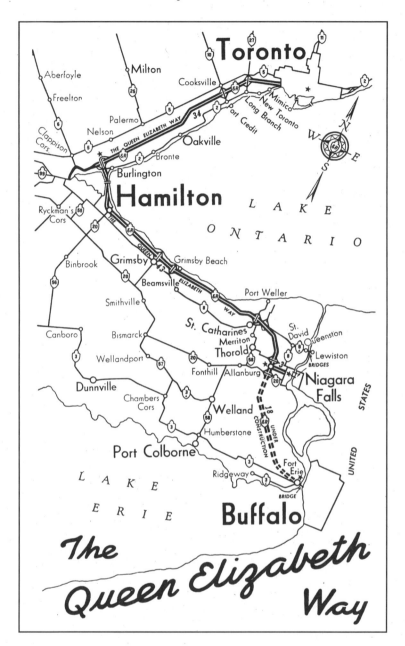

Figure 4.4 Route of the Queen Elizabeth Way.
Source: Department of Highways Annual Report, 1939.

Figure 4.5 The Henley Bridge at St Catharines as a Viking ship.
Source: Department of Highways Annual Report, 1939.

It was an exceedingly great departure from common practice to create a new road *tabula rasa*. According to general practice, the way to accommodate an increase in traffic was to widen existing roads, as with the new Middle Road. Little thought seems to have been given to the consequences of building a new road that bypassed existing settlements in order to provide speedier connections. Did the traffic planners assume land adjacent to the new road would remain agricultural and rural, given the limited access to the new road? Did they realize the new road would become a magnet for development? The answers to

Figure 4.6 Monument by Francis Loring at the Toronto entrance of the Queen Elizabeth Way.
Source: Department of Highways Annual Report, 1939.

these questions aren't known and, sadly, Department of Highways material for most of McQuesten's tenure as minister is missing.[14] More importantly, there is no record that these questions were ever asked. The impetus for the new roads was to find a way around congestion. 'These roads,' as some authors incorrectly and short-sightedly noted, 'were mainly intended for drivers wanting to by-pass the city.'[15]

One other point signals the change ushered in by these superhighways: they were seen as a provincial undertaking. The *Highway Improvement Act* required the City of Toronto, as the generator and attractor of traffic, to contribute to suburban roads, as already noted, and in 1936 the city paid $80,000 to the adjacent County of York to cover about half the cost of suburban roads around Toronto. As late as 1948, Toronto Mayor Hiram MacCallum complained that Toronto was required to pay 25 per cent of the cost of suburban roads, the same percentage as the county, with the province picking up the remaining 50 per cent.[16] But the province did not ask the city to make a financial contribution to the new Middle Road superhighway. These superhighways were a provincial investment.

The brilliant stroke for which Thomas McQuesten is probably best remembered is renaming the new Middle Road the Queen Elizabeth Way in honour of the visit by King George VI and Queen Elizabeth in 1939. The royal couple officially opened the new road – although parts of it had been functioning for at least a year – in a grand ceremony in June 1939 (see fig. 4.7). It was one of the largest and most progressive new roads that had been built in North America (see fig. 4.8).

Congestion on Highway 2 east of Toronto was severe, and that was where attention for another superhighway was focused. A decision was made in 1937 to construct a divided highway with controlled access from Highland Creek east to Ritson Road in Oshawa, where the General Motors factory was located.[17] This was a different kind of undertaking, because the superhighway had to be integrated into an existing settlement. The answer was to narrow the new right of way by omitting the centre boulevard, and to depress the road below grade, as had been done with a divided highway in Newton, Massachusetts, in

Figure 4.7 The Royal couple at the opening of the Queen Elizabeth Way in 1939.
Source: Department of Highways Annual Report, 1939.

1935.[18] A plan was prepared by ministry staff in late 1938 and presented to Oshawa City Council for approval, which was given on 13 February 1939. Construction began after the conclusion of the Second World War, and this stretch of highway still exists in much the same form (see fig. 4.9).

There is no departmental record available, but staff must have been much involved in planning for two other new superhighways – the Toronto Bypass and the Toronto–Barrie highway (more formally referred to as the Controlled Access Highway). Traffic congestion requiring the bypass was considerable, and much congestion clogged roads leading north to cottage country. Superhighways as the way of the future were certainly a matter of great interest to traffic engineers. At the 1939 New York World's Fair, General Motors sponsored a large exhibit on car culture called 'Futurama.' It proposed that within twenty years – that is, by the 1960s – America would be crisscrossed with a grid of fourteen-lane highways. Cars would travel by radio beams to control their spacing, and would easily

Figure 4.8 Traffic on the Queen Elizabeth Way, 1941.
Source: Department of Highways Annual Report, 1941.

achieve speeds of 100 mph in this automated setting.[19] Indeed,
following the Second World War, President Dwight Eisenhower
initiated a national highway construction program.

Both the Toronto Bypass and the Toronto–Barrie Highway
were set out in the 1943 Master Plan for Toronto mentioned in
chapter 3. The Toronto Bypass was referred to in the plan as
the 'Toronto Feeder,' which would 'act as an interceptor and
distributor for the traffic reaching the city on all existing and
proposed provincial highways.'[20] The plan also included the
proposal for an expressway along the waterfront and several
other 'super highways,' as they were labelled. In fact, agreement was reached with the Toronto Harbour Commission in
1944 on the location of the waterfront superhighway, although
it would take another decade and the leadership of Frederick
G. Gardiner as chair of the newly created Metro Federation to
make those plans real and get construction underway in 1956.[21]

Provincial staff had decided on proceeding with the Toronto
Bypass and the Toronto–Barrie highway by 1939, and they com-

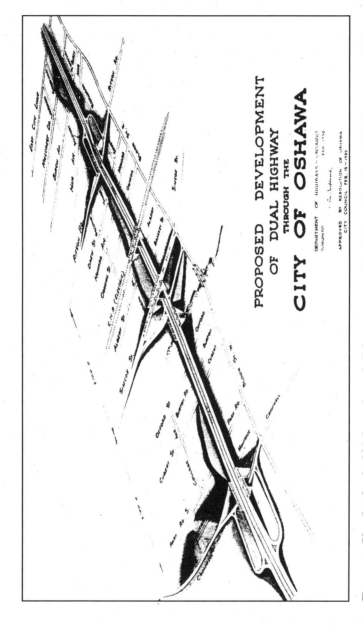

Figure 4.9 Plan for the dual highway through Oshawa, approved by Oshawa City Council, February 1939. This depressed road remains virtually the same sixty-five years later.

Source: Department of Highways Annual Report, 1938.

pleted the designs for both during the Second World War: the
engineering drawings were ready by 1943 or 1944,[22] and the
precise alignment of the roads was by then being finalized.[23]
The 1946 annual report of the Department of Highways stated,
'In preparation for the post-war construction program, detailed
soil surveys were completed on the location of the Toronto–
Barrie Controlled Access Highway between Wilson Avenue and
the Holland Marsh; and on the location of the Toronto by-pass
between Highway 27 and Bathurst Street.'[24] That report also
notes that engineering work had been completed on both highways.[25] The war effort delayed construction, of course, and for
several years after the end of the war there were shortages of labour and materials which also slowed the completion of the
roads. Property acquisition for the bypass was almost complete
by 1947, when the final parcels were being expropriated around
Bathurst Street where land values were rising as residential development expanded.[26]

Construction of the Toronto Bypass north of the city began
in 1949. It was built in sections, and it was not until 1956 that
one could drive on it from the Rouge River to the Humber River.[27] In 1953, the ministry decided to designate these kinds of
roads as the 400 series of highways, with the 400 designation going first to the Toronto–Barrie Highway, and 401 to the Toronto Bypass.[28] Unfortunately, it is not clear who selected the 400
appellation for these roads, or for what reason.

In 1957 John Robarts, still a junior cabinet minister and several years away from becoming premier, chaired the Ontario
Select Committee on Toll Roads, which concluded that major
highways in Ontario should be free to all travellers. This principle was used everywhere in the province except for the Burlington Skyway, built in 1958, where tolls remained in place until
1973. But a second and largely unstated conclusion was that the
cost of a new expressway system should be borne entirely by the
province. One conclusion of his report read:

The roads of tomorrow must be planned to serve the needs of the
Province, subject only to the budgetary limitations, otherwise there is
the danger that regional and local planning will be shaped to fit the

present road pattern rather than the road pattern shaped to accommodate proper and beneficial development.[29]

The warning appears to have had little effect: while the budget for roads seemed unconstrained – roads constituted the largest source of provincial spending in the 1950s – regional and local development in the Toronto area was largely shaped by roads, just as Robarts feared.

The Department of Highways also published *A Plan for Ontario Highways* in 1957. This document noted that 'cities are focal points of traffic generation and distribution,'[30] and it cited cities as marketing centres, centres of production, and as tourist destinations. But there was never a mention of the traffic that might generated by commuters, that is, those who lived outside of the city and drove downtown to work. It was as though provincial officials had a blind spot for the obvious (see fig. 4.10).

The behaviour of those living around cities showed no such qualms. They knew these new highways signalled that the fringes could now easily access downtown, and development proceeded accordingly. The Don Mills development was announced in 1951, and was quickly followed by the development of other suburban land close to the developed city. A few years later, housing subdivisions were being built to the west of Metro Toronto in what was called Toronto Township. The commuter traffic generated by the suburbs, which Highway 401 had encouraged, soon jammed the road.

In 1959, Metro staff produced the draft Official Plan for the Toronto area. It shows an expressways network that includes the recently opened Highways 400 and 401, and also locations for future Highways 403, 407, and 404, each assigned a number to make it clear these new roadways had been thought out with care (see fig. 4.11). This highway network was entirely a creation of planners. Unlike water and sewage systems, these roadways were planned far in advance of land assembly for development, and routes were established long before developers had purchased land for which they needed to lobby for development approvals or servicing. In many cases, suburban residents were a much more effective lobby for more roads.

Figure 4.10 Increase in downtown traffic, 1938–58. This document describes the increase in traffic entering the downtown area with the number of available parking spaces, and includes much (but not all) of an article published in the *Globe and Mail*, 7 July 1948.

Source: Normal Wilson Papers, City of Toronto Archives.

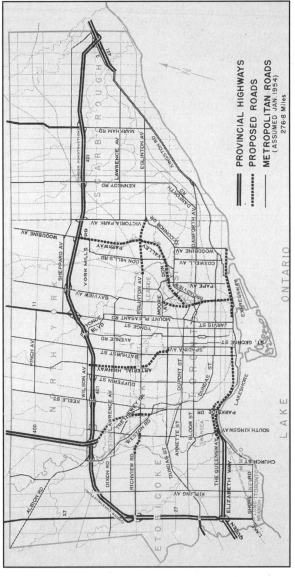

Figure 4.11 Plan of the places where Metro intended to build expressways, 1954. Metro later added to the plan the Crosstown, connecting the Spadina 'Arterial Highway' to the Don Valley Parkway; filled in the gap in what was to become the Gardiner Expressway along the waterfront; and added the Scarborough Expressway at the easterly end of the Gardiner.

Source: Metro Toronto Annual Report, 1954. Reprinted from Richard White, *Urban Infrastructure and Urban Growth in the Toronto Region, 1950s to the 1990s*. Used with permission of the Neptis Foundation.

By the early 1960s there was so much congestion around Toronto that drastic action was needed. The Toronto Bypass had
been planned to accommodate 35,000 vehicles per day, an
eightfold increase over traffic in 1946. But by 1961 it was used by
70,000 vehicles per day.[31] In 1962, the Ontario government established the Metropolitan Toronto and Region Transportation Study (MTARTS) within the Department of Municipal
Affairs to review transportation data and options. No sooner
had the study begun than in 1963 Minister of Highways Charles
MacNaughton announced that Highway 401 would be expanded into an express/collector system in the Toronto area, with a
total of twelve lanes – six in each direction. That would increase
the capacity if Highway 401 to 164,000 vehicles per day.

The mania for cars went further. On the west side of the city,
Highway 27 had been surveyed in 1940 with the expectation it
would become a divided road linking the Queen Elizabeth Way
to Highway 7 to the north, but in the early 1960s, it was decided
to rebuild the road as a second and alternative route to Barrie,
to relieve Highway 400. It would be called Highway 427, starting
as a multilaned controlled access expressway between the QEW
and Highway 401. East of the downtown, Metro Toronto Council had authorized as a matter of first priority in 1954 a parkway
running up the Don Valley. The Don Valley Parkway was
opened in the early 1960s, to be extended a decade later northerly into York Region as Highway 404. Considerably north of
the city, the first plans for Highway 407, paralleling the 401,
were firmly in place by the late 1950s, and quite possibly land
was already purchased, although construction would not begin
for another twenty-five years. In a speech in May 1970, Minister
of Municipal Affairs Darcy McKeough said, '[T]he parkway corridor, in which the route of the proposed Highway 407 will be
located, is an identifiable feature specifying a limit to intensive
development.'[32] To the north-west of the city, Highway 410 was
undoubtedly more than just a dream in the provincial eye.

Toronto was now surrounded by an expressway grid both existing and planned. To complete the network, the Crosstown
Expressway would, as proposed in the 1940s by Norman Wilson
and confirmed in the 1959 Official Plan, link the southerly ter-

minus of Highway 400 to the Don Valley Parkway. Another road, also proposed by Wilson and confirmed in the 1959 plan, would run from Highway 401 to the College Street and Spadina Avenue intersection, cutting through the city south of Casa Loma in a depressed trench, to become the Spadina Expressway. The Scarborough Expressway would proceed east from the downtown to join Highway 401 at Rouge River.[33]

Work on the Spadina Expressway began in the 1960s, and the infrastructure involved was mind-boggling. One intersection completed by 1968 – that between the Spadina and Highway 401 – contained no less than twenty-four separate bridges (see fig. 4.12). It was an amazing way to spend money, particularly since the promise to relieve congestion would never be realized. Almost immediately opposition to it arose downtown around the University of Toronto, and a classic fight between suburbanites wanting easy access to and from the downtown, and young professionals, living downtown and wanting to protect the places where they lived, ensued. The Metro structure, giving relatively equal weight to the regional and local viewpoints was sorely tested, as Metro Council supported the road and Toronto City Council opposed it. The matter was placed before the provincial government for resolution, and Spadina's southward trajectory was halted at Eglinton Avenue by Premier William Davis in 1971. Davis used stirring words: 'If we are building a transportation system to serve the automobile, the Spadina Expressway would be a good place to start. But if we are building a transportation system to serve people, the Spadina Expressway is a good place to stop.'[34]

With the Spadina Expressway dead, the Crosstown proposal faded away, never gaining enough support from anyone but engineers and Metro planners, since it proposed to slice directly through the Rosedale neighbourhood, home to the Toronto establishment. Metro Council finally agreed to abandon the Scarborough Expressway in the mid-1970s. The cancellation of the Spadina Expressway has never quite been accepted by suburbanites: forty years later, the complaint of congestion continued to be heard, with the suggestion that the Spadina should return.

Figure 4.12 Photo of the Spadina Expressway–Highway 401 interchange,
under construction, 1966, looking west. The Yorkdale Shopping Centre is in
the upper left, 1966. Photo by McCullagh Studios.
Source: City of Toronto Archives, series 3, file 386.

The provincial government continued to play a strong role in
transportation decisions in the Toronto region. The MTARTS
Committee recognized that cars were not the only answer to
transportation needs and in 1964, after two years of study, decided some kind of commuter rail system was needed. (That
story is told in chapter 5.) The success of the super-road system
continued to be called into question. Provincial staff were clear
that these large and expensive roadways were not resolving
transportation problems in the Toronto area, and in 1967 the
MTARTS study group issued the report *Choices for a Growing Region*, the main parts of which had already become public. The
report projected that the Toronto area population would climb
from 2.8 million in 1964 to more than 6 million by the millennium. The group thought the necessity of a regional plan was
clear, and the Toronto-Centred Region (TCR) Plan was an-

nounced in 1970. The plan appeared to reduce priority for the expressway approach, and Premier William Davis made many speeches about the limitations of expressways. 'In urban areas they do not usually work efficiently,' he said in 1972, 'since they tend to attract and encourage the use of automobiles to the point that they quickly become jammed over their capacities.' He proposed more transit options, including the magnetic levitation system, in which the province invested, although it did not survive the experimental stages.[35] But the good intentions about planning and transit never became operating policy.

The expressway system that the provincial government had built was its key planning tool. That system allowed access to land north of the city by Highways 400 and 404, contrary to the TCR Plan, and those lands were quickly assembled by large development companies. Highway 427 opened in 1972. Highway 410 from the 401 to Brampton was planned in the 1970s, and construction happened in phases in the 1980s. The Highway 404 extension to the Don Valley Expressway was constructed in the mid-1980s, pushing north as development occurred, finally reaching Newmarket by 1986. Highway 403 provided an alternative route to the west of the city. It was an impressive grid, but it had not been planned with care or forethought to shape urban growth. It was an example of how one element of a plan, as Blumenfeld had worried, received more attention than other elements, upsetting the balance that most people wanted to achieve.

Within that grid was a set of arterial roadways which, almost without exception, followed the concession roads that in the mid-nineteenth century had been surveyed and laid out at intervals of slightly more than one mile. These concession roads constituted a finer grid within the expressways, and they were widened into four-lane roadways with additional turning lanes, or six-lane roadways at enormous expense, at least half of which was paid for by the province. These arterials operated as through routes rather than as destinations. Commercial activity which was previously located on arterials was now set well back from the travelled road, prominently displaying the availability of car parking. This style of development quickly became ubiquitous and was called 'highway commercial.' Streets which had developed a commercial life before 1950 were either widened and destroyed as places of commerce and social interaction, or treated as quaint examples of the past, best visited on a Sunday afternoon. The commercial activity that serviced the new residential development was found in shopping plazas and shopping malls, with some retail and service activities also located within industrial campuses.

Just as the grid road system of the nineteenth century provided opportunities in those years for the development of farms and settlements, this larger-scaled grid servicing the automobile provided development opportunities for the twentieth-century, albeit it on a much different scale. The nineteenth-century grid spawned small lots, compact buildings, mixed use districts, and pedestrian activity. The mid-twentieth-century grid spawned large development parcels, single-use districts, and vehicular movement as a desirable activity, almost to the exclusion of transit and walking.

Development happened practically everywhere in the fringes and, since there seemed to be no constraints, most of that development was at very low density, consuming vast quantities of land. Cost was not a factor to local decision-making since the provincial government funded the construction and maintenance costs of the expressway and provided at least a 50 per cent subsidy for the reconstruction of the arterials. Developers were required to build local roads at their own expense as part of development approval. This development was also at the expense of the natural environment.

There are two significant natural features in southern Ontario. The Niagara Escarpment is a ridge of limestone running in a jagged, northerly line from Niagara Falls to the tip of the Bruce Peninsula and beyond. The Oak Ridges Moraine is a hillocky area north of Toronto, running from the Escarpment easterly to the Kingston area: it is where the glaciers dumped vast amounts of gravel and soil as they retreated at the end of the last ice age 12,000 years ago, and as an area that absorbed rainwater, was the birthplace of the streams and rivers flowing southerly to Lake Ontario. Both features were seriously threatened by the development roll-out in the latter half of the twentieth century. The Niagara Escarpment was eventually protected from development by strong provincial legislation, and has so far generally

survived, with only a few serious development intrusions, perhaps because of its distance from developing centres. That has
not been the case with the Oak Ridges Moraine. The creation of
the road system meant that surrounding land was attractive for
residential development, and indeed that development came,
particularly in the Yonge Street Corridor. The recharge functions of the Moraine have clearly suffered because it was not fully protected from development.

By the late 1980s it was again acknowledged that the road system around Toronto was severely congested. A Ministry of
Transportation study estimated that congestion in the Greater
Toronto Area cost Ontario's commercial and industrial sectors
$2 billion annually because of lost productivity and delayed
shipments.[36] There were many complaints about the length of
commuter trips, and constant pressure to revive the Spadina
Expressway. Provincial politicians responded by a selective widening of Highway 401, and staff wanted to build a new highway,
the 407 which had been notated in Metro's 1959 Official Plan,
but the cost of $20 million per kilometre was considered be-
yond the province's means. The breakthrough for staff came in
1986 when Premier David Peterson was given a helicopter tour
of the expressways around Toronto during rush hour. He saw
first hand what was called the '401 parking lot,'[37] a vast sea of
commuter traffic stalled in the evening rush hour. The decision
was made almost immediately to build Highway 407, and the
ground breaking occurred in 1987. The government felt it had
to look for innovations to help reduce the highway's cost. The
private sector was brought in to design and develop the road, in
the hope economies could be achieved, and indeed they were.
The ideas addressed by John Robarts in his select committee in
1957 were revisited, and the decision was made to create a toll
road. The road opened in the mid-1990s. It was seen by the government of Premier Mike Harris as an easy way to generate
money, and it was quickly sold for a song to the private sector,
which was given a free hand to raise tolls. The commercial story
of this expressway is not one that will be repeated here, since it
is told so well elsewhere.[38] For our purposes, it is to be noted
that Highway 407 is in exactly the same mold as the Toronto Bypass conceived in the late 1930s, just much farther afield.

CONGESTION ON GTA EXPRESSWAYS
1981 VERSUS 1998

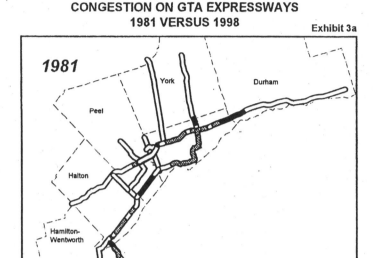

Exhibit 3a

Source: Perspective on Congestion in the GTA - Technical Report #12 for the GTA
Transportation Plan, Ontario Ministry of Transportation, 1997

Exhibit 3b

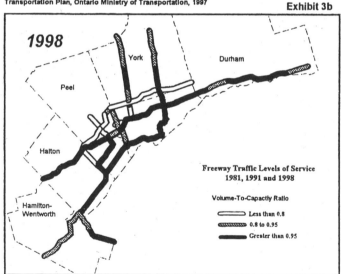

Figure 4.13 Congestion on GTA Expressways, 1981 versus 1998, where solid black represents an expressway operating at or over 95 per cent capacity.
Source: IBI Group and Hemson Consulting, 'Funding Transportation in the Greater Toronto Area and Hamilton Wentworth,' 9.

But new roads were not the solution. In the 1995 'State of the
Region Report,' Region of York officials minced no words
about the transportation crisis. Officials said that delays due to
gridlock added a 30 per cent surcharge to the cost of moving
goods. They wrote:

If commuters continue to use their cars to get to work at the same
rate they currently do, then by 2021 there will be a need for 100 additional arterial lanes constructed along corridor roads. Automobile
emissions in the form of carbon monoxide, carbon dioxides, volatile
organic compounds and dust will be spread across all of Southern
Ontario.[39]

The warning has not been heeded. Another study concluded
that, whereas 10 per cent of the highway system was congested
at peak periods in the 1980s, by the late 1990s there was 70 per
cent congestion, and GO Transit rail was operating at capacity,
with no room for expansion (see fig. 4.13).[40]
    At the turn of the millennium, one could hear the old, sad re-
frain from the 1970 Toronto-Centre Region Plan: 'Unstructured sprawl ... can create costly road and service systems, and
reduce the choice of transportation means, thereby decreasing
efficiency.' It had come to pass. The highways were clogged
with traffic, and congestion was rampant.

5

Transit and Commuting Alternatives

The strong initiatives taken by the provincial government to provide a road infrastructure to assist the development of fringe areas around Toronto thwarted the initiatives given to the creation of a public transit system as another good way to move people. Commuting by transit might have been touted by provincial officials as attractive, but it did not receive the attention required to make it an excellent service. After the GO Transit commuter system was established in 1965, the provincial government seemed to have little interest, other than pouring money into what it had created. Instead, it turned its energy into reshaping the Toronto Transit Commission – with the TTC's compliance and consent – from an excellent local transit service into a regional commuting service. Thus, the story of public transit possesses none of the leading-edge feeling that surrounded the building of the road system.

Even though roads were the favoured approach to addressing transportation problems in Metro's quickly growing hinterland, commuter rail was also being considered in the 1950s. The Toronto Board of Trade had established a Special Committee on Rail Commuter Services in 1953, and revived it in 1956 after the City's Board of Control expressed an interest in ways to relieve congestion. Discussions were held by Board of Trade members with the Canadian National Railways at which Board members let it be known their report would favour commuter rail. In December 1957, to pre-empt the Board's report, CNR president Donald Gordon made a speech indicating that the CNR was studying the issue, but that the commuter scheme was hampered by congestion at Union Station. The special committee reported in February 1958 on how a commuter service might be structured. Newspaper editorials favourable to the commuter idea appeared over the next few months, and Gordon made it clear that because the CNR alone could not bear the expense of running a commuter service – a subsidy would be needed.[1] However, the federal government apparently decided against providing a subsidy,[2] and the idea fell into limbo.

In 1964, the provincially led Metropolitan Toronto and Region Transportation Study (MTARTS) proposed a commuter rail system in the most economical manner possible – by using the existing tracks of the CNR and paying rent for that use.[3] The proposal was considered by government decision-makers in early 1965, and in May, Premier John Robarts announced the creation of GO Transit as a way to 'attract car commuters off crowded highways.' 'The problem that we face,' said the premier,

is that the main highway routes in this particular metropolitan area are becoming strained with over-capacity traffic during only about four hours a day, and at other times they have surplus capacity. What we are looking for is a better use of our transportation dollar through a balanced use of all modes of transportation in this rapidly developing area.[4]

The government estimated the deficit of GO Transit would be modest – about $2 million a year, based on $3.5 million in operating costs and $1.5 million in revenue. It noted that a mile of a six-lane expressway cost $4 to $6 million to build, and that an elevated road such as the Gardiner Expressway cost $16 million a mile. Compared to superhighways, GO Transit looked like a sure-fire financial winner, even if the province had to provide capital funding for equipment and ground facilities. The route proposed was along Lake Ontario, from Oakville to Pickering, a total of 60 miles with fifteen stations. Fares would priced according to distance travelled; parking at the stations would be free; and during rush hours, service would be every twenty minutes.[5]

GO Transit began service on the CN lakeshore rail line between Oakville and Pickering in 1967. In 1970, GO buses extended service from the commuter rail terminus east to Oshawa and west to Hamilton. Other routes were then added. Buses provided service in 1970 from Newmarket in the north to downtown Toronto, and in 1973 commuters from Malton, Bramalea, and Georgetown could travel by GO Transit rail to Union Station downtown. Additional routes, chosen because the tracks already existed, meant that the linear nature of the lakeshore route as a way to shape development was subverted by the larger, more dispersed catchment area which these other rail lines served. The expansion of these commuter routes encouraged suburban development in their catchment areas.

The province also saw GO Transit in a larger regional context, and hoped that it could be the beginning of a way to coordinate transit services in the Toronto area to form a regional network. In 1974, it established the Toronto Area Transit Operating Authority with the hope that this body could be responsible for planning and operating transit service in the same way that the TTC did within Metro. The idea was not well received in the fringes, perhaps because they feared being stuck with the very large transit subsidies required, and TATOA never was anything more than the agency which operated GO Transit. By the early 1980s the province had reassumed direct control of GO Transit.[6]

GO ridership grew from 4 million in 1969 to 12.7 million in 1976, and to 25 million in 1985,[7] with two-thirds of the riders using the lakeshore route (see fig. 5.1). GO Transit was so successful at attracting riders that the MTARTS notion of establishing an 'experimental rail commuter service'[8] was forgotten within a decade and GO came to be seen as a permanent service. The original financial projections were considerably off the mark: the expense of GO Transit was not modest, but considerable. The operating loss of GO Transit in the 1975–6 fiscal year was $12.4 million, with a further $14.5 million in capital expenditures for a total cost to the province that year of $26.9 million. Five years later, the operating loss was $31.9 million and capital expenditure was $51.5 million for a total annual cost of $83.4 million. In the mid 1980s the combined subsidy was $150 million annually, climbing to $220 million in 1988, before falling slightly.[9] The annual $2 million deficit projected in 1965 was a woefully optimistic.[10] In the 1970s, $2 million barely funded GO Transit for a month and, in the 1990s, barely a week. The subsidy per passenger on GO Transit in the late 1980s and early 1990s was more than $3, compared to a per-passenger subsidy on the TTC of less than $0.20.[11]

GO Transit's ridership success was a result of the growing population outside of Metro Toronto's boundaries, just as the increase in TTC ridership within Metro reflected the new

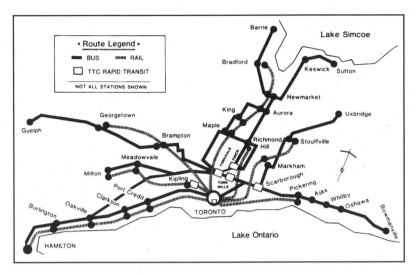

Figure 5.1 Map showing GO service routes, 1998.
Source: GO Transit Annual Report for year ending 31 March 1988 (Toronto: Queen's Printer for Ontario, 1988). Urban Affairs Library.

growth in the suburbs of Etobicoke, North York, and Scarborough. But the scale of the two operations was very different. In 1970 the TTC carried 324 million riders: GO Transit, barely 5 million. The TTC carried passengers on average less than two miles; GO Transit carried passengers five and six times that distance. That year the TTC paid its operating costs out of the fare box and, in fact, generated a small surplus: GO Transit had an operating deficit of about $1 a rider.[12] The challenge that both systems faced was the costly business of providing transit to low-density suburban communities, although a majority of the TTC's passengers at that time still came from the compact, mixed-use municipalities of Toronto, York, and East York. In 1971, when Premier William Davis announced that the Spadina Expressway would go no further south than Lawrence Avenue (later extended south to Eglinton Avenue), he offered Metro Council a transit carrot: the province announced it would pay half the capital cost of a Spadina subway line. Within a year the capital subsidy promise was increased to 75 per cent, and the province also agreed to pay 50 per cent of the TTC's operating deficit, which at that point was miniscule.[13]

The Spadina Subway had its own odd political context. Locating the subway largely in a ravine rather than under a main street where people lived and worked was rather odd. A vote at Metro Council in 1973 attempted to shift the line to run under Bathurst Street north of Bloor, so it might play the same role on Bathurst that the subway had done under Yonge Street – focusing development on an existing main street that already had a strong transit demand – but the motion lost by one vote, and construction of the subway in the ravine began. Many suburban politicians thought that a provincial reversal of its previous decision and approval of the Spadina Expressway was only a matter of time, and locating the subway in the ravine was seen as the best method of preserving the expressway's right of way. The provincial reversal never came. The subway was a problem for the TTC since the decision to build it had less to do with operating a transit system well than with using the transit operation to address other political problems.

As the low-density suburbs within Metro mushroomed, the TTC faced the problem of how best to provide service. Until the mid-1960s, the TTC had generally been serving a dense, compact mixed-use city. The gross densities of the inner three municipalities – Toronto, East York, and York – was 16,000 persons per square mile in 1951, falling slightly to 15,000 in 1976.[14] In the past, when the population of the surrounding suburbs was tiny compared to the compact city, the TTC made suburbanites pay a second fare when they crossed into the older city. The boundaries of the zone-fare system roughly followed the boundaries of the former City of Toronto, Township of York, and Borough of East York – generally the city as it was built by 1945 – which was one zone, and the area beyond, another. Thus travelling from the suburbs of Scarborough, North York, or Etobicoke required payment of a second fare when crossing into the older city. It was the TTC's rough and ready way of charging fare by distance. The double fare meant that suburban riders generally paid their way.

But in the 1970s the TTC was also expected to serve the sur-

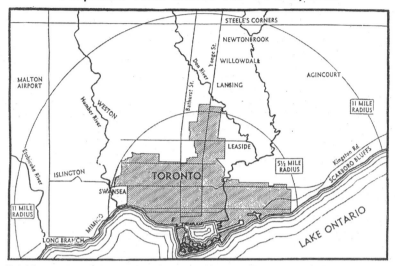

Proposed Fare Zones For TTC System

Map of Toronto and suburbs shows boundaries of the suggested fare zones which would come with increased fare as suggested by a consulting engineer to the Toronto and York Planning Board. Fare inside the 5½ mile radius would be 10 cents. Beyond the 5½-mile limit to the boundary of the 11-mile radius, additional fare would be seven tickets for 50 cents. The report suggests that suburban passengers be allowed to travel outbound for one fare of 10 cents, but inbound would be required to pay one of the 7-for-50 cents tickets, plus 10 cents. While part of the north Yonge section of the city is outside the 5½-mile limit, officials state the zone would be extended to give all city residents a single fare.

Figure 5.2 Proposed zone-fare system for Toronto Transit, 1948.
Source: Norman Wilson Papers, City of Toronto Archives.

rounding low-density single-use areas within Metro which were growing in size and political power. The gross densities of these new suburbs reflected the new building forms, and by 1976 the density was 6,600 people per square mile, less than half that of the inner city, a density not high enough to cover the full cost of transit service for those areas.[15] Political tension was building at Metro Council between suburban representatives who favoured cars and city representatives who favoured transit. In 1972 there was an open debate about the TTC's service to the newer suburban areas, and Councillor Karl Mallette, representing a ward in Scarborough, proposed that the two-fare zone system be abolished.

Admittedly, the zone-fare system had never been popular outside the boundaries of the inner zone. In September 1947, pol-

iticians from the twelve municipalities surrounding the city
asked the city to abandon the double-fare system but the TTC,
then controlled by Toronto City Council, wasn't willing to fore-
go the revenue needed to meet its costs.[16] Transportation consultant Norman Wilson undertook a comprehensive study for
the TTC in 1948, proposing to reduce TTC fares for the outside
zone, increase fares for the inside zone by $0.10, and impose a
$10 levy on automobile registration to create more revenue
(see fig. 5.2). The proposals caused a firestorm and were not
adopted.[17] The two-fare zone system continued. Then, more
than two decades later, the issue was back on the table, mostly
because the Spadina Subway promised to provide service to
suburban North York crossing the two-fare zone line, as did the
Bloor–Danforth line which extended into Etobicoke and Scarborough, and the Yonge line that also ran into North York. The
two-fare zone system worked well for buses and streetcars where
second fares could be demanded at transfer points located at
boundaries, but not for the subway which provided a continuous uninterrupted service across boundaries.

Under suburban pressure, the TTC agreed in 1973 to charge
just one fare for a ride anywhere in Metro Toronto. It was financial disaster for the TTC. The TTC's first operating deficit occurred in 1971 – it was tiny, just a penny a rider – but in 1973
that quickly climbed to $11.3 million and in 1974 to $23.6 million or $0.07 a rider.[18] The number of suburban riders rose,
and that increased the cost of the operation in relation to the
revenue, so that the operating deficit continued to grow, reaching $275 million in 1991.[19]

It was during the 1970s that the provincial government began
to show great interest in transit as a way to generate employment.
It encouraged using the new technology of the German firm
Kraus Maffei, which proposed to float a train on a cement track
by magnetic levitation, thus eliminating friction between the
train and the track for a ride that used less energy and made less
noise. Trees were cut down at Exhibition Place in west central
Toronto for a demonstration track and foundations were built,
but the finished track was never built. The government spent
millions of dollars on studies before it abandoned the idea.

The province then established the Ontario Transportation Development Corporation to develop and market new transit systems. The company was renamed the Urban Transportation Development Corporation – UTDC – to make itself sound less provincial when selling its wares to other jurisdictions. One UTDC project was to help the TTC find a replacement for the aging Presidents Conference Committee (PCC) streetcars, first purchased by the TTC in 1938. The last PCCs had been manufactured in Thunder Bay in 1951. Later in the 1950s the TTC purchased second-hand PCCs from American cities such as Cleveland and Cincinnati as those cities decided to scrap their streetcar systems. Working with the TTC, UTDC developed the Canadian Light Rail Vehicle (CLRV), a car which would operate on relatively long runs, mostly using its own right of way. The new vehicle was very heavy, mostly because of the undercarriage, wheels, and axles necessary to allow each car to achieve a speed of 70 miles per hour. The CLRV was introduced onto Toronto streets as a replacement for PCCs in the late 1970s, even though it would operate in mixed traffic rather than on the separate right of way for which it was designed. The new cars were not a good fit with Toronto tracks, already in poor repair, and they caused noise and vibration. Over the next few decades, the TTC was required to undertake an expensive program to rebuild the tracks.

In the 1970s UTDC also began to develop transit vehicles running on their own right of way, known as RT. UTDC saw RT as the market of the future and began work (which proved successful) to sell it to Vancouver for the International Exposition planned there in 1988. (The new technology is sometimes referred to as 'light rail transit,' but this is a misnomer since in the rest of the world an LRT runs on a street and does not require its own right of way.) It was reasonably thought that if an installation of RT technology was already working in Ontario that this would be a selling point. UTDC looked for an opportunity in the Toronto area. In the late 1960s, the TTC had proposed a new streetcar line that would run from the end of the Bloor–Danforth Subway east to Scarborough Town Centre, and hoped for something a bit grander than simply having the streetcar operate at grade, subject to all of the normal traffic constraints. A joint report by Metro and the TTC was issued in 1977 proposing a streetcar system where some of the line crossed other streets at grade and some of it relied on bridges, with its own right of way. The report mentioned UTDC's new technology favourably. The cost was estimated at $68 million, and diagrams showed how similar arrangements could cover Metro suburbs with similar lines.[20]

The UTDC had considerable influence on decisions about the Scarborough line, and ultimately the TTC agreed to accept UTDC technology, with much of the system on an elevated structure. When completed in the 1980s, the actual cost of the Scarborough RT exceeded $230 million, three times the original estimate. Ridership was low because the route passed through a low-density industrial area in a sprawling suburb, which meant there were few nearby potential riders. The operating deficit of the RT was significant – a subsidy of $0.38 per rider in 1986, about triple the subsidy for the rest of the TTC system.

Meanwhile, the TTC looked for ways to use the CLRV on its own right of way. In the 1980s a decision was made to create a transit right of way on Queen's Quay West through Harbourfront in downtown Toronto. To ensure this line would not interfere with commuter traffic, the city's traffic engineers decided it should be sunk under Bay Street from Union Station south to Queen's Quay in a $50 million tunnel. It was a harbinger of how senior city staff interpreted the TTC's role – transit should not interfere with commuter traffic. A second proposed route would run along Spadina Avenue, between Bloor Street and Front Street – one of the city's busiest bus routes. A group called Streetcars for Toronto, which had successfully organized opposition in 1972 to the TTC's plan to scrap all streetcar lines in Toronto, had proposed streetcars on Spadina back in 1973. That scheme faced the opposition of several merchants who feared transit might adversely affect car traffic. In the late 1980s the TTC decided to create streetcar tracks with their own right of way on Spadina, separated from car traffic by curbs. Traffic engineers for Metro Toronto agreed to the transit plan only if two lanes of automobile traffic could be available at all times. The transit right of way, the passenger islands, the barrier curbs, and the two lanes for moving traffic took up so much space that sidewalks had to be narrowed, and much of the curb-side parking eliminated. Residents and merchants objected vociferously. Bicycle advocates unsuccessfully demanded bike lanes.

The battle about the Spadina right of way went back and forth for almost ten years until finally the plan secured approval, and the finished line was opened in 1997. During construction, the sidewalks were narrowed even though, in the heart of downtown's Chinatown, they were the most heavily used sidewalks in the city. The right of way was constructed, but the transportation planners required that left turn lanes and signals be installed for cars and other vehicles. Many of the changes seemed more to accommodate commuters in cars than to offer better and speedier transit service. Ridership increased once the new streetcars were operating, but many said that was the result of the new residential and commercial developments south of Queen Street close to Spadina. One newspaper report in 2005 showed that it took longer to use the Spadina streetcar travelling from Bloor to just south of College Street during the day than to use the Bathurst streetcar going the same distance – and the Bathurst car had to fend for itself in mixed traffic, without the so-called advantages of its own right of way.[21] Despite claims by city staff to the contrary, transit didn't get the priority it was promised on Spadina.

During the 1980s and early 1990s the TTC was hemmed in by financial pressures, mostly the result of provincial decisions, but it was supported by an agreement that the operating deficit would be shared equally between the province and Metro, and the system continued to flourish. The TTC expanded service considerably into the suburbs of Etobicoke, North York, and Scarborough and, in 1990, ridership reached a high of 460 million, with an operating deficit of $290 million.

Premier David Peterson called a snap election in 1990, making a number of promises about transit in Toronto. He dug out *Network 2011*, the TTC's 1984 report which described its plan

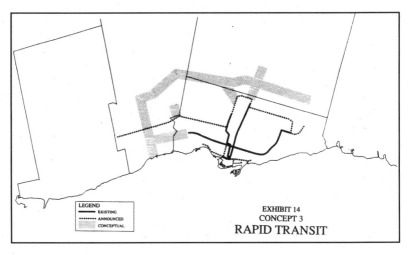

LEGEND
— EXISTING
········ ANNOUNCED
▓ CONCEPTUAL

EXHIBIT 14
CONCEPT 3
RAPID TRANSIT

Figure 5.3 Map of subway routes, 1990, showing planned expansions and
conceptual additions.
Source: IBI Group et al., *Greater Toronto Area Urban Structure Concepts Study*,
Background Report No. 3, Transportation Systems.

for a rapid transit network. Peterson took from it three ideas as
election promises: a subway under Sheppard Avenue just north
of 401, from Yonge Street east to the Scarborough Town Centre; an extension of the Spadina line from Wilson north and
west to York University; and the construction of an Eglinton
subway from Allen Roadway (the stub of the former Spadina
Expressway) west to Black Creek Drive. These were all routes
that stressed the regional role that the TTC could play delivering commuters between the downtown and the fringes, rather
than providing better transit within the existing city (see fig.
5.3). Peterson's government went down to defeat, and the New
Democratic Party under the leadership of Bob Rae emerged
with a slim majority.

What the public learned only later was that Peterson had
called the election knowing that an economic recession was on
the way. The province did indeed slide into considerable economic difficulty, which Premier Rae was forced to struggle with
in the early 1990s. Declining employment in the office towers
downtown was reflected in declining transit ridership and reve-

nues. The TTC looked for ways to save money. The easiest way to do this was simply to reduce service on downtown routes, with the expectation that riders wouldn't really notice than the ten streetcars or buses an hour had been quietly reduced to eight or seven an hour. Service on the long commuter routes such as the subways and the Scarborough RT was maintained. Fares were raised every year to increase general revenues, and that had negative impacts on ridership, particularly for those who were used to taking short trips. For those using transit as a commuting device covering considerable distances between work and home, the TTC was a good deal. The TTC saw itself more and more as a commuter service, much like GO Transit. Along with fare increases, the cuts to service downtown meant that downtown ridership fell. Work disruptions in 1989 and 1991 added to the transit woes. Ridership declined from 460 million in 1990 to less than 400 million in 1994.

Premier Rae looked for ways out of the economic downturn. One idea was the Keynesian method of using public expenditure to generate employment. Rae considered a number of ways to spend money on public infrastructure. He revisited the same agenda Peterson had advocated during the 1990 election. Mel Lastman, the mayor of North York, had been touting his scheme for a North York downtown on Yonge Street just north of Sheppard for a decade, and part of that plan involved building rapid transit on Sheppard. That pressure and Rae's penchant for public works investments to create jobs led to the decision in 1994 to approve the Sheppard subway. Rae also approved a subway under Eglinton, from the Allen Expressway west to Black Creek Drive. An Eglinton line had been touted since Richard Soberman's in-depth look at transit operations in the 1970s, the famous Metropolitan Transportation Review following the scuppering of the Spadina Expressway. In Report No. 64, *Choices for the Future*, Soberman outlined six transportation alternatives, of which a subway along Eglinton was the most prominent, being mentioned in five of the six suggestions.[22]

Metro Council and TTC officials were surprised at these commitments and were concerned about proceeding with all the lines at the same time. But Rae saw these new subways as a good way to help construction workers and their unions and to get the local economy back on its feet – things that he felt were critical for a successful re-election campaign in 1995. He went as far as to threaten Metro Toronto that if it did not authorize the new subway lines, the province would cut off operating subsidies. Construction of the Eglinton line began.

In June 1995, Premier Rae's government was defeated by Mike Harris and the Progressive Conservative Party. It was a major turnaround. Premier Harris led a government that intensely disliked the public sector and thought that the best way of proceeding was generally to reduce public expenditures, an approach that included public transit. Construction of the Eglinton subway was halted after a few hundred yards of earth had been excavated, and the hole was filled in. The Sheppard line was put on hold. Harris also moved to end provincial subsidies for public transit. In 1998 the Toronto municipal government was forced to cover the whole cost of the TTC deficit which by that time, with low ridership and much reduced service, amounted to $175 million a year. This was a major blow to the City of Toronto, which had relied on a provincial subsidy to cover 75 per cent of its capital expenditures and half of its operating deficit. The result was yet more retrenchment on the part of the TTC. The system was in great disarray. Between 1989 and 2001, fares doubled. Streetcar service was reduced by 30 per cent between 1976 and 2000, and bus service by 25 per cent. The number of riders on surface routes during the same period declined by about 30 per cent.[23] The TTC became the only major transit system in the world that did not receive subsidies from senior levels of government.

But North York Mayor Mel Lastman continued to chirp for his Sheppard subway. After local government was restructured into a 'megacity' and Lastman was elected mayor of the new Toronto in 1998, he was rewarded with the decision of the provincial government to share in the funding of the Sheppard subway, now truncated to run from Yonge Street east to Don Mills Road. The General Manger of the TTC, David Gunn, who had done much to repair an aging and ailing transit system, openly expressed his disdain for this new subway, indicating that the money would be better spent repairing the existing fleet and maintaining existing service. It was an argument he lost (he left the TTC a few years later). When the Sheppard Subway was finished and began operating in 2002, it was widely recognized as an expensive failure, given its high operating costs and low ridership.

In this way the TTC was being reshaped to become less of a good local transit service, and more of a regional commuting service. The fringes reciprocated: buses from beyond Metro delivered passengers to the ends of the subway lines, providing these distant suburbanites a terrific commuter service into the downtown area, largely subsidized by Torontonians. In 1998 the provincial government downloaded the combined capital and operating subsidy of GO Transit to the municipalities it served, an amount just over $100 million. The cost-sharing formula devised by the province was based on population, which meant that Toronto was required to pay about half this amount, yet another example of Toronto being required to subsidize the far suburbs while its own service was being degraded.

In 2002 the TTC again looked to another way to improve commuter service, this time by putting the St Clair streetcar route, running west from Yonge Street along St Clair Avenue to Keele Street, on its own right of way. The TTC first recommended the scheme as a way to save $600,000 a year by reducing the number of streetcars in the rush hours by 10 per cent, and making up for this by a quicker ride. The TTC made an alliance with the city's traffic engineers that two lanes of moving traffic would be guaranteed in each direction during rush hours so that the number of daily car commuters on St Clair would not be reduced. To both build the right of way and accommodate these two lanes of commuter traffic, the sidewalks would be substantially narrowed, curb parking reduced, and there would be difficulty making deliveries to stores on St Clair. After three years of bitter negotiations, these objections were brushed aside and the right of way was approved by City Council. It was the template for how the TTC thought it should proceed elsewhere.

In fact, the TTC's *Ridership Growth Strategy*[24] released in 2003, included a number of transit corridors similar to St Clair – on Eglinton, in the 'hydro corridor' just north of Finch Avenue, and on Jane Street. The emphasis on ridership growth seemed to be part of attracting more commuters from beyond the boundaries of the city with little emphasis on ways to increase ridership within the city. This emphasis was confirmed when the TTC advocated extending the Spadina line from the Downsview Station through York University to the edge of the Town of Vaughan. Greg Sorbara, the then provincial treasurer, represented this area and after he had secured agreement that the line would be extended into Vaughan, he ensured that this new subway – with a total cost exceeding $2 billion – received provincial support.

In the early years of the new millennium, the TTC's ridership again began to grow, but the growth was mainly on the subway lines serving those commuters living beyond Metro's borders. City riders complained that the morning subway cars were so crowded when they arrived at city stations that they often had to wait for two or three cars before they could get on. Surface transit was infrequent, and ridership declined. This was most visible on the Queen Street car, always the most heavily travelled streetcar route in the city. In 1976, the Queen car carried close to 70,000 people a day (even more than the whole of the GO Transit system); by 2006, ridership had fallen to just over 40,000. Other streetcar routes showed similar declines in ridership.[25]

While the TTC had seen its function in the 1950s and 1960s as providing a strong transit service for the people who lived in Toronto, it slid into a system that placed much more attention and emphasis on serving low-density communities in the distant suburbs beyond Metro Toronto at the expense of city riders as suburban development increased. It became a more local version of GO Transit. Some of that change was because of provincial seduction with subsidy dollars, but some was also because of compliance and consent by TTC leadership. The long-distance commuter system serving the fringe areas beyond Metro may have been improved somewhat as the TTC shifted its priorities, but the TTC's ability to offer good local transit service certainly suffered in the process. It was an example of how the power balance shifted so that financial benefits flowed to the more newly developed areas at the expense of the older, more compact, city.

6

Pipe
Dreams

Roads enable suburban growth, but that growth does not actually occur until water and sewage services are in place. The biggest challenge for the municipalities around Toronto related to the fact that there was no public institution capable of providing the services needed at the scale required. Metro Toronto's governing structure was eminently suited to building and financing these services inside Metro, but no such structures were available in the fringes. The provincial government and its agencies stepped into this void and agreed to assume responsibility for the provision of water and sewage in areas of growth outside of Metro. The pressures were such that the province only considered the financial aspects of these services once they had been promised, and the result was – unlike within Metro – that the cost of servicing was divorced from the approval of new growth: suburban growth occurred with very large subsidies from the provincial purse. One suspects that if more attention were paid to the cost of servicing and the kind of growth being encouraged on the edges of the Toronto urban area, a more efficient land-use form would have been obtained.

Sixty years ago Toronto's one million residents were settled almost entirely within the boundaries of the then City of Toronto, Borough of East York, and Township of York. As detailed in chapter 2, the remaining areas within the boundaries of the new Metro government were mostly rural and had few basic services. Twenty per cent of the 10,500 homes in North York, for instance, used outhouses, and a further 60 per cent were on private septic systems. The northerly portions of Etobicoke Township relied on wells for water. Clearly, the expected growth could not occur without expensive new water and sewage services being built.

Once Metro Toronto was established, its first priority was to provide water and sewage to all existing settlement areas within its boundaries, and then to create a plan to extend services to new areas within Metro as development occurred. Metro retained the leading engineer of the day, James MacLaren, and in 1957 he recommended how those goals should be accomplished.[1] His planning assumption was that by 1980, 2.3 million people would live within Metro Toronto and an additional 475,000 outside its borders. This meant more than a doubling of the population within Metro and more than a tripling on the fringes. His emphasis was on services within Metro Toronto, but MacLaren paid attention to what was happening beyond Metro's boundaries. 'The moral obligation on the part of Metro Toronto,' read his report, 'is to furnish water to these townships which the corporation actually isolates from Lake Ontario.'[2] This was the first sign that Metro would see its job as accommodating development north of Steeles Avenue. MacLaren continued: 'It is recommended, however, that the [Metro] Corporation exert stringent control by actual agreement with these municipalities upon the design and operation of their distribution systems if such are to be supplied with water by Metro Toronto.'[3] He estimated these surrounding townships would need 50 million gallons of water per day by 1980 – a relatively small amount compared to Metro's needs estimated at 317 million gallons per day by 1980.

Metro was responsible for paying the costs of construction and operation of its own sewage and water works. It could rely on the strong financial base of the City of Toronto to borrow the funds needed for construction. Indeed, one reason for establishing Metro was to ensure that growth within Etobicoke, North York, and Scarborough could be financed by levering the strong borrowing capacity of Toronto, without which it could not have occurred. With it, Metro's chair Fred Gardiner could fly down to New York and, in the course of a few meetings, borrow what was needed for infrastructure over the next year and be back in Toronto for supper. Beyond Metro, the townships with their small populations and agricultural base had no such financial capability or capacity. Perhaps that was part of the 'moral obligation' MacLaren talked about – not only was Metro located between Lake Ontario and the area north of Steeles Avenue, but also these very small municipal governments north of Steeles Avenue did not have the capability to finance water and sewage works. (See fig. 6.1.) The Village of Markham, for instance, wanted to construct a package plant in 1956, but when it asked the Ontario Municipal Board to approve the necessary borrowing to build the facility, the OMB refused, saying it was not financially viable for the town to take on this much debt.[4]

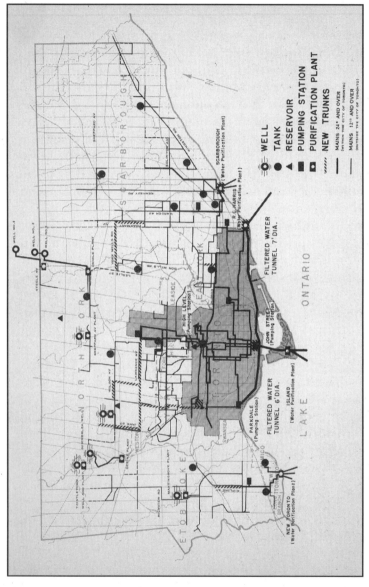

Figure 6.1 Map showing (shaded) areas with sewers in 1954, with plans for expansion and new trunk lines. Source: Metro Toronto Annual Report, 1954. Reprinted from Richard White, *Urban Infrastructure and Urban Growth in the Toronto Region, 1950s to the 1990s*, figure 2. Used with permission of the Neptis Foundation.

A snapshot taken by the Metro Toronto planners for the 1959 'Official Plan' shows the limited population in the fringe areas in the mid-1950s.[5] The western area had a population of 65,000, of which 7,000 lived in Port Credit, 5,000 in Streetsville, 1,000 in Toronto Gore Township, and the rest mostly within Toronto Township. The fringe north of Steeles Avenue to Richmond Hill had a population of 52,000, including 2,000 in Woodbridge; 14,000 in Richmond Hill (where a package plant had been built in 1951);[6] 4,000 in the Village of Markham; and 2,700 in Stouffville. Most homes and businesses operated on individual septic systems and water supply was from communal wells 80 feet deep. The eastern fringe was the least developed, with a population of 25,000 of which 1,600 lived in the Village of Pickering and 8,000 in Ajax where a sewage plant had been built to serve an armament factory during the Second World War. These fringe areas obviously had few communal water and sewage services because they didn't need them.

The real challenges were in these hinter lands where growth was expected, and the province knew it. Changes to the *Municipal Act* in 1943 allowed municipalities to finance servicing projects through user rates rather than property tax, but more was needed outside Toronto to help service the growth expected there. In May 1955 the provincial government appointed the Committee on Water Resources and Supply to consider how to serve growing areas of the province and, where services were below standard, find ways to improve or replace them.[7] The next year the committee gained the status of a commission, and in 1957 the passing of legislation made it the Ontario Water Resources Commission (OWRC). This legislation not only widened its mandate and but it also transferred responsibility for the approval of water and sewage systems from the *Public Health Act* to the OWRC. As the OWRC annual report for 1957 noted, '[E]mphasis is given to the construction of water and sewage for municipalities and new authority is given to control the pollution of waterways.'[8] From the start this was a sizeable operation: in 1957 the OWRC had a staff of eighty-two employees. The very existence of the OWRC indicated the province was not willing to allow servicing to proceed haphazardly; instead, it wanted to encourage a comprehensive approach to servicing, and it was not disappointed.

One complication was that while the OWRC was responsible for water and sewage, it was not responsible for land-use planning. In the Toronto area, that was the mandate of Metro Toronto and its widened planning jurisdiction which went far beyond Metro's boundaries. Municipalities in the fringe did not have planners on staff, and sometimes attempted to approve development with simply the consent of local public health authorities. The creation of the OWRC put an end to that practice, but it pitted the engineers of the OWRC against the Metro planners. OWRC was seen as the expediter; Metro planners as the naysayers. OWRC was 'a weapon for the fringe municipalities ... which wished to encourage rapid growth.'[9]

Each of the three fringe areas faced different developmental pressures and different environmental challenges. The servicing of each area will be dealt with in turn.

Servicing the Western Fringe

Toronto Township, just west of Metro Toronto, was a hotbed of development. Metro planners predicted in the 1959 Official Plan that the western fringe would grow from 65,000 to 265,000 by 1980,[10] and in the 1950s the services were already stretched beyond their capacity. The Town of Streetsville had had a water treatment plant since 1941, taking water from the Credit River, and emptying its untreated sewage into the same river until a package plant was built in 1950.[11] This plant was expanded as the town grew to slightly more than 5,000 in the early 1960s. (See fig. 6.2.) Then, as one report noted, the river was 'overloaded as the village expanded.'[12] Brampton, located on the Etobicoke Creek, tapped deep wells for water and disposed of sewage in the creek, but by the mid-1950s these systems had reached their limits.[13] In the early 1950s, Malton became the home of a new airport and of the large A.V. Roe aircraft factory, which employed 50,000 people. Named Victory Aircraft until it was purchased at the end of the Second World War, the factory obtained its water from nearby wells, but because a million gal-

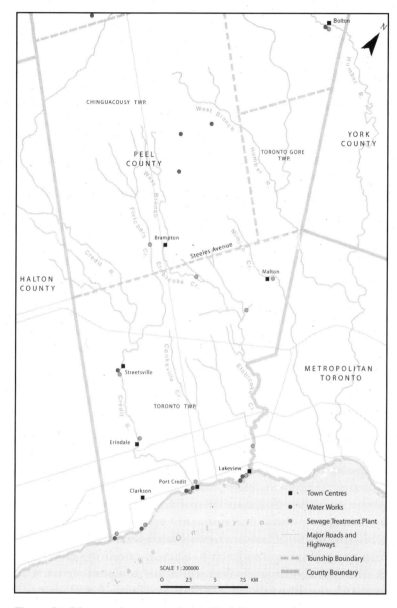

Figure 6.2 Water and sewer services in Peel County, 1963.
Source: Richard White, *Urban Infrastructure and Urban Growth in the Toronto Region, 1950s to 1990s,* figure 9. Used with permission of the Neptis Foundation.

lons of water a day had been extracted since the late 1930s, these wells were running dry.[14] A sewage plant had been built in Malton to serve the factory, but five years after the war's end, capacity was not large enough to satisfy the new airport.

Along Lake Ontario there was considerable industrial activity, first initiated by war needs and then spurred by the construction of the Queen Elizabeth Way. The Canadian Small Arms factory was in Lakeview, by the Etobicoke Creek at Metro's western boundary, and after the war it became the Canadian Admiral plant, manufacturing television sets.[15] The St Lawrence Starch Company was located in Port Credit, and further west were the British-American Oil refinery and the St Lawrence Cement factory. These industries not only needed water and sewage but also provided opportunities for jobs that created a demand for nearby housing and entrepreneurs were there to fill the need. G.S. Shipp began his illustrious career in land development – now carried on by his philanthropist son, Harold G. Shipp – starting in the early 1950s by cutting down an orchard to build the Applewood Acres suburban residential development near the Queen Elizabeth Way and Dixie Road. Next came Applewood Village, with a shopping centre, and then, continuing the apple theme, Orchard Heights and its Dixie Plaza, one of the very early examples of the new-style shopping plazas in Canada.[16] Murray Elia's first suburban development in the Town of Erindale was underway by 1957, where a decade later the University of Toronto would establish a satellite campus.

The most significant change came when E.P. Taylor began purchasing land here in 1954. Taylor had recognized enormous success from the development of Don Mills on virgin farmland in North York which had begun in 1951, and he quickly sought another opportunity. His Don Mills planner was Macklin Hancock who had grown up in Cooksville, and it was Hancock who suggested a site near the town of Streetsville for a new large development.[17] In all, starting in the mid-1950s, Taylor assembled 7,000 acres of land (3,000 hectares) stretching from the height of land just west of the Toronto–Trafalgar Township boundary east to the Credit River. Taylor paid about $1,000 per acre for

much of the site, and although almost two decades passed before development was underway, it was very prescient investment. The development was to become known as Erin Mills,
combining the Erin of Erindale and the Mills of Don Mills.[18]
(See figs. 6.3 and 6.4.)

 ′ Then, in 1957, Bramalea Consolidated Developments, an En-
glish company, began assembling 6,000 acres east of Brampton in
Chinguacousy Township, just beyond the limit of Metro's planning jurisdiction.[19] The development was billed as Peel's Satellite
City, whose projected population of 50,000 residents soon doubled to 100,000. It was championed by Cyril Clark, the long-term
reeve of Chinguacousy. The developer called it 'a jet age location
for industry and a new community for over 50,000 people,' noting it was only two miles from Malton Airport and sixteen miles
from downtown Toronto. Bramalea's Council boasted that it had
retained the planners responsible for New Towns in Britain and
Fairless Hills in Pennsylvania. In one report, it noted, 'Satellite
cities are one of the urban planners' solutions to the problems
created by the big city's mushrooming growth.'[20]

The problem for both these assemblies of land was a lack of
water and sewage services. Taylor and nearby developers retained the engineering firm Gore & Storrie in the late 1950s,[21]
and it recommended servicing the southern section of the
county by building a large sewer pipe north from the Clarkson
Sewage Treatment Plant close to Lake Ontario. (See fig. 6.5.)
But neither Toronto Township nor the County of Peel, the municipalities which would benefit from development, were experienced enough or financially strong enough to undertake the
construction of such a large piece of infrastructure.

Metro planners noted the development pressures in this area
in the 1959 Official Plan, which stated:

West of the Credit River, several large developers have assembled an
area totaling about 10 square miles and are developing plans for a
'New Town' in co-operation with the local and Metro Toronto Planning Boards. However, this will not be a completely isolated satellite
town, but will be continuous with the urban ribbon at the western end
of the Planning area near Clarkson.[22]

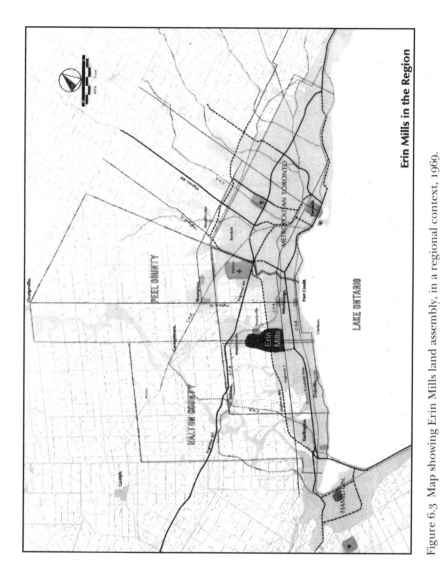

Figure 6.3 Map showing Erin Mills land assembly, in a regional context, 1969.
Source: Don Mills Development Limited, 'Erin Mills – New Town.'

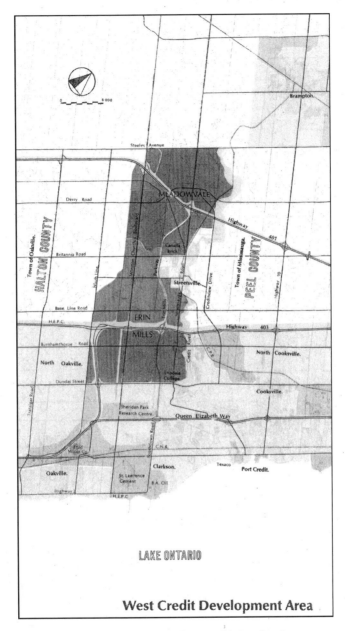

Figure 6.4 Map showing Erin Mills assembly in a local context,
1969.
Source: Don Mills Development Limited, 'Erin Mills – New
Town.'

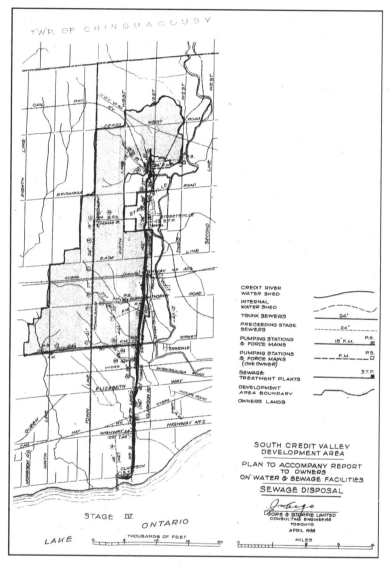

Figure 6.5 Sewage servicing plan by Gore & Storrie for the owners of the South Credit Valley land assembly (shaded), 1958. Servicing runs south through the Town of Streetsville, west of the Credit River, to the Clarkson Sewage Treatment Plant close to Lake Ontario.
Source: Gore & Storrie report to owners of the South Credit Valley land assembly.

The provincial government, through OWRC, did not respond with the comprehensive approach expected of it. Instead, it adopted a piecemeal, almost haphazard manner over the next seven or eight years. The OWRC agreed to fund an expansion of the Lakeview Sewage Treatment Plant and supply the pipes necessary to service existing development to the north along Etobicoke Creek. The area west of the Credit River would be served by an expanded sewage plant at Clarkson.[23] With the assistance of the OWRC, water supply also crept north, but the capacities of the systems were not enough to meet the development needs of Erin Mills or Bramalea. Fortunately, there was a growing recognition that the funds for such infrastructure projects needed to accommodate new development were more than a private matter; they were a public responsibility. In 1960, the federal Central Mortgage and Housing Corporation was authorized by a change in the *National Housing Act* to lend up to two-thirds of the cost of sewage treatment systems and to forgive up to one-quarter of the loan. A winter works subsidy was built on top of this arrangement. The package was known as the Municipal Infrastructure Program, and it continued for eighteen years, fuelling suburban construction and providing jobs. As well, CMHC had already convinced its federal masters to amend the *National Housing Act* to allow banks and financial institutions to provide mortgage financing for development.[24]

The population of Toronto Township doubled from 46,000 in 1956 to 94,000 in 1966.[25] The provincial politicians were not unaware of what a powerful animal this growth was. The dilemma was best captured in the mid-1960s by Premier John Robarts when he said, 'This government accepts the responsibility of guiding, encouraging and assisting the orderly and rational development of the province.' But he reflected on the difficulties of leading this initiative: 'I mean we were faced with all kinds of growth problems: transportation, education, hospital building. You know those were wild days in some respects. There was a period of 15 or 18 years, for instance, when we built a school and a half a day, every day.' Robarts' Treasurer, Charles MacNaughton was more succinct: 'All we're trying to do is shovel fog.'[26]

Sooner or later OWRC had to take more comprehensive action. That came in 1965, when the province announced that through the OWRC it would fund sewage and water services for Brampton and Bramalea and for the existing settlements and proposed development sites in Toronto Township. (See fig. 6.6.) One large sewage pipe would run up the Credit River to Brampton; another up the Etobicoke Creek and its tributaries even further north. It became known as the South Peel Scheme.[27]

Perhaps the biggest influence on OWRC's decision came from the Member of the Legislative Assembly for Peel, William Davis. Davis, a young lawyer from Brampton, had been elected MPP in 1959. He was clearly a rising star in the Conservative government of John Robarts, and was appointed Minister of Education in 1962. He was never shy about making Brampton a political priority, and undoubtedly OWRC knew that it would be politically advantageous to service not only the emerging Erin Mills (see fig. 6.7) and the newly established City of Mississauga, but also Brampton and Bramalea far to the north. In retrospect, Davis claimed that it was a considerable task to persuade the province to fund the South Peel scheme, and he was surprised with the degree of support it received. He thought the South Peel scheme 'gave planning an impetus' in the area since it required some form of planning cooperation between the municipalities.[28]

Metro objected to this servicing scheme and the development it would encourage since it did not fit well with its 1959 Official Plan, but to no avail. As noted by some commentators, the South Peel scheme was the 'jewel in OWRC's crown since it epitomizes the vigor, inventiveness and directness with which they exercised their mandate. It also marked a turning point in the ability of the OWRC to act without close provincial supervision.'[29] The discrepancy between planning and development was obvious, and it appeared to some that planning required more attention. Carl Goldenberg, whose *Report of the Royal Commission on Metropolitan Toronto* was issued the same year as the South Peel announcement, wrote:

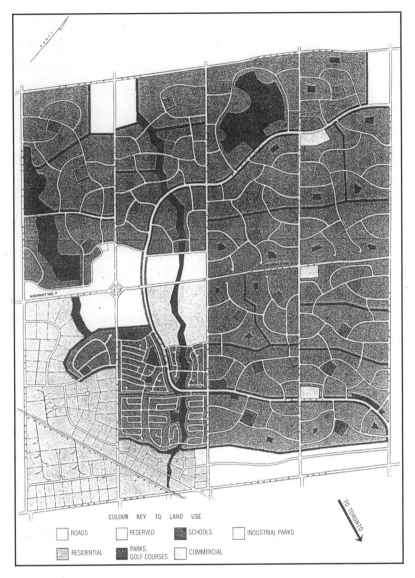

Figure 6.6 Master Plan for Bramalea, 1959. Note the discontinuous street system within the concession roads.
Source: Bramalea Consolidates Developments Limited, 1958. Region of Peel Archives.

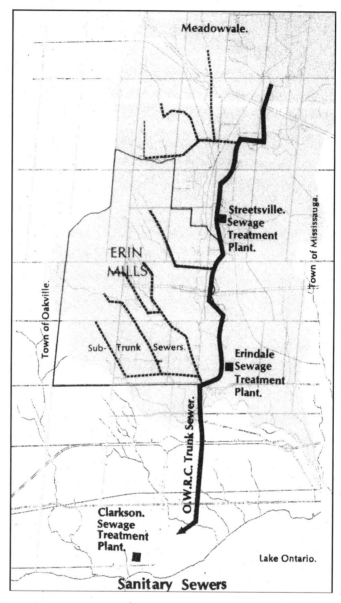

Figure 6.7 Ontario Water Resources Commission sewage services
plan for Erin Mills, 1969.
Source: Don Mills Development Limited, 'Erin Mills – New
Town.'

Considering the potential impact of further development in Brampton and Chinguacousy [Township], which would require the extension of water and sewage services from Lake Ontario through Toronto Township, I am of the opinion that, in the absence of other regional planning machinery, the area covered by Brampton and its vicinity should be included in the Metro Planning Area.[30]

That comment was something of a *cri de couer* about how disorganized the planning for servicing had become. Goldenberg was firm that Metro should not be the governing body for Toronto Township and Peel County, only its planner, in default of any other body doing the planning. He concluded, 'The extension of Metro to include the whole or part of Toronto Township would endanger the survival of Peel County which depends upon the Township for 62 per cent of the county levy.'[31]

In 1966, OWRC staff reported on the local servicing arrangements. The province would buy from the municipalities the existing limited servicing facilities in Peel County, the sewage treatment plants in Brampton, Streetsville, Clarkson, and Lakeview, and the pumping station and force main in Port Credit. It would also agree to build a new sewage treatment plant called Eastern, and enlarge the Lakeview plant. As well as looking after sewage treatment, OWRC would take responsibility for water supply. After several years of negotiation, a contract was signed in 1968 with the municipalities of Mississauga, Port Credit, Streetsville, Brampton, and Chinguacousy Township.

The price the province would pay for the existing facilities was to be established by evaluation, which settled at $6.3 million.[32] Hazel McCallion, then mayor of Streetsville (later mayor of Mississauga), remembers it being a generous windfall. Streetsville spent its funds improving the main street and burying hydro lines. The other municipalities also found their own popular projects for the money, except for the newly created City of Mississauga, which decided to bank most of it for a rainy day. When regionalization came in 1974, Mississauga found itself under attack by the region, which wished to grab the money – the city prevailed and retained the money only after a protracted legal fight. In any case, it was a no-lose situation for local municipalities: they were paid hard cash for facilities the province was replacing at its own cost.[33]

The province agreed to spend $35.7 million on water supply in three stages to 1981, and to spend $24.7 million on sewage treatment to 1981. The agreement specified that $0.31 would be the municipal cost for water for the first 1,000 imperial gallons per house per day and $0.20 in excess of the municipality consuming more than 1,500 million gallons per year. The sewer rate was $0.42 per 1,000 gallons per house per day, falling to $0.25 per 1,000 gallons once usage exceeded 1,500 million gallons.[34] There was a recognition that this was not a break-even rate for the province, but that it was being subsidized by the province. As Bill Davis noted many years later, 'It was heavily subsidized, no question. It was the kind of investment that provided an economic base for the growth that happened.'[35]

A South Peel Advisory Committee was established to smooth relations between the province and the municipalities. The municipalities seemed to use the committee as the chance to complain that the province was not paying enough for the facilities it was taking over and that payments were not made on a timely basis, even though the province was giving the municipalities a gift no one wanted to refuse. On cost recovery for new facilities, H.R. Brown, chair of the OWRC, attended a committee meeting in October 1971 to say 'the system is working on a deficit position for a twenty year period.' Brown said that for the province to break even, it would have to increase the price for water from $0.42 to $0.61, and to increase the charge for sewage from $0.25 to $0.36 per 1,000 gallons – about a 50 per cent increase. But facing local pressure, the OWRC couldn't bring itself to be so reasonable: it settled on a price increase of but $0.03, and even at that the municipalities complained, arguing it wasn't fair to levy the $0.03 increase all at one time.[36] The province was a prisoner of suburban growth, and it paid substantial subsidies to encourage it.

Robert Speck, The reeve of Toronto Township, enthused at the time of the announcement that the South Peel Scheme would open 8,000 acres to development.[37] Eph Diamond, president of the Cadillac Fairview Corporation which now owned the

Don Mills Development land assembly, trumpeted the arrangement: Cadillac Fairview had purchased the shares of Don Mills Development Corporation when the South Peel Scheme was announced.[38] The 1969 prospectus for the development stated:

The design of the water and sewage systems for Erin Mills is based on agreements reached last year between the OWRC, the Town of Mississauga and the Town of Streetsville. These provide for the province to construct major trunk facilities for water supply and distribution and sanitary sewage collection and treatment on lands tributary to the Credit River.[39]

The developer was responsible for subtrunk and internal sewers and piping, mimicking the successful arrangement Taylor had proposed in Don Mills. [40]

The South Peel Servicing Scheme was an initiative of OWRC engineers, and was not constrained by planners' talk. The engineers decided to build in extra capacity, on the theory that there was no appreciable extra cost installing a large pipe rather than a small pipe. Apparently they decided to order the largest sewage pipes that could be transported on the highway from the pipe manufacturer in Kitchener: the amount of land that could be serviced by South Peel depended, it seems, more on the capacity of the highway and trucking system than anything else.[41] (See fig. 6.8.)

The existence of the servicing scheme meant unbridled growth. A 1971 status report issued as part of the province's 'Design for Development' allocated a population target of 950,000 to the South Peel Servicing Area, even though only fifteen years earlier its population had been 65,000.[42]

The Northern Fringe

Metro planners predicted in the 1959 Official Plan that the north fringe would grow from 52,000 to 150,000 by 1980.[43] They were very worried about the ramifications this development would have on Metro, which was downstream and therefore the recipient of any degradation in water quality. The plan stated,

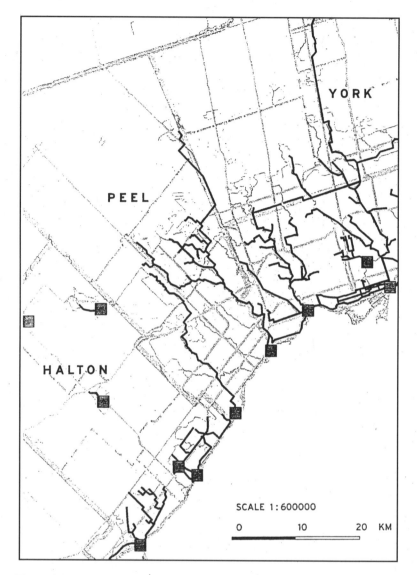

Figure 6.8 South Peel sewage servicing plan, as it existed in 1990. This also
shows sewage systems in the rest of the Greater Toronto Area.
Source: Richard White, *Urban Infrastructure and Urban Growth in the Toronto
Region, 1950s to the 1990s*, figure 14. Used with permission of the Neptis Foundation.

While the basic concept of the plan is that of a broad urban ribbon [hugging Lake Ontario], this is substantially modified by the existing urban development which has generally spread out from the core in the form of a semi-circle. From this compact urban area a 'finger' extends to the north along Yonge Street and will reach up to and merge with the existing 'satellite town' of Richmond Hill. To the northwest and northeast of the semi-circular urban area, the villages of Wood-bridge and of Markham are to develop into small 'satellite' towns of strictly limited size, close to, but not merging with the compact urban area.[44]

But the planners feared those municipalities would not provide good servicing, stating,

However, in these municipalities the state of development and the limitation of their financial recovery make [the] application [of sound planning and servicing] most difficult. As already noted they can be successfully applied only if development is kept to areas not too distant from Lake Ontario ... In areas distant from the Lake, a limited amount of development can be supplied with water from local surface and subsurface sources. In addition, a limited amount of water from the Metro system can be provided to urbanized areas beyond the Metro boundary, if and when required.[45]

The problem was spelled out clearly: 'Storm water, collected by a separate sewer system, will be discharged into the open streams which form the natural drainage system of the area.' Those streams ran into Metro watercourses.

The plan continued cautiously:

A few areas close to the Metro boundary will be served by extensions of the Metro system; notably Malton and Woodbridge in the Humber watershed and some sections of Markham and Vaughan Townships in the Don Watershed. The urbanized area further north along Yonge Street in Markham and Vaughan Townships is to be served by plants to be built by these two municipalities on the East Don River well upstream from the Metro boundary.[46]

In 1959, the OWRC agreed to a package plant on the Don River in the Village of Markham, permitting the population to double to 8,000.[47] To protect itself from what it saw as certain water pollution, Metro attempted to prevent the building of any upstream sewage treatment plant within three-quarters of a mile of Steeles Avenue. In 1961, it decided the easiest course of action was simply to extend its own services across Steeles; that at least seemed to offer some sense of control.[48]

The plan was an intelligent approach for handling the significant growth expected within Metro and its surrounding fringe. It laid out a strong strategy for building infrastructure and its structural components were repeated a decade later in the Toronto-Centred Region Plan. But it found little support outside of Metro. The reaction of the Richmond Hill Council was typical. Council began its commentary on the plan by noting there was considerable interest in the development of land in Richmond Hill, and 'it is possible that the municipality will seek to enlarge its area to accommodate future growth.' It noted that the Metro plan 'contains no mention of any expansion for Richmond Hill' and suggested that the plan be amended with a small addition of two sentences: 'The community of Richmond Hill at the northern end of the central urban area projection will probably assume a greater importance as its size increases. There is no intent in this Plan to restrict the Town to its present boundaries or to inhibit its efforts to improve it financial or assessment position.'[49] Metro planners did not agree to add the sentences to the plan.

It was an age-old problem. Planning is conservative and limiting, while development is energetic, entrepreneurial, and active. Rarely does a plan trump development activity. In the Toronto area, the development faction had the upper hand, which meant the OWRC was seen as the important player, certainly more important than Metro's planners. The OWRC seemed happier to respond to ad hoc pressures for development than to be bound by the confines of a plan. Added pressure for more services came from deteriorating water quality. A study in 1961 showed that the biochemical oxygen demand (BOD) level (which measures the oxygen required to decompose sewage) in the Don River just downstream from the Richmond Hill Sewage Treatment Plant was double the acceptable level. The OWRC concluded that it was 'a heavily polluted stream ... because of inadequately treated sewage treatment plant effluents.'[50] Three years later another study for the OWRC noted the 'low streamflow conditions in this tributary [German Mills Creek] of the Don River which complicates the use of the stream for waste water disposal.'[51] OWRC assisted in improving the treatment plant in Richmond Hill and building a new well for water supply for Richmond Hill and Markham. Indeed it rushed forward with remedial schemes in many of the growing settlements around Toronto.

The South Peel Scheme announced in 1965 led to considerable pressure on the province from York County politicians, who envied similar growth opportunities even though Metro planners had said it should not occur. They too, wanted the province to create a major sewage system in the area north of Toronto. The provincial government asked the OWRC to look at the request.[52] The OWRC study in 1965 concluded that there was no sewage capacity left in the upper reaches of the Humber and Don Rivers, or Highland Creek, and that a direct connection to Lake Ontario should serve the area north of Metro. It recommended that York County should have its own sewage system feeding into Lake Ontario, skirting the boundaries of Metro Toronto by piping through Pickering, to the east. The report also concluded that groundwater was not available in sufficient quantities to service water needs north of Metro, and it recommended that Metro's water system be extended northward. A study by Gore & Storrie for OWRC noted that this unusual sewage project would be expensive, but it was feasible, and in 1969 OWRC decided to proceed, indicating that the Pickering area east of Toronto could also be served by the treatment plant. It was known in its early days as the South-Central York Servicing Scheme.

Metro planners had been careful to say that only 'limited' development should occur here, and their 1959 plan had not proposed extensive development. OWRC took no note of these ideas: it barged ahead, another example of the provincial government acting on the basis of development pressure rather than on the basis of a land-use plan.

In May1970, after decisions had already been made on the South Peel and South-Central York Servicing Schemes, the provincial government released the Toronto-Centred Region Plan, which was its attempt to control development in the coming decades. A key intention of the plan was to ensure that development was related as much as possible to Lake Ontario both for ease of servicing and for ease of moving people and goods. The plan set a growth boundary to the north of Metro at the edge of Richmond Hill, beyond which land would be used for agricultural, not urban, purposes. This plan was unable to withstand the pressures already created by the OWRC. In 1971, a status report on the Toronto-Centred Region Plan was released by the ministry. It confirmed OWRC's position to encourage development in places that the plan had tried to discourage. It allocated a population of 400,000 to the Central York Area, stating: 'On the basis of these population allocations the OWRC has been instructed to explore the possibilities and costs of a major servicing scheme in the Central York Area.'[53] (See fig. 6.9.)

OWRC was, as one source noted, 'a world-ranking repository of expertise in water engineering, microbiology and public health,' but in spite of its activities it was also seen as being 'arrogant and unresponsive to local development planning.'[54] Many developers felt that it represented too much of a centralized planning approach, and in 1972, the OWRC staff and functions were relocated to the newly formed Ministry of the Environment. Water and sewage then became two of a long roster of functions given to the new ministry. At the same time, servicing growth in Toronto was seen as an important government initiative rather than simply as a program delivered by Queen's Park. This lofty status was reflected in a 1974 report from the Ministry of Environment:

These projects can no longer be considered as the proposals of a single Ministry of the government but rather as major provincial undertakings which will in fact materially reduce major sources of pollution from urban water-courses, direct growth and development as intended

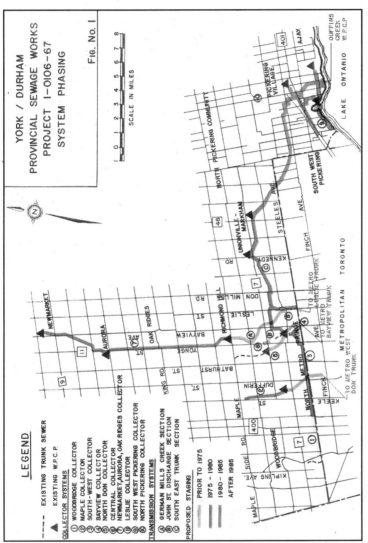

Figure 6.9 Phasing plan for the Central York/Pickering Sewerage Works, 1974.
Source: Province of Ontario, Ministry of the Environment, *York Durham Water and Sewage Service Systems.*

in the TCR Concept both north and east of Metro Toronto, materially reduce the pressures for serviced land for housing, permit the servicing of the North Pickering Development complex, east of Metro Toronto [an airport and a city of 200,000 had just been announced] and finally, as originally intended resolve the difficult servicing problems in the Central York Area.[55]

As recommended, this Central York Sewage Treatment plant project would remove nine existing plants, six on water courses flowing through Metro, which had been a continual source of concern.

The ministry retained James MacLaren to flesh out the details of the Central York Servicing Scheme. His May 1973 report documented the substantial development that would quickly occur throughout the hinterlands north of Metro.[56] The population of the combined Towns of Newmarket and Aurora was estimated to be about 29,000 in 1970, but MacLaren expected it would grow to 50,000 within thirty years – or as the recently created Region of York then optimistically said, 75,000. Richmond Hill was projected to grow from 28,000 to 67,000, but York Region saw the upper limit as 105,000. Markham and Unionville estimated increases from 10,000 to 21,000, but York Region's estimate was 63,000. The remaining area, known as the North Metro fringe (which included Vaughan and Thornhill), was projected to grow from 16,000 to 95,000 – or, in York Region's more optimistic estimate, to 136,000. In each case, York Region expected unbridled growth.

MacLaren concluded that 'the ultimate population' – that is, the total build-out population to be served in York Region – was somewhere between 263,000 and 416,000. By way of contrast, the 1959 Metro Plan had proposed a population in the north fringe of no more than 150,000. In 1971 the TCR Plan allocated 250,000 for an urban population for York Region, yet by 1973 that had been increased to 416,000, and in 1976 to 457,000 with another 100,000 in rural areas.[57] (In 2005 York Region's population was more than 900,000.)

MacLaren proposed that the province proceed with the major sewage treatment plant to be built east of Metro Toronto at

Duffin Creek. As an interregional servicing scheme, MacLaren thought it appropriate that the Ministry of the Environment rather than local governments undertake it, and the hope was that the Duffin Creek plant would be in operation by 1977. The scheme would relieve the overloaded package plants in the small communities north of Toronto, and permit them to grow. MacLaren recommended a sewer down Yonge Street following the course of the Don River, until just north of the Metro boundary at Steeles Avenue where an interceptor pipe coming from the west would head east beyond Metro's easterly boundary and then south to the Duffin Creek plant on Lake Ontario. The sewer would have a 24-inch width at Aurora, expanding to 36 inches by the time it had run south to Richmond Hill, becoming 48 inches at the boundary of the Town of Markham. It then became a 78-inch interceptor sewer running east through Unionville, continuing into Pickering, and then south to Duffin Creek. This was the underlying idea of the 'Big Pipe' in the York Durham Servicing Scheme. (See fig. 6.10.)

Two other alternatives to the Big Pipe were possible. One was to expand Metro's capacity to handle the demand for sewage and water to the north, but that was rejected as not feasible within reasonable financial constraints. The other – to restrict development in York Region by intensifying development and densities within Metro – was not explored.

In 1972, the ministry signed an agreement with Metro and the newly created York Region that allowed Metro to temporarily treat sewage for 10,000 people in the area immediately north of Steeles Avenue in Woodbridge and in south Thornhill.[58] In late 1974 it contracted Metro Toronto to supply water to Vaughan, Richmond Hill, and Markham. Also that year, the ministry signed an agreement with York and Durham Regions to close the eight package plants in York and to construct the Big Pipe to funnel sewage to the new Duffin Creek plant. So began construction of the Big Pipe in earnest. Like the South Peel scheme, this servicing arrangement was provided by the province at a discount, and York Region received heavy subsidies. One author states user fees paid for $69 million of the total cost of $297 million (23 per cent), but that estimate is not docu-

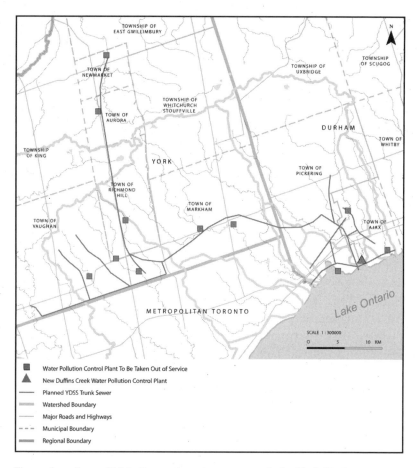

Figure 6.10 James F. MacLaren Associates proposals for York Durham sewage system, 1973.
Source: James F. McLaren Associates report to Ministry of Environment, 1973. Reprinted from Richard White, *Urban Infrastructure and Urban Growth in the Toronto Region, 1950s to the 1990s,* figure 12. Used with permission of the Neptis Foundation.

mented,[59] and independent documentation is not available. It's fair to say that users probably paid less than half the cost.

There was one constraint to the Central York scheme – the provincial planners. In South Peel the OWRC engineers had a free hand, but the OWRC had been disbanded before Central

York was underway, and development in Central York was hampered by the population forecasts of planners who wished to limit servicing to ensure their forecasts were met. Planners pushed hard to limit pipe size, and were successful enough to create a complicated decision-making process about how servicing would be allocated among competing demands in the region. As it has turned out, the planners' constraints have had little impact, and as the Central York Servicing Scheme was built, supply apparently kept up with demand over the following decades.[60] However, unlike the impact of the South Peel scheme, which seemed to allow unlimited development, Central York's Big Pipe Scheme, raised questions of shortages, and there was always an issue of who would be awarded an allocation of services. This often pitted developers against each other as they vied for whatever capacity remained in the Big Pipe. They worked out elaborate schemes to show that there was always extra capacity to accommodate extra development. Further, the existence of nearby services always led to ideas of more development in York Region. Various schemes were created by local politicians to show how surrounding lands that had previously been thought unserviceable because of their distance from the Big Pipe could now be served. For example, in King Township, politicians set out to show that because of failed septics water quality was a problem that could only be rectified by piped services and entry of the Big Pipe into the township. Once politicians successfully made the argument about poor water quality – even though the evidence was spurious, and perhaps cooked – the township was in a perfect position to decide that land should be opened for suburban development.[61] The function of the Big Pipe was to provide the impetus to replace farm land and other rural uses with suburban subdivisions.

Thus, York Region looked for other ways to increase capacity. While claiming that its water supply from the Big Pipe and aquifers was significant enough to meet all needs, it decided in 1994 that it should look for more water. A study with the private company Consumers Utilities was undertaken in 1997 to find it. Although the 1994 York Region Official Plan stated that its policy was to ensure that water and sewage for major urbanized areas 'was Great Lakes based,'[62] the study concluded that new supplies of water should come from Lake Simcoe,[63] which was not one of the Great Lakes.

The Big Pipe did not respected watersheds. The height of the land between Lake Ontario and Lake Simcoe is located just south of Aurora. This would imply that water should not be shipped across this height of land, since it would substantially interfere with natural watersheds. But the Big Pipe has fed Lake Ontario water as far north as Newmarket and has taken sewage from the same place. In 2003, a senior staff person in York Region's Works Department stated what he thought about this interference with the watershed. He first said that the department saw no problem, then added 'You must realize that it is all the same water. The water in Lake Simcoe connects through Georgian Bay, Lake Huron and Lake Erie, with the water in Lake Ontario, anyway.'[64] He was expressing a novel interpretation of the motto 'Everything is connected to everything else,' perhaps adding the coda 'Don't worry, be happy.'

Development in York Region has come a long way from the suggestion by Metro planners in the 1959 Official Plan that services to Central York should be very limited. Instead, development has occurred with almost no regard to that plan, and the water and sewage services provided by the province have proved to be the factor determining growth in the area (see fig. 6.11).

The Eastern Fringe

Projections in the 1959 Official Plan for the east fringe were modest compared to those for the west and the north: the population would triple from 25,000 in 1959 to 85,000 in 1980. The community of Ajax, situated on Lake Ontario, had been used for training and for the imprisonment of German soldiers during the Second World War. During this period, a small sewage treatment plant had been built, which is probably why it became the location for a new style of suburban development in 1951.[65] The Town of Pickering, just to the west of Ajax, also had a small package plant. The 1959 Official Plan saw most of the growth occurring in and between these communities and con-

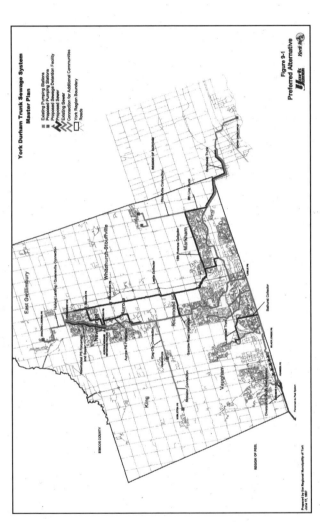

Figure 6.11 York Durham Trunk Sewer System, Final Master Plan Document Preferred Alternative, figure 9-1, 1997. This preferred alternative was proposed in the Class Environmental Assessment prepared for the Region of York by Proctor and Redfern Limited and MacViro Consultants Inc. It shows the existing and recommended sewer system for York and the limits of built form in the region as of 1997. The existing sewers are in grey. Proposed sewers are Leslie Street Connector (the main north-south line to the east); 16th Avenue collector; Gamble Road Interceptor; Aurora PS Forcemain; Newmarket PS Forcemain; Holland Landing/Queensville Connection; Nobleton and King City Connection; Stouffville Connection; Langstaff Trunk; 9th Line Trunk and South East Trunk. York Region Council decided not to proceed with the sewer between Nobleton and King City, but instead to provide Nobleton with an independent facility.
Source: Department of Works, Region of York, Final Master Plan Document, 1997.

cluded that 'Ajax-Pickering may also be regarded as a fairly large satellite town'[66] to Metro. With the development of Ajax, demand for services increased, and in 1959 the OWRC agreed to enlarge the sewage plant on Duffins Creek serving Ajax. By 1973, demand seemed to be increasing, and the MacLaren report on the Central York Scheme predicted strong growth for Pickering. One factor may have been the decision of the provincial government to encourage growth to the east, particularly through the proposed North Pickering Airport and its related community of 200,000 residents.

The fact that growth east of Metro was sluggish compared to the activity to the west and north meant little: the decision to proceed with the Central York scheme provided more than adequate capacity for the eastern fringe, given that is where sewage and water services would be located for the northern fringe. The east was encouraged to grow mainly because there was demand for growth in the north.

Development Charges and Services

Municipalities might have found that they had to bear no direct financial responsibility for building and operating these large systems because of provincial willingness to fund them, but they did have to worry about local pipage and other parts of the infrastructure. It was only natural that they looked for others to pay these costs. As developer of Don Mills, E.P. Taylor realized in 1951 that the Township of North York would be concerned about the financial implications of sewage and water improvements necessary for this development, which is why he guaranteed funds for the sewage treatment plant, as well as covering the costs for the trunk lines needed for transporting water.[67] He also paid to install local pipes, which quickly became standard practice. After Taylor's successful gambit, municipalities realized developers could be tapped for money, and levying charges on developers for the costs of servicing incurred by their proposals became common practice.[68] Reeve Oliver Crockford of the Township of Scarborough took the lead in the early 1950s and imposed a levy of $3 per foot frontage on each lot to help

pay for the package plant on Massey Creek. Other Metro municipalities quickly followed, which meant the heavy infrastructure
– the trunk lines and the plants – was paid for by taxpayers and
the new local infrastructure was paid for by developers. By the
late 1950s, Metro had worked out a servicing levy of $100 per
housing unit. The townships around Toronto adopted similar
policies to cover the local costs of their infrastructures.

By the end of the 1950s, the average levy on developers by
municipalities in the Toronto area was about $400 per lot, and
in general this money was used to cover capital costs for sewage,
water, and roads. The provincial government provided the legal basis for the charge by an amendment to the *Planning Act* in
1961, and it restricted the levies to be used for water, sewage,
and roads. The legislation seemed to encourage municipalities,
and the amount of levies in the fast-growing suburbs quickly
climbed as municipalities realized the easy opportunity of getting what was basically free revenue. In the 1970s the levy was
$1,000 or more per lot, and in 1985 it averaged $3,500 a lot, although one municipality had a levy of $7,500 in 1985 and anoth-
er had a levy of $8,800 in 1988. In the fringes, municipalities
generally found that development approvals had a lot to do
with municipal revenues, and nothing to do with costs.

In the 1990s the provincial government again intervened,
this time on behalf of developers. Legislation was passed that
required municipalities to do a study that would relate infrastructure costs to development so that the levies would reflect
municipal needs rather than political dreams. Levies were
somewhat moderated for the development industry. Some municipalities prized themselves on low taxes because of high development levies, but when development opportunities came
to an end in the late 1990s, as they did in Mississauga, residents quickly learned they had been living in a protected
development levy bubble when property taxes increased enormously.

By the mid-1970s, it was possible to draw three conclusions.
First, the province had assumed the role of chief supplier of
sewage and water services in the developing areas surrounding

Metro Toronto. Functions of servicing had previously been seen as a responsibility of local government, as indeed was the case in Metro Toronto, but in the fringes, the province assumed this role.

Second, the province took a comprehensive approach to ensure that water quality would not suffer. This was a noble objective, but it had unintended consequences since the land-use planning mechanisms were divorced from the servicing mechanisms. Provincial attempts at planning comprehensively failed miserably. The Toronto-Centred Region Plan, which bore so many similarities to Metro's 1959 Official Plan, had proposed very limited development for the Region of York, but that was set aside in favour of a muddled series of decisions responding favourably to development pressures. After worldwide oil prices almost doubled in 1973, the province found itself in a financial crunch. The lack of ready cash considerably weakened the province's planning backbone since it did not wish to constrain growth, the one thing that it saw would bring in more money. The new era was bereft of any vision of compact urban form or land-use structure in the mid to long term. Almost any kind of development was permitted over the next thirty years. Since comprehensive servicing was in place, development occurred wherever developers pushed for approvals, and in a form that was devoid of simple concepts like efficiency, sustainability, cost-effectiveness, or urbanity – concepts which had been the staple of government announcements for a decade. The Big Pipes were open to any developer.

Third, the province was the chief funder of water and sewage services for suburban development in the fringes beyond Metro. It took responsibility for financing and constructing sewage treatment and water purification plants and the trunk sewers necessary to distribute these services to their catchment areas. This did not mean that the province alone paid for all of the hundreds of millions of dollars needed over the next three decades. Substantial revenues were collected annually from benefiting municipalities in the form of water and sewage charges paid by homeowners, but those revenues were not equal to the capital and operating costs paid by the province, as we have already seen with the South Peel scheme. It remains unclear exactly how great the subsidy absorbed by the province actually was – perhaps one-third of the total cost, which would represent well over $500 million – perhaps more.

By assuming financial responsibility, the province freed municipalities from having to worry about whether the development they were approving could sustain the cost of the infrastructure. One has the sense that this was never a concern for the municipalities involved – they assumed that whatever they approved would find water and sewage services, and if it didn't, the development industry would influence provincial decision-makers enough to expand services.

In contrast, Metro Toronto planned and financed its own water and sewage services. It was responsible for creating a planning and financial framework in which decisions were made. There was no division between the development decision-maker and the servicing decision-maker. It appears that the subsidies available to the provincially sponsored projects were not available within Metro, although a detailed financial comparison has never been undertaken. Metro received the 15 per cent subsidy from the federal Municipal Infrastructure Program, which continued until 1978, but it did not benefit from the write-down by the province of the water and sewage infrastructure provided in the fringe.

Thus, in the fringe, there was a disconnect between land-use decisions and servicing decisions, just as there was a disconnect between the cost of infrastructure in the fringe and the incomes necessary to support it. One suspects that without heavy provincial subsidies for this infrastructure, suburban growth in the fringe could not have occurred at this pace or in this form – even by 2001 the densities of the fringe areas abutting the former Metro were less than half those of the suburban areas within the former Metro.[69] Low-density suburban development, the very development form which the provincial officials had railed so strongly against in the 1960s, was subsidized by the province.

7

Reshaping
Governance
in the
Fringes

While it was obvious to most observers that the local government structure in the fringes was not capable of planning for and controlling growth, the provincial government proceeded slowly in making changes. Services preceded structures, and local politicians resented what they saw as provincial intrusion about the shape of their governments. Again, the good lessons from the Metro structure seemed not to have been learned, and even though attractive alternatives were advanced for reforming local government, the province decided simply to paste two-tiered structures over different areas in the fringes. This did not result in local happiness nor in good local government.

The formative event in the restructuring of local government in Canada in the 1950s was the creation of the two-tiered metropolitan government for Toronto in 1953, as recounted in chapter 2. The new Metro had the financial capacity to borrow large sums to build the needed infrastructure for growth, the staff expertise needed to make sophisticated decisions, and reasonably adept political leadership. But the areas outside of Metro, such as Toronto Township which was growing explosively, had none of these attributes. That was one reason why the province decided it had to provide sewage and water services.

The success of Metro in its first decade sparked much interest in restructuring other local governments in Ontario. The existing municipal structure of townships at the local level, and the way the townships were melded together in a council at the county level, was seen to be inflexible and moribund. It may have been an appropriate structure to cope with the issues facing sleepy rural communities, but it was not geared to deal with the dynamics of growth or with the complexities of urban governance. In 1961 the Ontario Municipal Association, the body representing local governments in the province, recommended restructuring at the county level in order to improve both access and services. This interest in restructuring was also reflected in the Legislative Assembly with the creation of the Select Committee on the Municipal Act, chaired by Hollis E. Beckett. Beckett, of the governing Progressive Conservative Party, had served as the elected member from the Borough of East York since 1951.

'The need for larger units of local government,' read the Beckett committee report, 'is most pressing in dealing with regional problems and boundary adjustments of urban municipalities.'[1] The committee thought that larger units of local government provided opportunities for better coordination; more qualified and specialized staff; financial strength; less competition between small municipalities for assessment; and more equality in taxation. The section of the report dealing with these matters was headed 'Local and Regional Government,' leaving little question that what it was asking was that the two-tiered regional government established in Metro be more broadly embraced. Further, since a stronger structure was necessary to provide good government for growing communities, the choice in any urban locale was either for the province to establish regional government or step in with a special purpose agency or board. The preference was for local decision-making: 'In order to restore responsibility to the elected representatives and increase the possibility of economical and efficient administration of municipal services, larger units of government are necessary in the province today.'[2] In addition, 'as a practical start the committee recommends the adoption of the county, in whole or in part, as the basic unit of regional government.'[3] Proposals were also included to allocate powers between the regional and local governments on a basis to similar to that practised in Metro Toronto.

In 1965, Carl Goldenberg submitted his report as chair of the Royal Commission on Metropolitan Toronto. Metro Toronto seemed to be working well and Goldenberg proposed a relatively minor change, reducing the number of local governments in the federation from thirteen to four, although, following discussion with local officials, a compromise was reached to settle for six local governments, a structure which remained successfully in place for over thirty years. But the real problem was outside Metro where Goldenberg realized the need for better planning and servicing capacity, particularly to the west. 'If more extensive urbanization is contemplated, with the consequent need for a wide extension of Metro services,' he wrote, 'incorporation in some form with Metro will have to receive serious consideration.'[4] But he dismissed the idea of Metro expanding at that time, instead proposing three regional governments around Metro to the west, north, and east.[5]

In 1967, the provincial Smith Committee on Taxation issued its three-volume report. While the issue of local government seemed removed from tax policy, the committee's review of property tax, the main independent revenue source of municipalities, encouraged it look at municipal reorganization, to which it devoted a long and fulsome chapter. It began, 'A pressing cause of local reorganization throughout the post-war world has been the dramatic shift of a growing population to urban and metropolitan centres. Ontario has proved no exception ...'[6] Noting that studies for regional government in several communities were underway, it continued: 'Whether or not a result of the Toronto experiment, it is becoming increasingly apparent that the spread of regional government to other parts of Ontario is a matter of considerably more than academic interest.'[7] The committee recommended that southern Ontario be divided into twenty-two municipal regions, six of which covered the largest urban areas in the province – Hamilton, Kitchener/Waterloo, Guelph, London, Windsor, and Ottawa.[8] (See fig. 7.1.) It concluded, 'Through the medium of a rationalized regional government system, we believe we offer a dynamic opportunity for the material enhancement of local autonomy throughout Ontario. We look to provincial action that will augment, not curtail, local initiative.'[9]

A special legislative committee chaired by MLA John White considered the Smith Committee recommendations, and it came to an all-party agreement in late 1968 in favour of the regional government model. That year a general government policy was adopted 'of modernizing the structure of municipal government throughout Ontario in an effort to return more responsibility to local government. An integral part of this reform program is the establishment – on a phased basis – of regional government.'[10] A year later the Ontario Economic Council argued that regional government in fact provided a defence to local autonomy. The council indicated its concern regarding 'the gradual shift towards the centralization of political power to the

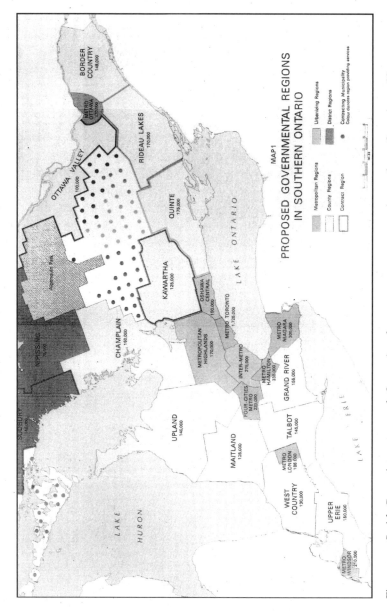

Figure 7.1 Smith Committee proposals for regional government structures in southern Ontario, 1968.
Source: Ontario Committee on Taxation, *Report*, vol. 2.

provincial level which indicates that local autonomy is no longer an operative principle of political organization in Ontario.'[11]

The expectation was that regional government could do two
things at once. It could provide more effective local government through regionalized property tax assessment and financial expertise, and at the same time it could provide more local
autonomy. This duality seems to have been at the heart of
Metro's success, and many wished to replicate it, even if by for-
mula rather than adapting the ideas to local circumstances.
Thus the mayor of Port Arthur, a city located on Lake Superior,
pushed hard in the mid-1960s to bring together the five large
municipalities in the Lakehead to become a single regional government. In September 1965, the Minister of Municipal Affairs
appointed Eric Hardy to study local government options in the
Lakehead, and his recommendations resulted in 1969 legislation that created the regional government of Thunder Bay.
Studies were underway in 1968 for regional government structures in Hamilton-Burlington, the Waterloo area, Sudbury, and
Oshawa. Regional government was introduced in Ottawa–Carl-
ton effective 1 January 1969, and in Niagara on 1 January 1970.

But the development pressures around Toronto didn't make
things easy for the provincial politicians and their staff. Local
politicians vied for the power and fame they expected new development would bring, and the fancy theories of structural reform often were subverted. The Metro fringes had their own
peculiarities.

The Western Fringe

The area west of Metro faced enormous growth pressures. In-
dicative of the scope of the problem was the fact that in 1966 fifty subdivision applications for Toronto Township alone were
submitted to the Toronto Planning Board – almost one a week.
Here, the local government structure was fractured among Toronto Township, which covered the southern half of Peel County, and the small, feisty and cohesive Towns of Port Credit,
Streetsville, Clarkson, and Cooksville. Under the leadership of
Reeve Robert Speck, Toronto Township considered asking for

city status in 1963, but by one vote township council rejected
the idea.[12] The preliminary work of the Royal Commission on
Metropolitan Toronto led some to think that perhaps the commission would propose that Toronto Township be swallowed by
Metro. The townships council stated firmly it had no wish to be
so consumed and indeed Goldenberg rejected that kind of approach.[13] But, as already noted, Goldenberg did worry about
the lack of serious land-use planning or servicing in the western
fringe, and suggested extending Metro's planning powers to
cover an even larger area:

Considering the potential impact of further development in Brampton and Chinguacousy Township [the reference is to the Bramalea
proposal, then beyond Metro's planning jurisdiction], which would
require the extension of water and sewage services from Lake Ontario
through Toronto Township, I am of the opinion that, in the absence
of other regional planning machinery, the area covered by Brampton
and its vicinity should be included in the Metro Planning Area.[14]

He generally recommended regional governments for the
fringes, but these areas were only peripheral to his main
interest, which was Metro Toronto itself. His proposal was not
adopted.

The Towns of Port Credit and Streetsville proposed amalgamation with Toronto Township. Thinking this was a viable
possibility, the treasurer of Toronto Township, M.D. Hender-
son, prepared a consolidated budget to show what the financial
picture might look like in an amalgamated world. But Reeve
Speck was anxious for the power that came with a separate status, and he rejected this advance. He had originally supported
amalgamation as 'some protection of us being swallowed by
Metro Toronto,' but when that threat passed, he pursued other
avenues.[15]

That same year, 1965, the provincial government appointed
Thomas J. Plunkett to review local government in Peel and Halton Counties. Plunkett was then acting as a consultant in Montreal (he later became an eminent academic in municipal
politics at Queen's University). He noted, as a start, that while

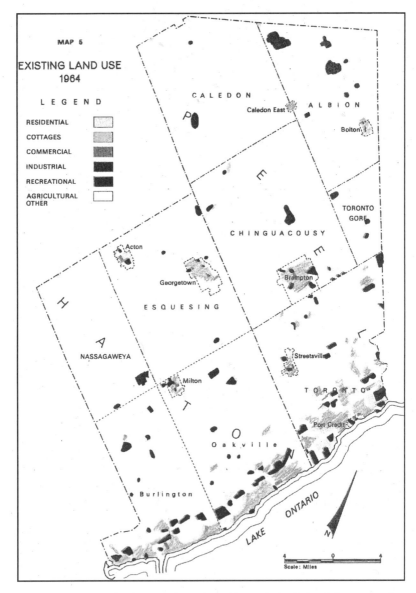

Figure 7.2 Existing land use and municipal boundaries in Peel County, 1964.
Note how limited development is – most of the land in the southern
townships remains rural in use.
Source: Thomas J. Plunkett, *Peel-Halton Local Government Review*, Appendix B.

the population of Peel County was 47,600 in 1951, it had grown to 141,000 in 1964, and was expected to be 362,000 in 1980. (Peel's population in 2000 exceeded one million.) Nor was Halton County to the west a laggard – it had grown from 41,700 in 1951 to 76,000 in 1964, and was expected to be 217,000 in 1980. (In 2000, Halton was home to almost half a million.) Plunkett noted there were ten local municipalities in Peel County and seven in Halton, and came to a blunt conclusion: 'The existing infrastructure does not reflect either the character or pattern of development and the boundaries of municipal units in most instances no longer serve any meaningful purpose.'[16] (See fig. 7.2.) He reviewed the options for change: revamp the tired county structure; create a two-tiered metropolitan structure; provide one government for the whole area. He opted for a fourth model, consolidation, arguing it would eliminate competition between municipalities for industrial assessment and would ensure 'reasonable local capacity to provide services.'[17] But one twist was Plunkett's criterion for structural reform, namely, 'recognize the development pattern and character of the area and establish boundaries coterminous with effective planning areas.'[18] This criterion meant that the governance structure would relate to development expectations, which added an entirely new dimension to structural proposals.

His proposal was to create two new governments: one, to the south along the lake would be the Urban County of Mississauga; the other, to the north, would be the Rural County of Peel-Halton (see fig. 7.3). (Plunkett had not bought into the fashionable language of 'regional government,' continuing with the more traditional 'county.') Brampton, which was located on the dividing line, would be included at the northern edge of the urban government area for obvious reasons. The Town of Milton – even then ambitious for growth although located far to the north of water and sewage services – would be in the rural area. Although Plunkett called these units 'counties,' reflecting the Beckett committee's idea of building on what was in place, they were single-tier governments, and all existing local governments would be destroyed. The merit of the Plunkett scheme was that it defined with great clarity the function of each new county government – one was to be urban, the other rural. Such clarity in linking form with function is unusual in local government, and one can only imagine what would have happened if this idea alone had been adopted. That some form of local decision-making, such as the federated model of Metro Toronto, could not be retained, proved a major flaw. As well, Plunkett had been unable to respond to the rapacious development appetite that had been unleashed with the expectations of the South Peel servicing scheme. All local leaders expected development as a natural future.

Ambitious local politicians, who sensed wealth and fame if their particular communities grew with them at the helm, attacked Plunkett as 'the Montreal planning consultant' and sniffed that while the southern 'urban super-county' would grow to a population of more than a quarter million, the 'rural super-county' would be home to a paltry 15,000 residents. 'For one hundred years Peel has been growing into the county it is today,' a 1967 centennial publication boasted. 'Will it disappear in the next two or three years to be only a part of two super-counties?'[19] Even the Minister of Municipal Affairs was forced to reject Plunkett's advice, saying, 'He isn't Moses leading the Israelites, and he isn't God.'[20]

Hazel McCallion, then a rising star in the Town of Streetsville, which wished to welcome the development of Erin Mills on its borders, said she never had any problem with the Plunkett proposals. In fact, she considered them relatively well thought out, but noted 'the strong pressure came from Bill Davis.'[21] Bill Davis had been elected in 1959 as the Member of the Legislative Assembly for Peel and made no bones about how he wished to stand up for Brampton. Plunkett's proposals left Brampton contained by a new rural regional government to the west, the north, and the east, effectively preventing its growth in those directions. Further, Brampton was relegated by Plunkett to the edge of things rather than to the centre.

But that was only part of the problem. Davis admitted forty years later that the boundary between the urban and rural municipalities proposed by Plunkett could easily have been pushed farther north. He said the significant problem was that Plunkett

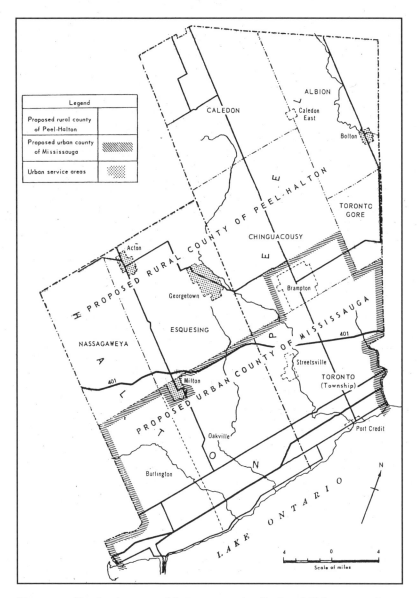

Figure 7.3 Plunkett's proposal for restructuring Peel and Halton counties: an urban municipality to the south and a rural municipality to the north, a precursor to the Toronto-Centred Region Plan still four years away.
Source: Thomas J. Plunkett, *Peel-Halton Local Government Review*, Appendix B.

tried to redesign the boundaries to run east–west rather than the historical axis of north–south.[22] Even more significant was the destruction of the existing seventeen municipalities, which represented the loss of power bases for so many local politicians.

Local politicians in Peel County tried to sort out their differences by creating a Regional Government Review Committee, which first met in July 1966.[23] After some discussion, there was a tentative agreement that the number of local municipalities in Peel County could be shrunk from ten to five. Reeve Speck carried a motion through committee to that effect, as well as an agreement to expand the functions of the regional upper tier, once established, beyond those assigned to the county. Speck also pushed to improve the status of Toronto Township itself so it could become a town, since the application for city status had not fared well. Town status was finally granted by the Ontario Municipal Board in March 1967.

Speck needed a name for the municipality with a new town status, clearly not wanting to be known as Toronto Town. He asked voters to choose between Sheridan and Mississauga. The former came from the name of the former village given prominence by the provincial decision in the early 1960s to establish the Sheridan Research Park on the QEW in hopes it would parallel the Massachusetts Institute of Technology outside Boston. The latter came from the name of the First Nations band that had once controlled the area. Voters chose Mississauga in late 1967, and the Town of Mississauga was born on 1 January 1968, with a population of 100,000.

In an attempt to forge some agreement about future structures, Halton County politicians were asked to join with their Peel counterparts. A committee was struck, and it reviewed the newly adopted regional city legislation in Winnipeg as well as the Metro Toronto model, which was strongly favoured. The committee retained Metro's former clerk, William Guardhouse, to help draft a legislative proposal. The committee voted on a proposal that any legislation should contain a provision that no local municipality should have more than 49 per cent of the votes on regional council, but that failed. This, apparently, was the device Bill Davis intended to use to protect Brampton from being outvoted by Mississauga. (Whether any one municipality could have a majority of votes on regional council was still an issue in Peel forty years later.)

In 1968, Streetsville, a growing community of 12,000 residents, undertook what it called a 'Boundary Study,' recommending that the town's boundaries should expand to the north, south, and west to incorporate the proposed Erin Mills.[24] The proposal found little support with Bill Davis who was manoeuvring in the background. Local politicians met in October 1968 with Darcy McKeough, Minister of Municipal Affairs, in the presence of Davis. McKeough promised to present a proposal for regional government in January 1969, which he did: he proposed combining Peel and Halton Counties into one regional government and shrinking the number of local governments from seventeen to seven. This met instant opposition, and a submission by County Council to the government claimed it was 'rejected mainly due to the concern of the vastness of the proposed region and the danger of it being too large to govern without being "remote from the electorate."'[25] A brief from Hamilton's Board of the Canadian Institute of Management argued that the 'one region' proposal made sense, and that the Peel-Halton area, with a population of 370,000 in 780 square miles was much the same as the newly created Niagara Region with 340,000 residents in 720 square miles.[26]

McKeough's proposal was quickly abandoned. Hazel McCallion, who had just been elected mayor of Streetsville, obtained the support of Streetsville Council to annex 10,000 adjacent acres – 7,000 acres from Mississauga and 3,000 from Oakville – to give new life to the 'Boundary Study' proposals (see fig. 7.4). Mississauga responded by applying to annex Streetsville. Lou Parsons, first elected to be a member of Mississauga Council and then, in 1972, to be warden of Peel County, led negotiations to find regional proposals that the province could move ahead with. McCallion responded by proposing to annex even more land. Parsons, an ally of Davis, proposed a Peel region with three local municipalities. McCallion and Streetsville Council fought the proposal on the basis that there was no

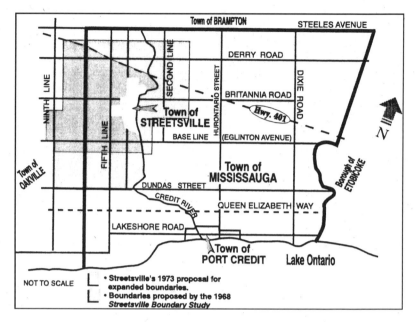

Figure 7.4 Plans for expanding the boundaries of Streetsville. The proposed
1968 expansion to the west is darkly shaded; the 1973 proposal to expand to
the north and east is lightly shaded.
Source: Thomas Urbaniak, *Farewell, Town of Streetsville*, 108.

good reason to include Caledon, a rural area, in the new government. She thought Streetsville should not be swallowed by
Mississauga, but should continue to have its own local government which could be suitably enlarged.

The provincial treasurer, Charles MacNaughton, waded in
with a speech in December 1972: 'Would our forefathers expect
us to continue their system after all the changes we have experienced?' he asked rhetorically. 'Can we expect our children to
live under a system that was not designed to cope with these
problems?'[27] He continued,

In an area that is growing as fast as Southern Ontario, we must
broaden our planning programs to provide service more economically and to preserve our good farm land and attractive green space.

We must stop the wasteful and costly process of continuous urban sprawl ... By giving an area-wide government the responsibility for major services, and for selecting strategic development sites, the overall costs can be reduced through economies in the use of the area's financial and land resources.[28]

These were the old arguments trotted out once again – large-scale regional government will save us from sprawl, protect natural features, and protect farm land. But the function of the regional model seemed to be to create a government structure large enough to approve more suburban development.

John White, now provincial treasurer, announced in May 1973 that legislation would be soon introduced to create regional governments in both Peel and Halton. In Peel the proposal was to have the three local municipalities that Lou Parsons, and most certainly Bill Davis, had advocated: one south of Steeles Avenue, combining both Mississauga and Streetsville, with a 1971 population of 175,000; a central area, including Brampton and Bramalea, with a population of 72,000; and a northern area (Caledon), with a population of 17,500 (see fig. 7.5).[29] The Halton regional government would have four local governments, including Oakville, Burlington, Milton, and Halton Hills. The legislation came into effect on 1 January 1974, and those structures remain in place today.

The Northern Fringe

The situation to the north of Metro was as complicated as it was to the west. The problem was noted by Carl Goldenberg in his study of Metro government. He found that Richmond Hill submitted a brief (as did Pickering to the east) arguing that it was entitled to financial assistance from Metro to meet the costs of serving as a dormitory municipality.[30] That a dormitory community needed compensation from the city was a wild claim since suburbs generally sponged off the central city, and Goldenberg rejected the claim. He hinted at the possibility of Metro annexing Vaughan and Markham to ensure that services were in place there, but backed away from this idea and instead proposed a

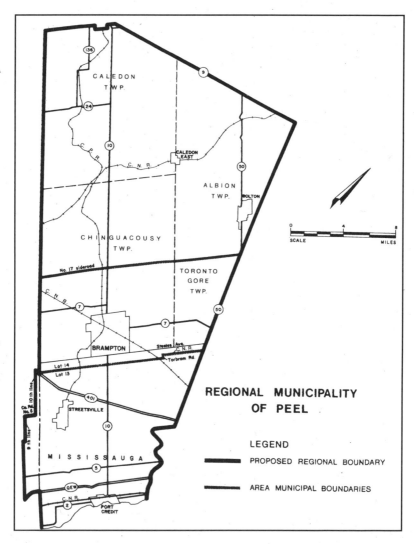

Figure 7.5 Provincial proposal for restructuring Peel County into a regional government with three local governments, as set out in legislation enacted in 1974.
Source: Ministry of Treasury, Economics, and Intergovernmental Affairs, 'Proposal for Local Government Reform in the Area West of Metropolitan Toronto,' January 1973, 16. Available at the Urban Affairs Library (352.07135 05637.2).

regional government for the north and a servicing scheme very much like the York-Durham Servicing plan.

Since at least 1966 there had been an informal committee of municipalities in York County called the 'Southern Six,' consisting of the Townships of Vaughan and Markham, the Towns of Richmond Hill and Markham, and the Villages of Woodbridge and Stouffville (see fig. 7.6). These were the municipalities closest to Metro, and the most likely to face very strong development pressures. They had combined their efforts in 1966 to try to convince the OWRC to investigate joint water and sewage possibilities without success.[31] (It came four years later.) The Smith Committee report in 1967 proposed transmogrifying York County and areas to the west into the Metro Highlands regional government. (See fig. 7.1.) In February 1968, York County Council created a committee of senior staff to review the Smith recommendations. This staff committee generally supported the Smith proposals, as long as the boundaries of the region could be coterminus with York County so that the county itself became a regional government. Staff thought this was important 'to minimize the disruption of rapid growth and economic development.' The committee's vision for York Region was, in hindsight if not apparent at the time, ridiculously innocent: 'By present technological standards the County is best suited for farming, estates, recreation and small towns and villages – an area best suited for low density uses of land and to ensure conservation of resources and minimize pollution.'[32] The quote is similar to what provincial officials had said in 1950 about the Don Valley, just north of Toronto.

The Minister of Treasury, Economics, and Intergovernmental Affairs, Darcy McKeough, intervened in early 1969. He met with Richmond Hill Council in April and later presented some ideas for a regional government. They were studied by an inter-municipal committee, which reached no conclusions. The County of York waded into the matter with its own report, which stated, 'The County unit can provide an efficient and practical means of achieving local needs as opposed to the disadvantages associated with central control by senior governments far removed from the local scene.'[33]

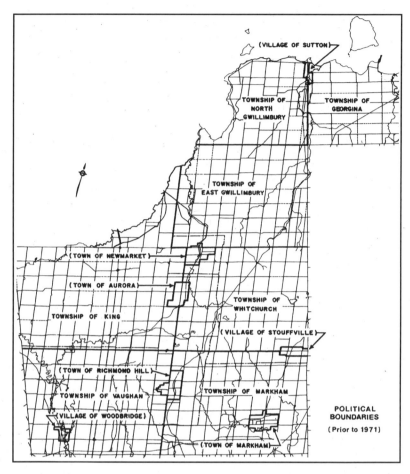

Figure 7.6 Municipal boundaries in York County, prior to restructuring in 1971. It is an odd mixture of small settlements with municipal status and large rural townships. Note the 'Southern Six.'
Source: Region of York, 'Insight: Local and Regional Government in York Region,' 20.

Meanwhile, the Toronto Board of Trade proposed that Metro expand to take control of the whole 700 square mile planning area, expanding from 240 square miles within Metro. In the municipal election in December 1969, voters in Woodbridge (and in Pickering to the east) authorized amalgamation with Metro Toronto. This foment forced McKeough to move quickly. The day after the government released the Toronto-Centred Region Plan in May 1970, McKeough was in the area north of Toronto selling his reorganization. 'Under the existing system, a number of the municipalities in the region are unable to perform even the most basic tasks of providing local services,' he said. 'This weakness forces municipalities to make decisions that are not in the best long-run interests of their own communities. To expect this municipal system to meet the challenges of the future without basic reform is unrealistic.'[34]

He then turned to the issue of regional government in York, saying, 'Any major expansion of Metro Toronto would leave an inadequate base for local or regional government in the remainder of York (County),' so that was not on the table.[35] He noted that Richmond Hill councillors asked that five southern municipalities leave the County of York – an echo of the Southern Six grouping – but that, he said, would be 'a step towards the ultimate absorption of the southern area into a greatly enlarged Metro Toronto.' Further, he doubted that one local government would be capable of governing 'such vast and complex urban communities ... There is a rational limit to be established to the intensive physical development of the urban core to the south,' he said.

To do this [that is, establish the limit on growth in Metro], it will first be necessary to encourage growth in other sectors of the TCR [Toronto-Centred Region]. Secondly, the parkway corridor, in which the route of the proposed Highway 407 will be located, is an identifiable feature specifying a limit to intensive development. Therefore at some time in the future after the incorporation of a regional government in York, lands south of the parkway corridor will be brought under the full municipal jurisdiction of Metro Toronto.[36]

McKeough proposed that the boundaries of Richmond Hill, Aurora, and Newmarket be considerably expanded; that the Townships of Vaughan, Whitchurch, East Gwillimbury, and Georgina become towns, with only King remaining a township; and that together they all be structured into a regional government with local and regional powers distributed much the same

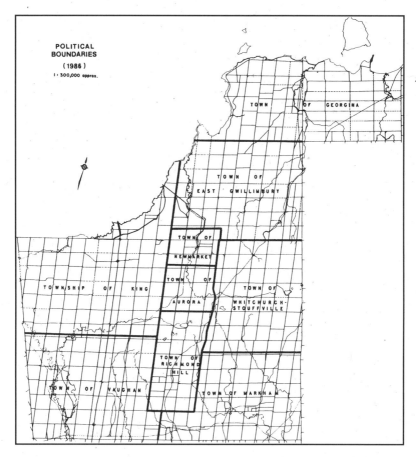

Figure 7.7 Regional government proposal for York County, showing the nine
lower tier governments that made up the region in the 1971 restructuring.
Source: Region of York, 'Insight: Local and Regional Government in York
Region,' 22.

as Metro Toronto (see fig. 7.7). In an interview thirty-five years
later, McKeough said he remembered the Southern Six config-
uration, but rejected it since it would interfere with existing
boundaries. He says he has since realized that if transitional
funds had been offered to local governments, the opportunity
for different and better kinds of changes would have presented
itself.[37]

On 19 May 1970, by a 4–3 vote, Richmond Hill Council opposed the proposal as 'premature,' and as not fitting 'the pattern for development in the Toronto-Centred Region Plan.'[38] The council may have read the Toronto-Centred Region Plan correctly, but it was fighting a losing battle. One questions whether council wanted to constrain development more than it wanted more power to approve development. Legislation was introduced in 1970, taking effect in 1971, that reconfigured local government and gave birth to the Region of York with a population of 171,000. The Toronto Planning Board lost its planning authority over the area, and York County Council ended its life with a resolution it called 'the resolution on immortality.' It stated in part:

Whereas it would seem that the Ministry of Municipal Affairs recognizes the evolved excellence of this the County of York; and whereas it would further seem in the Honourable Minister's opinion an impossible task to replace this venerable body, and rather than hazard a chance on replacement, [he] has chosen to implement a system of reorganization.[39]

All future meetings were adjourned.

Why did McKeough decide that this whole area would be under one regional government? Regional government was touted on the grounds that larger was better, that it would reduce competition for assessment, and that it provided a strong base for growth. By including this whole area up to Lake Simcoe in one regional government, did the government signal that the whole area would be a single area of development? If not, why were there no legislative triggers about where suburbanization could occur, and which areas were to remain in a rural state? This structure seemed to assume that growth would continue right up the Yonge Street corridor, as indeed has happened. The government had the opportunity to propose a local government structure which would help to contain and direct growth; instead, it chose a model that allowed it to – well – sprawl.

But regionalization rather than local government restructuring, which addressed problems of growth directly, was the order of the day. A 1973 White Paper from the Ministry of Treasury, Economy, and Intergovernmental Affairs put it this way: 'Costly urban sprawl and wasteful competition must be halted. To do their job, local governments must be broader and stronger. They must be able to control and guide growth within whole regions of the province. At the same time they must have broad basis of assessment.'[40] The benefits of regional government had already been established to the government's satisfaction in Niagara, York, Sudbury, Waterloo, and Ottawa Carleton. One tax advantage was that 'industry can be guided into the most logical sectors of a region without depriving other sectors of tax revenue.'[41]

According to the mantra, regional government provided better responses to growth, a skilled administration, better delivery of security services such as police, and improved effective dealings with other governments. What was not noted was that a larger, stronger regional government was even more liable to promote growth and sprawl. The solution was promoting a problem.

The Eastern Fringe

The last section of the Toronto area for the province to deal with was east of Metro (see fig. 7.8). This area had suburbanized much more slowly, although after the war there had been a spurt of growth in Ajax. Oshawa, with a population of 100,000, was an economically strong city on its own because of the General Motors plant, and Whitby, with a population of 26,000, was a small and stable community. Although the spillover from Metro in the 1960s was expected to be relatively limited, it was expected to happen soon. Metro politicians made strong statements in favour of annexing Pickering, adjacent to the Metro border, and Pickering residents voted overwhelmingly to support annexation in 1969, a proposal that was endorsed by Metro staff, then Metro Council, on 6 November 1971.[42] The province responded by funding a joint study with Oshawa and other local municipalities in 1969 to look at different structures, but the study went nowhere,[43] with one person even calling it a 'spectacular failure.'[44] Several other proposals were locally generated, including one to consolidate twenty-four municipalities into eight and impose a weak regional government. Another would regionalize just the areas closest to Metro where growth was most anticipated. The most attractive proposal bore the same form-follows-function characteristics as the Plunkett recommendation for the area west of Metro: create one regional government from Pickering east to Haldimand that would run along the lake in a ribbon fashion. But it found no substantial support.

In 1972 the provincial and federal governments announced plans to build the Pickering Airport and a new city in north Pickering, whose population was to become 200,000. The intention was to try to divert growth from the west to the east of the city. In support of this initiative, the province moved quickly. In 1974, from the twenty-one existing local governments, it created the Region of Durham with eight local governments. Like the regions created to the north and west, Durham's boundaries were extensive rather than strategic. When created, Durham Region's population was about 200,000. Today it is 600,000, and the planned population in 2021 is anticipated to be one million, even though the airport has not been – and may never be – built and the community in north Pickering remains in a prenatal form.

The model for the reorganizations in the fringes was Metro Toronto, but the conditions there were entirely different. Levels of staff expertise were not present in the fringes at either the local or county levels as they had been twenty years earlier in Metro, so there was little for the new structures to fall back upon once established. Since the provincial government had assumed responsibilities for water and sewage services in the three fringe areas, there was little to moderate the urge to approve subdivisions without limits at either the local or regional level. And the importance of engaging passionately the competition between the regional and local viewpoints so critical to Metro's success was lacking: local politicians seemed swallowed up by the desire for regional development and the local inter-

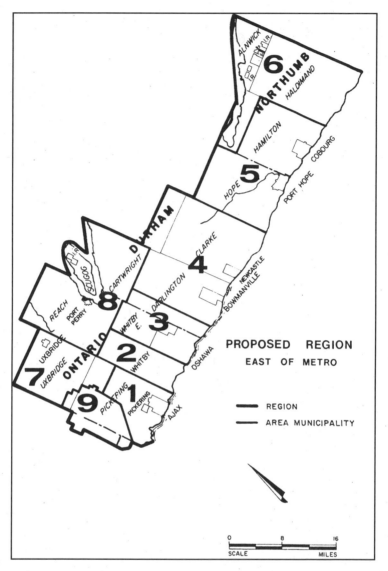

Figure 7.8 Proposal to restructure government to the east of Metro Toronto, showing one regional government hugging the lake, consisting of nine local governments.
Source: Province of Ontario, Department of Treasury, Economic, and Intergovernmental Affairs, *Proposal for Local Government Reform in an Area East of Metro Toronto.*

Figure 7.9 Regional and local government structure in the Greater Toronto Area, 1990.
Source: Report of the GTA Task Force, January 1996.

ests were only vaguely defined. Unlike in Metro Toronto, where local interests in the municipalities of Toronto, York, and East York had matured and found expression for up to 100 years, the small communities of the fringes possessed weak and insubstantial cultures, which in any case had been submerged for the decade or so before the reorganizations by development frenzy. For these reasons the new structures were not capable of providing the directions needed, and they proved to be weak devices for governance in the following decades.

Intergovernmental Relations

These new structures were not static, and relationships between
them and the province evolved. The provincial government had
assumed responsibility for regional transportation – the 400
series of highways, commuter transit (GO Transit) – and for the
provision of water and sewage infrastructure. The main function of the regional governments in the fringe areas was to process development applications for growth. This was achieved
through the provincial planning regime set out in *The Planning
Act*, which required that each region prepare and approve an
official plan that set out growth expectations over the next twenty years, the areas where growth would occur, and how those
areas would be serviced. The official plan also had to 'have regard for' a list of general planning policies determined by the
province. Until the early 1990s, regions were required to submit
official plans to the Ministry of Municipal Affairs for approval,
as well as plans of subdivision. Disputes were to be resolved by a
quasi-judicial administrative body, the Ontario Municipal
Board.

This procedure sounded good in theory, since it provided for
local initiatives within a provincial framework, subject to provincial oversight. But in practice the system was a shambles.
Provincial policy consisted of bland generalities that allowed
virtually anything to happen. The rule was not that policy had
to be followed, but that a municipality had to 'have regard to' it,
which could be done by knowingly deciding to do something
contrary to that policy. Official plans turned out to be flabby
documents without teeth, useless for anything except providing
a rationale for whatever decision was made by the local or regional council. And if the official plan did not permit a development that council wanted to approve, then the plan was simply
amended, which happened with great regularity. Or, in the
case of Metro Toronto, the council simply never adopted a plan
until 1980, twenty-seven years after Metro was created. The
OMB seemed to see its role as approving developments that the
municipality had refused, so it was a court of last resort for the
developer, not for the citizen or the municipality.[45]

It is fair to say that the planning regime established by the provincial government has served little purpose except to slightly delay development approval. It is very hard to make a case that consideration of suburban development applications was improved substantially – some say in any way – by the Ontario planning regime. The province could have sharpened its policies to require decisions more directed to sustainable development, but it did not. As with the regional government structure that the province had established, the planning regime was an attractive framework that abetted suburban development.

Those new structures and processes also destroyed the co-ordinating mechanism that had been in place. Metro Toronto had been the planner for the 720 square miles of the Greater Toronto Area (see fig. 2.2). A land use regional vision had been outlined by the Metro Toronto planners in the 1959 Official Plan, a vision confirmed a decade later by the Toronto-Centred Region Plan. But that regional framework was destroyed with the creation of regional government around Metro and the shrinkage in Metro's planning jurisdiction. Any other co-ordination fell away when the Toronto-Centred Region Plan was so quickly abandoned.

A new coordinating mechanism was suggested by the Royal Commission, headed by former premier John Robarts, which was appointed in 1974 to review Metro yet again. The commission made a number of recommendations for the internal restructuring of Metro, none of which were adopted; more importantly, it addressed the issue of regional coordination. It said the region needed 'processes for co-ordinating public responsibilities on a larger interregional scale' and recommended a Toronto Region Co-ordinating Agency. The key to this new agency was that the local and regional representatives would be working with a provincial minister who would be responsible for the Toronto area. The commission was suggesting a powerful instrument to ensure that provincial, local, and regional interests had a regular forum for decision-making and a mechanism to ensure that the provincial government, with an especially assigned minister, paid some attention to the most vibrant area in Ontario.

But the provincial government had no interest in sharing a regional role. Darcy McKeough, the minister responsible, said that these issues were entirely within the provincial purview, and declared, 'Assigning a role to an agency which is not entirely responsible to the Province would confuse attempts at a clearer definition of responsibilities between the provincial and local levels of government.'[46] The province had clearly not learned the important lesson of Metro, namely, that forcing a body or agency to hold two points of view at the same time enhanced rather than obscured both. The broad regional perspective was to be taken by no one, and so the situation would lie, in limbo, for more than a decade.

8

The Challenge of Unbridled Suburban Growth

By the early 1980s, it was clear that the muddled strategies used by the provincial government after the demise of the Toronto-Centred Region Plan a decade earlier had not resolved the clearly expressed concerns about sprawl. The fringes around Metro Toronto bristled with low-density growth. Over the next two decades, the provincial government began a number of initiatives to address problems, but none of them have been seemed effective. The new suburban areas continue untamed, and perhaps untamable.

When Metro Toronto was created in 1953, the population in the fringe areas around Metro was less than 100,000. By the late 1950s, it had climbed to 140,000, with an expectation that by 1980 it would reach 500,000,[1] and by 2000, more than 600,000.[2] Those estimates proved far too modest. By 1990, the population projection for the fully developed fringe areas had ballooned to between 2.8 million and 3.4 million.[3] By the end of the 1990s, the actual population of the urbanized area – Metro and the fringes – was close to 5 million, of which half was located within the former Metro Toronto, and half outside.

Almost all of this new growth has occurred at a density of between six and ten residential units per acre. In the late 1980s, the Metrus Group, one of the area's largest development companies, proposed a compact medium-density development in Brampton called the Heart of Springdale, in which a 100-acre site would have mixed uses and residential densities in the order of twenty units per acre. The development felt a lot like the Riverdale community in downtown Toronto that was built in the early twentieth century, with row houses, apartments over shops, and back lanes. But municipal staff objected, claiming the streets would be too narrow, particularly with so much on-street parking, and would be clogged with snow. By retaining existing trees, they thought the developer was not providing enough open parkland for playing fields, and that back lanes were more of a problem than a solution. Staff opposition made the municipal council nervous enough that it rejected this development. It was virtually the only time a serious alternative to low-density suburban growth was proposed by the development industry, and it's rejection meant others would not risk a similar approach. Developers and their financial backers found it much easier to submit the traditional suburban subdivision created by Don Mills.

The Toronto urbanized area had more than tripled, from 193 square miles in the 1950s to 656 square miles by the end of the 1990s, but the population had only doubled.[4] The contrast between the fringes and the older urban area was pronounced. Residential density in the former City of Toronto in the 1990s, built-up mostly by the start of the Second World War, was 7,000 units per square mile; in the rest of the Metro Toronto (including the outer suburbs of North York, Etobicoke, and Scarborough which were built largely between 1950 and 1985), it was 3,300 units per square mile. Density in the fringes was 1,800 units per square mile or one-quarter of that found in the former City of Toronto.[5] The population comparison was similar: 20,000 residents per square mile in the former city; 8,000 in the rest of Metro; and 4,700 in the developed portion of the fringes.[6]

One study showed that in the former City of Toronto there was an average of 49 residents and jobs per urbanized acre, and in Metro Toronto as a whole, 23. In the fringes the ratio was much lower: Mississauga, 14; Brampton, 16; Markham, 13; Vaughan, 9; and Richmond Hill, 9.[7] The mixed residential/non-residential density in the more central city was five times what it was in most parts of the fringes.

About one million new housing units were constructed on greenfields in the Toronto area between 1940 and 2000, and for developers, one happy outcome of this growth was that housing prices rose as development proceeded. This sounds counterintuitive, given that the extraordinary growth in housing stock should have meant a moderation in housing prices, but the growth in the number of units was obviously not sufficient to meet demand. One powerful study blamed land speculation for the rise in prices,[8] and a full-scale debate began about the causes behind the increases.[9] The average house price in the Toronto area in 1950 was $14,000, but by 1981 it had reached to $90,000 and by 1991, just over $234,000. The ratio of house price to income jumped considerably, as shown in table 8.1.

Table 8.1 House prices and incomes in the Greater Toronto Area.[10]

	Average house price	Median household income	Ratio of house price to income
1953	$14,000	(average) $5,400	2.6:1
1963	16,000	(average) 6,542	2.5:1
1971	30,426	11,841	2.6:1
1981	90,203	31,238	2.9:1
1991	234,313	55,000	4.3:1
2000	258,000	59,000	4.4:1
2005	384,000	60,000	6.4:1

Price was one problem: another was transportation. Most people travelled by private automobile. In the city's core there was five feet of road per person; in the outer suburbs, eighteen.[11] A resident in the city's core could expect to travel four miles a day by car, and a further two miles by transit; a resident in the fringes would travel an average fourteen miles per day and two miles by transit.[12] As Richard Gilbert has pointed out, 'The ascendancy of the automobile in the 1940s and 1950s in North America stimulated development at much lower densities made possible by widespread personal motorized transport; but the lower densities created corresponding dependence on such transport.'[13] It was a closed circle: the low densities required automobiles, and the automobiles encouraged more low densities.

Because the urban densities were so low, it was not cost effective to serve suburban areas with good public transit. The long travel routes meant subsidies would be very high on a per-rider basis, and the time involved for each ride would be oppressively long. Although GO Transit provided some commuter capacity (at a very high public cost), most residents in the areas beyond Metro Toronto were forced to rely on private transportation, and that involved great costs to the individual as well as a considerable expenditure of time. In the late 1990s, it was estimated that the cost of driving from Newmarket to downtown Toronto by private automobile was somewhere between $600 and $1,200 per year and took just over one hour each way. For residents living in fringe areas closer to the city, the cost was somewhat lower, but the time involved – whether from Richmond Hill or Mississauga – was about forty-five minutes for a one-way trip. The private cost of using GO Transit was considerably less than the cost of driving, but the travel times on transit were much longer, and longer again if one had to transfer from GO Transit onto the TTC.[14] Any reduction in house price because of distance from the city's care was more than offset by an increase in travel cost.[15]

On top of the personal cost was congestion. As already noted, the expressways seemed to fill with cars as quickly as they were built, and then the congestion spilled over to the arterials. By the year 2000, many of these roads were operating at or above capacity, hence the gridlock which so many people experienced daily. Estimates were that most roads would soon be at or above 95 per cent capacity during rush hour.[16] Congestion has resulted in very high lost opportunity costs for all of the individuals affected and in hard business costs for those moving goods. York Region officials have stated that gridlock has added a 30 per cent surcharge to the cost of moving goods; the provincial government has said that congestion in the GTA cost the commercial and industrial sectors $2 billion a year.[17] The government also believed that if development patterns continued without improvement in public transit, that vehicle emissions would increase by 42 per cent.[18] These are the marks of a failed transportation system.

This congestion has also created considerable concerns about air quality, given the automobile's incomplete burning of carbon-based fuels. Because most of the travel throughout the fringes was by automobile, there were substantial negative effects on air quality. The measurement of air quality as published daily in the *Globe and Mail* newspaper showed that the air quality index in the fringe was lower (that is, worse) than in downtown Toronto, even though most people felt that because of the 'wide open space' in the fringes air quality should be better there. However, automobiles produce nitrogen oxides (a source of acid rain and smog) and carbon monoxide (another component of smog), and these negatively effect living organisms, including humans. It has been thought that in the

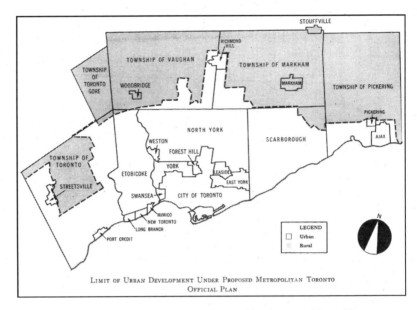

Figure 8.1 Limits of development as proposed in the 1959 Metro Toronto Official Plan.
Source: Carl Goldenberg, *Report on Metro Toronto*, 160.

Toronto area about 1,700 people per year die prematurely because of poor air quality.[19]

What has been most apparent with sprawling development has been the extraordinary amount of land it consumed. Toronto was surrounded by Canada's largest array of Class 1 farmland in the 1950s up until the 1970s. It was often said that more than three-quarters of Canada's Class 1 farmland could be seen by the naked eye from the top of the CN Tower in downtown Toronto on a clear day. Throughout the early 1970s, Stephen Lewis, then leader of the Ontario New Democratic Party, announced with some regularity how many acres of good farmland were being converted into subdivisions every hour and every minute. The public was aware of the problem, but apparently not eager to address it.[20]

There was also the issue of the costs of sprawl. Building a sewer pipe to serve twenty homes each with a frontage of twenty-five feet might cost the same as building a pipe to serve ten homes with frontages of fifty feet – but the cost per house was half in the former scenario. The per-unit cost of collecting solid waste from the houses on larger lots was greater than those on narrower lots since the vehicles and the personnel had to travel twice as far to service the same number of houses. As well, the cost of building roads was more expensive than for a more compact form given the need for wider roads to accommodate the extra automobile traffic in the lower-density areas.

Perhaps the best work on the economic impact of different urban forms has been by Dr Pamela Blais, who works with data from the Greater Toronto Area. She states,

An urban form [in the GTA] that relies to greater degree on re-urbanization, more compact development, and mixed land use would decrease the capital investment required for roads, transit, water and sewer services by an estimated $10 billion to $16 billion, and decrease operating and maintenance costs by $2.5 to $4 billion ... When external costs such as those associated with emissions, publicly-borne health care, and accident policing are added to the capital and operating and maintenance cost savings, a conservative estimate would suggest that a total of about $700 million to $1 billion per year could be saved in the GTA by accommodating future growth in more efficient urban patterns. ... Further substantial savings could be achieved by altering the standards to which infrastructure of all kinds is built, to allow more efficient, flexible, sustainable and cost-effective alternatives.[21]

In short, low-density development has imposed much higher capital and operating costs than has more compact development. That extra cost was in the order of $1 billion per year in the GTA, or more than $1,000 per family per year for those living in the fringes. As already noted, the water and sewage services in the fringes had been substantially subsidized by the provincial government and the superhighways had been built entirely at government expense, so the extra costs of low-density development already built had been borne by all of society. One is reminded of the principle that subsidies often deceive the beneficiaries, hiding from them the burden they impose on others.

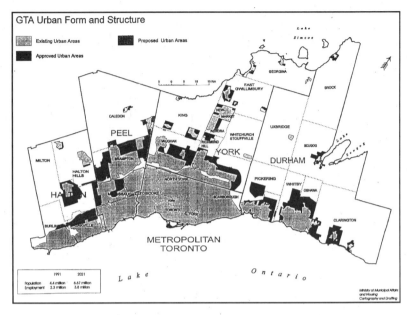

Figure 8.2 Limits of development as of 1991, with areas approved for development and proposed for development.
Source: Ministry of Municipal Affairs and Housing.

Over the years, various provincial ministries have felt an obligation to respond to these issues, since they are the ones who review municipal official plans and subdivision agreements on behalf of the government and are drawn into the ramifications of suburban sprawl. Not surprisingly, it was the Ministry of Agriculture in the 1970s that first responded with a policy regarding farmland; it issued the Agricultural Code of Practice in 1976 and the *Food Land Guidelines* in 1978. These documents expressed concern with the amount of farmland being converted into residential use and questioned whether so much land needed to be consumed in such a manner. But these policies were not strong enough statements to prevent suburban sprawl; they were simply ministry guidelines.

Similarly, in 1978, the Ministry of Housing issued a *Land Use Policy Near Airports* addressing noise impact issues and restricting the height of structures in close proximity to airports. The

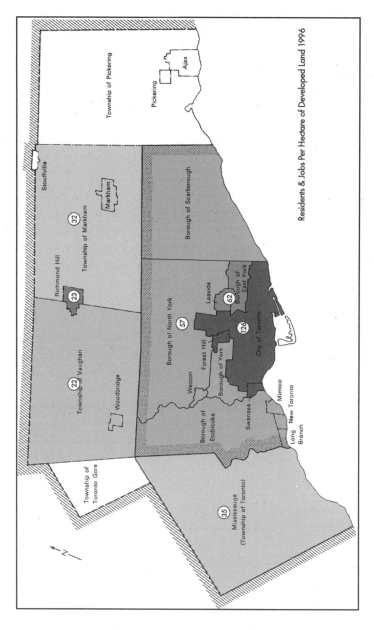

Figure 8.3 Residents and jobs per hectare in selected parts of the Greater Toronto Area.
Source: Pamela Blais, *The Economics of Urban Form*, 2.

Table 8.2 Travel characteristics by urban zone in the Greater Toronto Area, 1996.

Area	Percentage of households with no car	Daily km per person by car	Daily km per person by transit	% daily trips by transit walking or cycling
Core	51.9	6.8	3.6	60
Core ring	31.5	10.2	3.9	37
Inner suburbs	17.4	13.4	4.0	24
Outer suburbs	5.8	23.2	2.5	12

Source: Data from the Transportation Tomorrow Survey, 1996, prepared by the Centre for Sustainable Transportation. Cited in Pamela Blais, *The Growth Opportunity*, 11.

next year, the Ministry of Municipal Affairs and Housing released *Guidelines on Noise and New Residential Development Adjacent to Freeways*. Both guidelines were developed by ministries with their own sense of urgency and without a consultative process that brought other parties onside. They were not treated as formal documents on which local governments could rely during the planning process. In all, about two dozen policy guidelines were adopted between the mid-1970s and the early 1990s, some general in nature, some very specific. Amendments to the *Planning Act* in 1983 had proposed that the provincial government enact comprehensive policy statements, but only four such policies were implemented over the next decade: the protection of aggregates (given the need for extraordinary amounts of gravel for road construction and new buildings)in 1986; the restriction of development in flood plains in 1988; a weak and general policy entitled *Land Use Planning for Housing* in 1989;[22] and protection of wetlands in 1992.

These policies and policy guidelines had little effect on the suburban onslaught. They did little to change the proposed subdivisions, save in details around the edges of wetlands and water courses. They did not address the public concern galvanized in late 1988 by a series of eight articles published in the *Globe and Mail*'s series 'Behind the Boom: The Story of York Region.' The reporters for this series, Jock Ferguson and Dawn King, outlined how the development industry was doing its business in the area directly north of Metro Toronto. They described a regime of friendships between politicians and staff as well as the making of political donations, which apparently led to the necessary approvals and sewer allocations in Vaughan, Richmond Hill, Markham, Aurora, and Newmarket.[23]

The need for better provincial direction and better regional and provincial coordination in the Toronto area where most growth was occurring was widely apparent. In 1988, then premier David Peterson responded by establishing the Office of the Greater Toronto Area (OGTA). The hope was that this office, under the leadership of long-term provincial civil servant Gardner Church, could harness provincial resources, help flesh out important regional policies, and encourage municipalities to work together. Church headed a group of staff seconded from various ministries. In turn, they established the Greater Toronto Coordinating Committee, consisting of the heads of all councils in the area whose mandate it was to define important issues that would help to overcome continued sprawl. Under the auspices of the committee in 1989, the *Urban Structure Concepts Study* was completed.[24] It looked at options for the future: continued sprawl, centralizing development, and creating development nodes, echoing the Metro Plan from 1980.[25] It opted for the nodal approach, concluding that it resulted in a more efficient servicing costs. The study did not receive formal endorsement, mostly because the committee was generally dysfunctional – that is, there was no incentive for local politicians to change their ways. They liked the power that came with approving growth, and developers liked low-density subdivisions. The OGTA had some success getting local governments in the Toronto area to agree at least in principle to ideas of nodal development, intensification, and protection of agricultural land, although less progress was made translating these ideas into local policies strong enough to influence development decisions.

The OGTA initiative continued after 1990 when the government of Bob Rae assumed office. Several years later the new minister responsible for the OGTA, Ruth Greer, committed the OGTA to finding a new waste site for municipal garbage, rating some forty sites as possible locations for the dump. Most munici-

Table 8.3 Cost comparison for different development patterns in the Toronto area, indicating the significant extra costs incurred by low-density single-use development.

	1990 dollars			1995 dollars		
	Spread	Central	Nodal	Spread	Central	Nodal
Total 25-year costs – regional roads, expressways, transit, sewer/water, local roads, and services						
Capital costs	$49.8	$35.5	$41.0	$54.8	$39.1	$45.1
O&M costs	$13.0	$9.2	$10.7	$14.3	$10.1	$11.8
Total 25-year costs	$62.8	$44.7	$51.7	$69.1	$49.2	$56.9
Total capital/O&M cost savings compared to spread	na	$18.1	$11.1	na	$19.9	$12.2
Average annual costs						
Capital costs	$2.0	$1.4	$1.6	$2.2	$1.6	$1.8
O&M costs	$0.5	$0.4	$0.4	$0.6	$0.4	$0.5
Auto-related external costs – 'basic' estimate	$0.3	$0.1	$0.1	$0.3	$0.1	$0.1
Total avg. annual costs	$2.8	$1.9	$2.1	$3.1	$2.1	$2.4
1) Total avg. annual cost savings compared to spread	na	$0.9	$0.7	na	$1.0	$0.7
Annual average external costs – 'enhanced' estimate	$1.1	$0.4	$0.6	$1.2	$0.4	$0.7
Total avg. annual costs using enhanced estimate	$3.6	$2.2	$2.6	$4.0	$2.4	$3.0
2) Total avg. annual cost saving compared to spread using 'enhanced' estimate of external costs	na	$1.4	$1.0	na	$1.4	$1.0

Source: Pamela Blais, *The Economics of Urban Form*, 42.

palities did not want the dump located in their jurisdiction and that provided a reason why many municipalities lost interest in continuing to work with the OGTA. Thus, the OGTA became more ineffective.

With the *Globe and Mail* articles in hand, Rae's government also decided to proceed with a royal commission to investigate what it assumed to be corruption in York Region. After some internal discussion, that idea was transformed from an investigation into wrongdoing to a review of planning legislation in order to address the more general question of suburban sprawl and the related impacts of low-density development. The initiative was announced in 1991, and was formally known as the Commission on Planning and Development Reform in Ontario, or more colloquially as New Planning for Ontario. It was chaired by John Sewell who sat with two other commissioners: George Penfold, a professor of rural planning at the University of Guelph; and Toby Vigod, an environmental lawyer who had recently been the executive director of the Canadian Environmental Law Association. The commission addressed two questions: the key objectives that land-use planning should attempt to achieve, and the process of a good planning system. It held widespread consultations throughout the province and recommended substantial policy changes. Most important for the matter at hand, it proposed policies the provincial government should enact in order to constrain low-density suburban growth. Its proposals would prevent leap-frog developments, require new development areas to be logical extensions of existing development areas; require compact development and a mix of uses and densities; mandate planning to minimize the consumption of land; and density levels that would encourage good public transit. Quality agricultural lands would be protected for agricultural use, and significant natural features would be protected from development. In terms of process, the commission recommended that provincial policy become a template to which land-use decisions by municipalities and the province must conform. Within the policy framework, it removed the overlapping of government roles and provided clear lines of remedy if decisions did not conform to stated policy.

The commission found this strong policy package had widespread support in the community. Rae's government agreed and it enacted these policies in early 1995 and required all municipalities to conform to them in their planning. It looked as though the provincial government might have found a way of tackling the behemoth and containing the sprawl.

The Rae government also decided to begin addressing extraordinary congestion problems in the Toronto area. Studies had shown that an enormous amount of traffic moved during peak hours between Metro Toronto and its fringes. Cordon counts done by Metro Toronto in 1991 showed that during the afternoon peak period, between 3:30 and 6:30 p.m., more than 150,000 outbound commuter trips were made across Metro's western boundary and close to 100,000 inbound; more than 130,000 outbound commuter trips crossed Metro's northern boundary and 107,000 inbound. Eighty-five per cent of these trips were by automobile and less than 15 per cent by transit.

Two kinds of transit service were offered for cross-boundary trips – GO Transit and the limited local services operated in adjacent fringe municipalities that linked up directly with TTC service. The province wondered whether it would be possible to increase transit usage between Toronto and the fringes by better integrating transit services. The Transit Integration Service Task Force was established in 1993 by the province with the hope that it would show how better coordination could increase the share of cross-boundary transit trips. The task force consisted of provincial and local officials that met over a period of a year and reported in early 1994. The report began by noting the significant traffic congestion, which it called a 'deepening crisis,'[26] The report proposed a comprehensive integration of transit services to be implemented by early 1996 so that a 'seamless' service could be offered in the Greater Toronto Area. This would require fare integration, possibly through a 'smart card' that would store fares electronically and that could be read by any transit system in the GTA, and through the integration of services.

The problem with this idea was that it attempted to bring into one relationship a very large elephant and some very tiny mice.

The TTC attracted over 400 million riders in 1992; the next largest operation was Mississauga Transit with an annual ridership
of 20 million. The other services were smaller still (Brampton,
5.5 million; Markham, 2.6 million; and other municipalities less
than one million riders). The extraordinary difference in the
scope of operations had financial implications. The TTC's subsidy per rider was about $0.23 in 1992, whereas the subsidy per
rider in Mississauga was more than $0.50. Subsidies per rider
were even higher for other systems. Toronto's fear was that integrating these disparate systems would direct money and energy away from the TTC into these less efficient services. Thus,
while the report of the Transit Integration Task Force registered
high on the scales as a 'good idea,' there was no eagerness in
Toronto to proceed quickly with integration. This remained a
stumbling block for more than a decade.

In the last few months of the Rae government in 1995, the
Greater Toronto Area Task Force was created to explore how
better area-wide coordination could occur on the governance
side. Anne Golden, then president of the United Way of greater
Toronto, was appointed chair. The idea of governance reform
was in the air and various reports were underway. The City of
Mississauga, led by Mayor Hazel McCallion, immediately responded to the Golden Task Force by releasing its own publication entitled *Running the GTA 'Like a Business.'* Mississauga
touted itself 'as a leader in management and financial practic-
es' since its creation in 1970, and in its report said 'the GTA is
no longer economically competitive in today's global environment,' claiming that 'a business approach' was the 'key to Mississauga's success.'[27] The report proposed abolishing the five
regional governments, and combining the thirty-three local
governments in the Toronto area to create what it called '10 to
15 cities.' It suggested that a Greater Toronto Area Services
Commission be appointed and not elected, and that it be responsible for all area-wide services, including transit, waste disposal, water and sewage. The report made little mention of the
serious problems caused by low density growth, but instead
talked vaguely about integrating 'land use and transportation
planning.' It proposed support for a 'nodal form of develop-

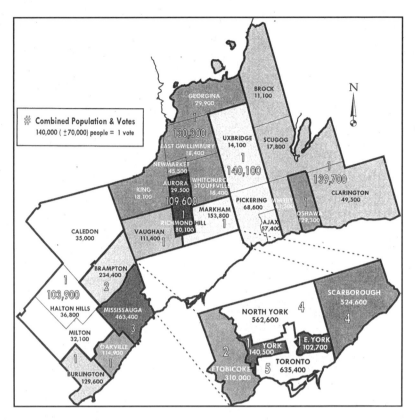

Figure 8.4 Proposal by the Golden Task Force to restructure government in
the Greater Toronto Area.
Source: GTA Task Force, 1996, 173.

ment' and an '"ecosystem" approach to sustainable development.'[28] It was exactly the kind of ill-thought out proposal that
was bound to cause trouble.

   In January 1996, after being pressured by the new government in Queen's Park to wrap up its work quickly, the Golden
Task Force reported on the need for a new regional government that would cover the whole of the GTA (see fig. 8.4) in order to resolve what was referred to as 'a fundamental lack of coordination.' 'Greater Toronto's five regional governments,' the
report claimed, 'lack the collective sense of purpose and mo-

mentum to address issues that could be handled more effectively on a region-wide basis.'[29] But more important, perhaps, than
its recommendations on governance was the chapter entitled
'Shaping the City Region.' This section documented the cost of
low-density development, showing that $1 billion a year could
be saved in operating and capital costs over each of the next
twenty-five years if a decision was made to favour compact development over low-density development.[30] It argued that 'more
compact development allows 'more efficient use of transit systems and at the same time reducing congestion on existing
roads 'fosters a higher quality of life,' and protects 'valuable rural as well as urban land.'[31]

The Golden Task Force proposed the creation of a new
Greater Toronto Council that would consist of representatives
from the local municipalities, be led by a chair appointed by
council, and have an executive committee of six members. It
would be a two-tiered structure applied across the GTA, and it
would create a regional plan for the area.

It was an ambitious set of recommendations, trying valiantly
to respond to the lack of direction and coordinated decision-
making that had been apparent for the past twenty-five years. It
showed some promise in taming the suburban behemoth, but
sadly the behemoth was already a large and unruly animal with
a mind of its own.

9

A Triumph
for Suburban
Values

I t is generally acknowledged that the shape of buildings affects human life and behaviour. Architects have agreed that
good design improves human outlook and behaviour; bad design gets in the way. In her book *Utopia on Trial*,[1] Alice Coleman
recounts how the design of council housing in the United Kingdom has had a major influence on social interaction (mostly for
the worse), and that alterations to that design have resulted in
surprising and well-documented changes in human response.
Oscar Newman showed the same kinds of response to physical
design in *Defensible Space*.[2]

The design of settlement areas also affects human behaviour,
although it has not generally been well acknowledged. Low-
density suburban areas create different responses than more
compact, medium-density areas. As well, there will be different
kinds of social relations and expectations in these different areas.[3] Since the built form in the Toronto area before the mid-
twentieth century differs so greatly from that after mid-century
in compactness and density (to name two factors), it was likely
that differences in outlook and political aspirations would sooner or later become evident. What are the differences? Examin-
ing the experience of getting to work each morning from each
of these different areas gives a good idea of how urban form affects our daily lives. Here are two scenarios, starting with the
suburban experience.

It's 7:30 in the morning. You get into your car, turn on the radio to
your favourite station with the traffic updates, and back out of the
driveway. You drive down the road – there are few other vehicles on
these wide streets – making your way to a collector then onto the arterial street where traffic is beginning to pick up. You flip the radio dial,
then back again. You edge onto the expressway where traffic is now
heavy. You push into the flow – there sure are strange drivers out
there – and keep your eyes peeled for cars doing funny things, darting
in and out of the traffic.

Traffic slows, and you do too, but not too quickly because you're
worried about that jerk on your tail who seems to be too close. It's you
against the world. Some mornings it feels like everything is being
done to delay you, but it's not always that way. You just have to pay

attention. You can't take your eyes off the traffic for a single moment even though you aren't going nearly as fast as you'd like to be going. At least the guy on the radio seems to have empathy, between the ads.

You've been on the road for thirty-five minutes now. Things are about normal, you aren't late. But you've got another fifteen minutes to go. You pass a car parked at the side with a guy pulling up the hood – thankfully it's not you with that problem which, you know, also comes with a big repair bill. You approach your exit, jiggle and jaggle with the traffic to get to the appropriate lane, then make the exit and come to a halt at the first stoplight off the expressway. Traffic's always bad here. You put up with it. But you get through the light, make your turns, and finally get to the parking lot where you park, and make the ten-minute walk into the building. You're ready to start work, and how are you feeling? Well, you've begun the day with forty-five nerve-racking minutes of you-against-the-world, and you've survived that much. The day can't be much worse. What have you experienced? Competition with other drivers; fear of making a mistake; tension from the pressure of speed; a reinforcement of your own private world. As they say in the ad, 'You deserve a break today,' and they're right.

Here's the city experience:

You walk out of the house, down the front walk, and along the side-walk. The neighbour's kids – you can never remember the names of those kids, is it Jane? Jamie? Joanie? – have left their bikes on the lawn. No big deal. None of the other kids on the street are likely to steal them. The morning paper's still on the porch of Harold's house. He's usually taken it in by this time. Is he okay? That's right, he said he was catching an early flight to New York this morning, back tonight. You go up and push the paper over to the side of the porch so it isn't obvious that he's not there. You do it quickly.

You walk around the corner, along a block, and there's the bus stop. Three other people are waiting. Two of them are familiar, and you nod and say, 'Nice day.' They respond with some pleasantry. You think – who's that teenager with the wild shirt? Haven't seen him before. He's looking mean and tough. These kids.

No bus. You remark to the guy next to you. He complains vaguely. There's a brief mention of last night's hockey game. The bus comes, you get on. Can't find a seat, you stand and fold the paper so you can read. There's Gayle a few seats back. You both wave and do expressive eyes. Her kids and your kids know each other, but your families aren't any closer than that.

You look around. All these different people are on the bus. A couple over there are speaking – is it a language from the Middle East? There are three Chinese ladies together, chatting quietly to your right. About half the people on the bus have skins that aren't white – a real rainbow. The teenagers going to school are goofing off, as usual, and that mean-looking kid has found some friends. It turns out he's the joker in the crowd, and they are as surprised as you were to see him. He must have slept over at a friend's house in the neighbourhood.

Sometimes the bus slides along, sometimes it seems to creep. There's nothing anyone on the bus can do about that. We're all in it together. Complaining won't do a thing about the slow speed.

You get off the bus to transfer to the subway, and the journey continues. As you get closer to your destination, you see one of your colleagues. You put the paper aside and chat about the latest news. You both joke over the cartoon on the editorial page, which you knew he'd like to see. Finally, it's your stop. You get off, and walk along the street to the coffee shop where you always buy a coffee to take into work because – well, because you like to say hello to the woman in the shop and anyway the coffee at work is never all that good.

What have you experienced getting to work? A bit of neighbourhood life, including an anonymous favour to one neighbour; nodding acquaintance to several people in your community; a chance to interact in a non-threatening way with people much different than you in language, colour, and age; the recognition that you are part of the community on the transit, not apart from it.

It's fair to argue that these brief fictions are the quintessential city and suburban experiences of getting to work. They define the values created by different kinds of developed space. Transit works well – that is, it is popular enough with residents that most people ride it – where buildings are compact, densities are moderate to high, uses are mixed, and blocks are short. Those attributes are all found in the city as it was developed before mid-century. Transit in Metro Toronto attracted about 400 million rides a year in the late 1990s, which means, on average, every man, woman, and child living in Toronto rode transit almost 200 times each year.

Transit does not work well, and is not popular, in sprawling communities where densities are low, uses are separated, and blocks are long. Suburban transit ridership is in the order of five to ten transit rides per person per year. Transit operates here at a very significant deficit (given the length of most rides, riders can't possibly pay anything but a small percentage of the cost of their ride). Service is infrequent, and because of suburban design, it's usually a long and uncomfortable walk from a home to a transit stop, or from transit to anywhere else. In low-density suburbs, most sensible people travel by private car.

Transit promotes a sense of community: people are not competing with one another, but they are all on the same bus, sharing a common experience, reinforcing the idea of community. Transit promotes tolerance – individuals experience people who are different ages, speak different languages, wear different clothes, and have different colours of skin, and know they are not a threat. One starts tolerating others because there is no choice, but quite quickly, toleration becomes a matter of standard behaviour. Transit promotes civility. One is expected to be civil to those around you, sometimes crowding very close, and most people are civil, respecting the space of others, sometimes even going out of their way to demonstrate respect. Teenagers do give up their seats to older people. The disabled do get priority. Riders do generally respect other riders.

The private car promotes different values. It promotes a sense of individuality, as one must drive more against, than with, the rest of the world. Every day one proves how good one is. Driving promotes a sense of competition with other drivers for space on the road, and it is of the intense kind: each driver must pay very careful attention to what the other drivers are doing, and be prepared to react quickly if something is out of line. It's a bit of a jungle – one cannot relax for a minute. Driving in a sealed car also promotes a sense that everything is at a distance. The car is a bit of a cocoon with its personalized heat and sound system, and noise can't leak into it too easily. The speed at which you move means the world passes by quickly.

The private automobile promotes the values of individuality, competition, distancing. Transit promotes the values of community, tolerance, and civility. Obviously individuals can and do take actions that transcend these qualities. Some people on transit are really impolite and cause trouble. Some drivers are very considerate, and you notice it. For those in a bad relationship or a bad job, the drive to and from work can be the best part of the day. For some transit riders, the crowding is uncomfortable, and leaves them in a snit by the end of the ride. Sometimes transit breaks down and causes enormous inconvenience. But these cases are infrequent, and the more usual outcomes are the ones described.

As one author writes:

What has disappeared in the postwar city (the low-density suburbs) is a casual public street life, where nothing in particular may be discussed but through which the social and political vitality of a local place is maintained. The street life needs small-scale, mixed and concentrated land uses, described over forty years ago by Jane Jacobs ... We are less connected to our neighbours and to the ebb and flow of activity on the street. There's been a loss of simple sidewalk contact: casual but essential greetings as we pass each other, the occasional chat about potholes or a troublesome dog, the odd remark about our children or our parents. These contacts, as Jacobs points out, may not be significant in themselves, but they provide a context for solutions when problems do arise, such as increases in vandalism or burglaries, proposals for a new development in the neighbourhood, or a misfortune suffered by a local resident.[4]

These values are played out in the life of communities. Compact cities generally have strong social programs because the transit experience encourages people to have a strong sense of empathy for others. Compact cities seem more willing to find public ways to pay for things than to ask that every service pay its own way from user fees. Compact cities are more willing to tolerate differences because the transit experience has shown that differences are rarely a threat and are mostly interesting and energizing.

Community values are quickly reflected in the politicians they elect, and different urban forms create differing political expectations. This was certainly experienced at Metro Council. As the low-density communities in Etobicoke, North York, and Scarborough grew in the 1960s and 1970s, elected politicians from those areas expressed views that often conflicted with those held by representatives of Toronto, York, and East York. The differences were clear in the struggle over the approval of the Spadina Expressway, on which Metro Council was divided. Suburban representatives almost uniformly supported the expressway; city politicians almost uniformly opposed it. That issue was finally settled by the provincial government.

Many other issues saw similar politician divisions. City politicians supported establishing group homes for offenders or the mentally ill in residential neighbourhoods on an as-of-right basis, whereas suburban politicians generally opposed such as-of-right uses until a solution was imposed in 1984.[5] The City of Toronto embraced an active affordable housing program with the city itself a leading developer, but that was never the case with the suburban councils, which felt that Metro's housing for senior citizens was about as far as their residents were willing to go in terms of government intervention in the housing market. The City of Toronto offered all recreation programs free of charge to children on the basis that they served a powerful social good; suburban councils charged for recreation programs for kids. And from the mid-1970s on, the city and the suburbs clashed over the extent of the subsidy for transit from the local property taxpayers: city representatives supported frozen fares and increased subsidies (to encourage more ridership), while suburban representatives wanted frozen taxes and increased fares.

As already noted, Metro's success lay partly in its ability to provide a forum for these differing points of view and in its process for trying to resolve them. Voices similar to those from Metro's suburbs began to be heard in the fringes as they developed, and without the constraint of the Metro structure, they were often rambunctious and forceful. They gained considerable confidence as they grew into communities, particularly Mississauga whose population soon surpassed that of Metro's suburbs. Further, Mississauga mayor Hazel McCallion proved to be an expert at negotiating solutions favourable to her municipality and the more she was re-elected (being first elected in 1970 and most recently re-elected in 2006), the more powerful she became. The new confidence of this rising fringe was best expressed in the 1995 Mississauga reports, which proposed how restructuring should take place in the Greater Toronto Area. The reports were issued under the general title *Running the GTA 'Like a Business.'*

It was only a matter of time until the new communities of the fringes found a strong political voice that was louder than that of the older, compact city. That happened in 1995, with the the provincial election of the Progressive Conservative government of Mike Harris and the defeat of Premier Bob Rae.

Harris had been very clear about his priorities – lower taxes, fewer government services, fewer social programs. He called it 'The Common Sense Revolution.' It appealed to and reflected the values of the new suburbs and was seen as an antidote to the muddled approach of the Rae government with its old, downtown values. In the June election, his party swept every seat in the fringes (by then referred to as the 905 area, reflecting the telephone exchange), and half the seats in Metro Toronto. His majority gave him the opportunity of putting in place an agenda that expressed these new values and attacked the older city.

The Harris government moved immediately to implement the most controversial parts of its agenda, such as reducing welfare rates by more than 20 per cent. It introduced Bill 20, the *Land-Use Planning and Protection Act,* gutting the Rae recommendations that had flowed from the Commission on Planning and Development Reform and putting in their place weak, general polices that gave municipalities a free hand in decision-making while removing considerable provincial oversight. Municipal plans and decisions no longer had to conform to provincial policy. Bill 20 permitted low-density suburban sprawl to become the hallmark of this government's land-use vision. In March

1996, the provincial budget included a land-transfer tax rebate for those who purchased a new home, a simple way of subsidizing the expansion of suburbia. A short leash was placed on members of the Ontario Municipal Board, the provincial body that reviewed municipal land-use decisions – the terms of OMB members were shortened to a few years and progressive members were not reappointed. The OMB's new role seemed to be simply to approve development that in recent years had been stalled or rejected by local councils.

As recounted in the next chapter, the Harris government then began a major attack on municipal structures within Metro Toronto by forcing unwanted amalgamation, followed in January 1997 by announcements that it would be ending operating subsidies for public transit as well as downloading onto municipalities subsidies needed to support affordable housing and terminating subsidies for municipal public health programs and libraries. Transit and affordable housing were programs that were part of the infrastructure of Metro Toronto and absorbed considerable amounts of money, so there was extensive opposition within Metro Toronto to these changes. But in the fringes there were relatively few social housing units and public transit was quite limited, so there was not as much negative reaction there. It seems fair to say that the changes were directed at the older city and were intended to disrupt its activities.

In 1997 and 1998, the structure of the property tax system was radically altered. Property tax had always been a municipality's chief source of revenue, and although the province controlled the legislation that determined its mechanisms, most property tax revenue that was generated flowed to the local council. Under the new arrangement, the provincial government seized about half the revenue derived from commercial property taxation and used it to fund public education, which it had removed from the local level. It justified this change with the promise to level and equalize commercial property tax rates across the province. But the legislation based the commercial property tax rate on the existing local rate, and those rates varied widely from one municipality to the next. They were highest in the former Metro Toronto and remained that way under the new regime. The tax rate paid by commercial properties in Mississauga, for example, was 40 per cent lower than in Toronto. It was odd to find a provincially levied tax that varied from municipality to municipality, but this was the new reality. The low-density fringe areas were rewarded at the expense of the more compact city.

In 1997, the province introduced the pooling of the costs of social service payments, which it was downloading onto municipalities. This required the regions around Metro Toronto to share in the costs of those payments with the whole region. Since the vast majority of social service recipients living in the Greater Toronto Area lived in Metro, the effect of pooling was to require regional governments to increase property taxes in order to pay for Metro's social service costs. It was a fiendishly clever way for the province to provoke anger and enmity between the regions and Metro. Peel Region distributed to all residents a flier entitled Behind the Eight Ball that more or less told people to be angry at Toronto for this extra burden on property taxes. (See fig. 9.1.)

In June 1998, the Harris government introduced Bill 56 to establish the Greater Toronto Area Services Board and the Greater Toronto Transit Authority. Both bodies were intended to institutionalize suburban power in a way that swamped the central city. The stated functions of the Services Board, as set out in section 22(1) of the legislation, were 'to promote and facilitate co-ordinated decision-making among and adopt strategies for the municipalities within the Greater Toronto Area with respect to the provision and optimal use of infrastructure.' The idea of the Services Board had been most fully advanced by the City of Mississauga, in its report *Running the GTA 'Like a Business.'* It proposed a GTA Services Commission to control transit, waste, water, and sewage, suggesting that the commission could save up to $1 billion a year from changes in service delivery, particularly by contracting out or by using public–private partnerships.[6] The specifics of Bill 56 came from a report prepared for the province by Milt Farrow, a former provincial official who had been asked in December 1996 to report on the matter. His report, issued in June 1997, argued that the Services Board would improve coordination.

The function of the Transit Authority was to operate and fund a regional transit system. The bill came into effect in January 1999, and it downloaded provincial public transit responsibilities in the Toronto area by giving to the Transit Authority responsibility for GO Transit and allocating its costs among the regional governments in the GTA. Half the subsidy for GO Transit was allocated to the newly amalgamated City of Toronto. After it downloaded transit subsidies to municipalities in the 2000 budget, the province used its newly freed financial resources to allocate $1 billion to highways, making similar allocations for highways in its 2002 and 2003 budgets. Much of this money was to expand the express highway system in the GTA – extending Highway 407 to the east; Highway 404 to the north; Highway 427 to the north; and planning a new highway corridor to the west past Hamilton and through the Niagara peninsula to the American border. The province set a target of ensuring that about 90 per cent of the province's population was within ten kilometres of a major highway corridor.[7]

Continuing public concerns about out-of-control development in the Toronto area did not go away, and in early 2001 Premier Harris tried to steal a page from environmentalists by announcing a Smart Growth strategy. Smart Growth was the term used by those who wanted to replace sprawling subdivisions with compact development, but Harris used the term in a slightly different way. In a speech to the Toronto Real Estate Board in January 2001, he said,

Our made-in-Ontario vision of Smart Growth will foster growth ... not stop it. Our plan is based on three main principles. A strong economy. Strong communities. And a healthy environment ... Our plan will encourage growth that offers people choices about how and where they want to live. That offers transportation choices. That builds vibrant communities where families can lay down roots. Where children can grow, play and go to school. And where parents might even be able to walk to work.

The third part of our made-in-Ontario plan involves a healthy envi-

Renseignements importants. S'il vous plaît, veuillez faire traduire.
Informação importante. Por favor traduza.
Ważne informacje. Prosimy o korzystanie z pomocy tłumacza.

ਸਾਰੀ ਸੂਚਨਾ | ਮਿਹਰਬਾਨੀ ਕਰਕੇ
ਇਸ ਦਾ ਤਰਜਮਾ ਕਰਵਾ ਲਵੋ |

They're YOUR property taxes!

The provincial government removed half of the cost of education from your residential property taxes.

In return regional governments assumed the costs of many former provincial programs … **That's downloading.**

The costs of transferring education costs to the province were supposed to be **equal to the costs of the programs downloaded to local government … That's revenue neutral.**

But, in 1998 the Region of Peel raised **$66 million** through **your** property taxes to pay for programs in Toronto because downloading was **not** revenue neutral there … **That's pooling.**

And **you** don't have any say in what Toronto will spend this year, or next year! Toronto politicians aren't accountable to you. If Toronto wants to raise service levels, introduce new programs or keep Toronto's residential property taxes artificially low, guess who's going to pick up part of the tab?

You are!

Pooling added $196 to the average Peel homeowner's property taxes in 1998 …

Nobody enjoys paying taxes. But, reasonable people understand that property taxes are necessary to pay for important services like police, fire, child care, roads and garbage collection. Property taxes pay for services that benefit **our** families and **our** communities.

However, pooling service costs and property taxes with Toronto **does not** benefit our community or our families.

The average Peel homeowner, with a house assessed at $200,000 paid a Toronto pooling subsidy of $196 in 1998. **Your** property taxes went to support services in the City of Toronto such as housing and social service programs.

Think of it as having dinner with a neighbour in a restaurant. You, the Peel taxpayer, order the chicken entrée, a house wine and decide to skip dessert.

Your neighbour however, orders shrimp cocktail, lobster and steak, dessert **and** champagne. So far, no problem, as long as you each pay your **own share** of the bill.

But, by introducing pooling, the province has decided that you must not only pay for your meal, you have to chip in for part of your neighbour's lobster and champagne!

Losing your appetite yet?

Why Toronto has YOU behind this ...

For $66 million, there are a lot of things Peel could do to meet the needs of our growing community -

Hire 400 new police officers,
Fund 450 nursing home beds,
Create 2,000 new day care spaces,
Resurface 110 km of our roads,

OR

Save $66 on your property taxes

A new program you didn't even ask for...

Pooling is like adding a new program to the Region's operating budget. Before pooling, a Peel homeowner's property taxes* paid for four main services ...

Housing and Human Services	*$452*
Police	*$373*
Regional Roads & Waste Management	*$170*
GO Transit, Ambulance and other	*$117*

With pooling, we've had to add **$196** to the average property tax bill ... **Toronto** is our **fifth** program. If we didn't have to pay for pooling, you'd have **$196** in your pocket or over **$60 million** worth of Regional service improvements. Either way, it would have been **your** choice!

* Regional taxes only based on a house assessed at $200,000.

Who Did What to Whom ... and Why?

When the provincial government took back half the costs of education, **you** probably expected your property taxes to go down.

Instead, the province turned over $124.4 million worth of **their** programs to the Region of Peel, cut operating grants by about $43 million and reduced tax revenue by $2.4 million.

When Peel compared the costs of downloading against the reduced education tax the impact was in **our** favour. Peel taxpayers were in line for a significant tax decrease ... over $60 million in fact.

Unfortunately, the province's plan didn't work for Toronto. It meant Toronto property taxes would go up ... **big time**. So, the province created **pooling** – a program designed to spread the burden of Toronto's tax problems across municipalities from Burlington to Oshawa.

In 1998, pooling cost Peel taxpayers $66 million. That's several million more than the decrease we might have enjoyed had pooling never been invented.

Although Peel managed to avoid a tax increase due to pooling **in 1998** ... there's no guarantee we'll be able to avoid it in the future. So, stay tuned because ...

Pooling costs may get higher!

Region of Peel

Figure 9.1 Peel Region pamphlet to residents making the City of Toronto the enemy for the provincial decision to download and pool social expenditures.

Source: Region of Peel, Archives R913, Records of the Office of the Chairman, Accession 2004. 016.001 – Unit 4 – Tax/Service Pooling 1999.

ronment. It means cleaner air and water. Conserving the open, green spaces we have. Revitalizing and cleaning up land that has been contaminated or abandoned, or brownfield rehabilitation as it is being more commonly referred to.

Five panels reflecting a range of regional interests were appointed, and the panel for the central region, chaired by Mississauga mayor Hazel McCallion, reported in mid-2002. The recommendations, as expected, were weak and stuck to vague generalities, proposing a new body to carry on the research and generally refusing to criticize the ramifications of ongoing low-density suburban growth. Meanwhile, the community reaction to the continued encroachment of suburbia on the Oak Ridges Moraine in the Region of York, particularly in Richmond Hill, boiled over.

The Oak Ridges Moraine is a hilly area left by the glaciers as they retreated to the north about 10,000 years ago. The Moraine is rich in sand and gravel. Rainwater filters through it, feeding aquifers and giving birth to tributaries and streams, augmenting the Humber and Don Rivers flowing south through the city.[8] The Moraine is beautiful, and an important ecological resource. Local activist Glenn de Baeremaeker received support from a foundation to work with residents to protect the Moraine from development. He called meetings of residents living in Richmond Hill, and found a ready reception. In 2000, several hundred residents would attend meetings, but as more and more developments were approved, those gatherings exploded into angry sessions of more than one thousand people who wanted an end to the sprawl which was destroying the Moraine.[9] In 2001, the provincial government passed the *Oak Ridges Moraine Protection Act* to provide temporary relief. It took a few years and a change of government (when the Conservatives were defeated by the Ontario Liberal party in 2003) for stability to come to the Moraine, and it was clear that no more development on the Moraine would occur.

The Greater Toronto Services Board and the Greater Toronto Transit Authority, the two bodies established by Bill 56 in 1998, proved unworkable. They had been established by the province as a way to shed financial responsibilities, but that was not an agenda that appealed to local government. These bodies provided no clear provincial plan for the Toronto area, and thus they were unable to forge a working relationship with municipalities in the GTA. The law was quietly repealed in 2001, and the bodies were abandoned.

The 'Common Sense Revolution' of the Progressive Conservative Party came crashing down in October 2003, when the Liberal Party led by Dalton McGuinty was elected. In eight years, the Conservative Party, first under Premier Mike Harris then under Premier Ernie Eves, had done much to fuel low-density residential and commercial growth in the Toronto area. The combination of eliminating existing controls on suburban growth, however feeble, providing subsidies for sprawl, and disabling Toronto's metropolitan government allowed low-density development to spread farther than once thought possible. Toronto was now a city that resembled Vienna surrounded by Los Angeles, and without the remarkable metropolitan style of government that had served it so well for fifty years.

10

The Death
of Metro

I f there was one symbol of the importance of regional land-use planning and decision-making in Ontario, it was the Metro Federation. Metro was the government charged with a regional vision, the body responsible for land use planning on the fringes of urban settlement from 1953 until the early 1970s, the organization that created a regional plan in 1959, the structure that became the model for regional governments established in the surrounding areas. The Metro Federation was the institution that gained an enviable reputation throughout North America with the scope and structure to work well.

Metro represented the values of centralized decision-making and regional strengths, particularly because it gave a legitimacy to local decisions. As a government that 'worked,' it was despised by Premier Harris and his colleagues, with their Common Sense Revolution and their perceived mandate to reduce the size and influence of government. As well, Metro was not loved by those in the fringes, who envied its wealth and disputed its values. As noted in chapter 9, the tensions between the new suburban areas and the older City of Toronto at the heart of Metro bubbled throughout the last half of the twentieth century. Sometimes they fought over transportation routes and modes, such as the Spadina Expressway. Sometimes they fought over housing, and whether low-income households, rather than suburban homeowners, should receive public subsidies. There were disputes about how land should be developed, until the ability of the Metro Planning Board to plan for the fringe areas beyond Metro was abolished in the early 1970s. The older city looked askance at the subsidies the suburbs received for water and sewage, services which generally had to pay their own way in the city. It would only be a matter of time before the growing suburban areas found themselves in the position to take action to weaken and damage their rival, the older city, and the Metro Federation. Once the interests of the suburbs had gained the upper hand through the election of Premier Mike Harris' government in 1995, there was nothing holding them back from an all-out attack.

The creation of the Greater Toronto Area Task Force in early 1995, under the government of Premier Bob Rae, focused de-

bate about structural issues in the GTA. This was a matter of
wide public interest, but on which there was no clear way forward. The task force had the opportunity to clarify the issues
and help direct public debate, but unfortunately, it did not take
up that role. It decided it would not hold public hearings, as
had occurred at the Ontario Municipal Board in the early
1950s. Instead, individuals and organizations were asked to submit their opinions to the task force for private consideration,
and those opinions vied with the two dozen research papers
commissioned by the task force (listed in its final report), but
privately, in the private deliberations of the Task Force members. Perhaps the Task Force decided on this course after the
Harris government had been elected in June 1995, and it realized the hostility of the new leaders to its work. But it meant
there was no public process to address these large governance
questions.

Various people and organizations sought influence in this
murky situation. Metro Council, which began as an indirectly
elected body but had gained independent status with legislation allowing direct elections in 1988, feared its demise from
whatever the task force recommended, and it established an internal process of its own to review alternatives. By the summer
of 1995, it suggested that one regional government should be
established for the whole of the urbanized area in Toronto and
its environs, with a northerly boundary that generally followed
the southern edge of the Oak Ridges Moraine, and a western
boundary that followed the eastern edge of the Niagara Escarpment. The five existing regional governments would be replaced with one, and the forty local municipalities would be
restructured into fifteen local governments. It also urged that
the duties of the three levels of government – the province, the
region, and local government – be clarified.[1]

A group of GTA mayors and regional chairs released an action plan in September 1995 called *Leading by Example.*[2] It proposed property tax reform; a review of provincial financial
support so that the province would assume the costs of welfare,
child care, and other soft services; a local (not provincial) process to review municipal boundaries; and a more permissive

Municipal Act. It suggested significant reforms to education governance and a process to review decision-making in the GTA. This restructuring was expected to result in financial savings. This group renamed itself the Greater Toronto Coordinating Committee, and in January 1996 produced two financial documents. One report, *Rethinking the Fundamentals*, concluded that the province took away $2.4 billion more in tax revenues from the GTA than it provided in services, redistributing the surplus to the rest of the province, and that provincial allocations to municipalities within the GTA were lower than to municipalities in the rest of the province. The second study, *Documenting the Fiscal Facts*, showed the significant differences in service levels throughout the GTA and in provincial funding.[3] For instance, the Region of Durham received a grant of $2,513 for every public school student; Peel, $993; York, $845; and Metro, nil. Once again, the fringes were being subsidized at the expense of the city.

The Metro Toronto Board of Trade released its position in October 1995. It, too, suggested one regional government with broad sweeping powers for the whole urbanized area. It recommended that school boards be abolished, that local municipalities be reduced in number, and that the property tax system be reformed.

In January 1996, the GTA Task Force released its report. It recommended a region-wide Greater Toronto Council that would be responsible for regional infrastructure and for land-use planning to create more compact development. Property taxes should be reformed, as should provincial finance support to local governments, and a new legislative framework for municipalities should be enacted. But given the limited process, this was just one more report, rather than a summing up of a public debate. The new provincial government made it clear it didn't have much sympathy for the recommendations.

The four most powerful mayors in the GTA – Hazel McCallion of Mississauga, Mel Lastman of North York, Barbara Hall of Toronto, and Nancy Diamond of Oshawa – had been meeting for several months to create some consensus, and on the heels of the GTA Task Force report, they released their own docu-

ment, *Moving Forward Together*. The four mayors took the position that local governments served everyone well, and regional
government in any form was 'not necessary.' 'The co-ordination
and delivery of cross-boundary services can better be accomplished through a management board representing member
municipalities.'[4] The mayors opposed the idea of pooling assessment for regional expenses as recommended by the task force,
and committed themselves to reducing the number of local governments through amalgamation.

The GTA Task Force report was also attacked by the head of
staff for Metro Toronto, Robert Richards. In a speech on 14
February 1996, he complained that a Greater Toronto Council
as recommended by the task force would be 'too weak to carry
out its responsibilities,'[5] given that it consisted of local representatives. Richards noted that the task force had not discussed
community services, which he thought a serious omission, and
that nothing was done to reduce duplication by different local
and regional governments. He seemed to opt for existing structures – or at least the continuation of the Metro government.

It is fair to say there was confusion among municipal leaders
and there was no consensus about how problems in the GTA
should be addressed. Meanwhile, the Harris government
moved forward with its own agenda. It introduced Bill 26, the
Savings and Restructuring Act, at the end of November 1995, an
omnibus bill to 'promote economic prosperity through public
sector restructuring, streamlining and efficiency.' The bill
amended more than two dozen public statutes, including the
Municipal Act. Among other things, Bill 26 enabled the province to appoint a commissioner who would report on restructuring specified municipalities and whose recommendations
would be final, binding, and without appeal.

As some municipalities found, the commissioner had the
power to abolish them without any recourse whatsoever. It was
under Bill 26 that the County of Victoria and its eight local governments, with a total population of less than 70,000 sprinkled
over a vast area of the Canadian shield, was arbitrarily abolished
and replaced by one government known as the City of Kawartha
Lakes. The same fate befell the County of Kent and its twelve lo-

cal municipalities. Massive public outcries in both areas fell on deaf ears, and Bill 26 prevented any legal challenges. The Harris government was clearly determined not to be constrained by local opinion.

In April 1996, the government introduced Bill 34, an *Act to Amend the Education Act*. The legislation allowed the province to seize property taxes from commercial properties in Metro Toronto (and in Ottawa–Carleton) to pay for education costs. It was an exceptional proposal, both because property taxes had always been seen as within the sole purview of municipalities, and because public education costs within Metro were paid for entirely by Metro taxpayers, whereas in the fringes – as already pointed out – they were subsidized by the province. It was a direct attack on businesses located in Metro Toronto which were being asked to pay more property taxes even though their property taxes were already 40 per cent greater than in the areas surrounding Metro. In a rare move the Toronto Board of Trade and the mayor of Toronto made a joint announcement of concern. Their 10 April 1996 press release read:

This unprecedented move by the Provincial Government to take property taxes raised by the City of Toronto and other municipalities in Metro, is contrary to the requests of the City and the Board of Trade to provide tax relief to the beleaguered business community in the core of Toronto.

'I have stated since I was elected that nothing is more important to preserving the health of the downtown core than the creation of an equitable tax system across the GTA. Taxes that are four times rent are unacceptable and a real barrier to growth,' stated Mayor Hall. 'We have repeatedly told the Province that they must work towards a level playing field for Toronto businesses or we will no longer be the economic engine of the country. Bill 34 goes in exactly the opposite direction.'

'I think it is unfair to go after school boards whose provincial subsidy has already dwindled to zero to help cushion the cuts to other boards that still depend on provincial handouts,' said Board of Trade President Murray Benyon.

The Mayor and Murray Benyon point out that the untenable tax sit-

uation is a result of the fact that Toronto and other Metro municipalities pay for 100% of all education costs. The imbalance is created
because municipalities in the suburbs receive education grants from
the province that allow them to keep their property taxes lower.
Therefore, taking additional property taxes out of the core will only
exacerbate the problem and Metro Toronto's businesses will remain
uncompetitive compared to the surrounding regions. The 'hole in
the donut' scenario found in many North American cities is known to
be linked to high taxation in the centre core.[6]

The province apparently paid no heed to the criticism, but carried on with Bill 34 which received royal assent in June.

The province threatened to introduce legislation imposing
market value reassessment (MVA) on municipalities. This
caused great consternation, since assessments had been frozen
in Toronto for more than forty years, and MVA would cause
major shifts in tax burdens, particularly imposing much higher
costs on the downtown neighbourhoods City Council had been
protecting and enhancing since the early 1970s, while reducing
taxes on houses in the near suburbs of Scarborough, North
York, and Etobicoke. The government held off on this change
for almost a year. What it did do was appoint David Crombie to
report on how to sort out provincial–municipal relations.
Crombie had been a popular mayor of Toronto in the 1970s, a
federal cabinet minister, head of the Waterfront Royal Commission, and was generally seen as a progressive voice for the city.
He was appointed chair of the 'Who Does What' panel to look
at local governance, services, and restructuring. At first it
seemed the panel might provide useful direction in defining local and provincial roles, but in the fall of 1996, it become clear
the provincial government had made up its mind to sweep the
City of Toronto and the Metro federation out of the way. When
the *Who Does What* report was issued on 6 December 1996, it was
evident Crombie's role was also to justify serious restructuring
of government in Metro Toronto. The panel's recommendations about local and county governments in the province were
bland and unexceptional, but it could not agree on Toronto, so
Crombie came forward with his own thoughts. He recommend-

ed 'consolidation in Metro that creates a strong urban core for the GTA,'[7] in short, forced amalgamation of the six municipalities within Metro.[8] He also proposed a Greater Toronto Services Board to provide regional services for the GTA.

Alan Tonks, chair of Metro Council, proposed a similar solution, perhaps because he had been promised a prominent part in any restructuring. On 28 November, Tonks released a letter he had written to Al Leach, Minister of Municipal Affairs, saying

it is clear to me that a unified city is an essential first step to the eventual implementation of a GTA regional government ... It is obvious to me that a unified city is best positioned, in terms of both administrative and fiscal ability to take on the responsibilities flowing out of the 'Who Does What' process and your government's reductions in transfer payments to municipalities.

Tonks said that the savings, 'by going the unified city route,' would be between $187 and $208 million per year.

These savings are just from the inefficiencies of integrating those services that are currently provided by six or seven separate administrations. Do we really still need seven Treasurers, seven legal departments and so on? I don't think we do. The savings from eliminating politicians, chief administrative officers and other headquarters functions alone probably amount to $78 million or more annually.[9]

Where did this idea come from? It is not found in any of the submissions made to the GTA Task Force, nor was it voiced in any public discussion of options. Former Metro chair Paul Godfrey, a close friend of many in the Mike Harris government and a major political influence in city politics since his term as Metro chair from 1973 to 1984, apparently suggested the idea of amalgamation to Minister Leach sometime in the summer of 1996. Premier Harris had no earlier penchant for amalgamation. On 19 September 1994, a year before his government was elected, Harris said, in the small agricultural centre of Fergus, 'I disagree with restructuring because it believes that bigger is bet-

ter. Service always costs more in larger communities.'[10] Two
years later, however, there were other issues in play. The Harris
government found the City of Toronto Council bothersome.
The council had challenged the province on plans for market
value reassessment, for downloading costs to municipalities, for
cutting welfare, for proposing to end rent controls. Why not destroy the troublesome Toronto City Council by amalgamating it
with the other local governments in Metro?

That was certainly the rumour and the fear in late fall 1996.
Provincial officials indicated they wanted to restructure local
government in time for the municipal election scheduled for
November 1997. In fear and trepidation, the mayors of the six
local governments in Metro tried to work out a response to
what they saw as their imminent destruction. On 29 November
1996, they released the report *Change for the Better*, which suggested the number of elected municipal officials in Toronto be
reduced from 106 to 54, and that the two-tier system within
Metro be abandoned in favour of stronger local governments
and a local municipal coordinating board that would oversee
the delivery of regional services within Metro. The mayors proposed that, in a few years, regional services be taken over by a
Greater Toronto Area Coordinating Board with responsibilities
for sewers, water, waste, and transit. They estimated cost savings
of $135–$165 million a year. They rejected the 'unified' approach, stating 'we do not believe that a city of 2.3 million people is a local government.'[11]

There was widespread concern among activists in Toronto
about the coming change. Toronto Mayor Barbara Hall invited
residents to respond to the *Change for the Better* report, and while
the council chamber was filled with citizens for several evenings
in early December – more than fifty people spoke at the 2 December meeting, which lasted more than five hours – Hall was
unwilling to lead a large movement that would confront the
government when the expected legislation, in whatever form it
might be, was revealed. At the 9 December meeting in the
Council Chamber former mayor John Sewell said he was calling
a meeting for 16 December, to create a citizen's movement to
confront the provincial reorganization.

Minister of Municipal Affairs Al Leach made public his proposal on 17 December 1996, when Bill 103, the *City of Toronto Act,* was given its first reading. He proposed the forcible amalgamation of the six local governments and one regional government in Toronto.[12] Following the lead of Alan Tonks a few weeks earlier, Leach argued that amalgamation would save money, using the example of the six fire departments in Metro with six chiefs. If they were amalgamated into one department, said Leach, there would only be one chief, and therefore money would be saved. To justify his proposal, Leach said that twenty-five reports had been prepared on governance in Toronto in recent years. That was true, but apart from the very recent report by Crombie's 'Who Does What' panel, none had suggested or even discussed, total amalgamation as a solution. Leach released a report by the consultant firm KPMG, arguing that amalgamation could have potential savings of up to $100,000,000 a year, but the consultant with KPMG who wrote the study was reported by the *Globe and Mail* as saying, 'There has been no amalgamation, of which I am aware, in the current fiscal environment that would demonstrate the certainty of savings in Metro Toronto.'[13]

More worrisome was the proposal in Bill 103 to immediately strip decision-making powers from the six local councils and from Metro Council, lodging those powers with an appointed Board of Trustees responsible to the provincial government. The Board would make all important decisions about money, policy and staffing, effectively replacing the democratically elected local governments in Toronto. It was little more than a provincially appointed junta. Leach immediately arranged the delivery to Toronto homes of an advertising flier claiming the megacity was a done deal. This was untrue, since Bill 103 had not yet been passed, and the speaker found Leach in contempt of the legislature, although the finding came with no penalty. Leach had not misrepresented the government's intention with the flier that was being distributed; it intended to play hard ball and pass Bill 103 quickly. On the day the bill was first introduced into the legislature, Harris appointed the Financial Advisory Board proposed in the bill, as though the bill was already law. It took a court decision on a legal application by the City of Scarborough to quash those appointments and declare them illegal.

The 16 December meeting organized by Sewell attracted several hundred, and a group quickly came together.[14] Its second meeting on 23 December after the bill was released, attracted more than 300 people. The group decided to call itself Citizens for Local Democracy (C4LD) and its slogan was 'Restore Local Democracy to Toronto.' A steering committee was patched together, both of those who volunteered at the meeting and of others asked to join in order to round out the interests represented (see fig. 10.1).[15]

The group decided that there was enough interest in this issue that meetings should continue every Monday evening in downtown Toronto. The meeting on 30 December drew an even larger crowd, and the first meeting in January 1997 attracted more than 800 people. The steering committee had to find a location capable of handling such a large number of people, and it turned to the two largest churches in downtown Toronto, the Metropolitan United Church and St James Anglican Cathedral. Both churches agreed to provide their sanctuaries for meetings free of charge. There was an atmosphere reminiscent of Eastern Europe, as politics were practised in a church packed with citizens and political banners. Most meetings in January and February attracted close to 2,000 people. The problem for the steering committee was to determine how these gatherings would be programmed and, at the same time, how to use this resource of people to organize citywide opposition to the megacity.

The City of Toronto retained its own consultants to counter the province's claims. American Wendall Cox argued that smaller governments are more accountable, more responsive, and more attuned to local opinions than larger governments, which are more susceptible to special interests. He also showed that larger governments have higher unit costs than smaller governments, and said that the most efficient local government had a population over 200,000 and less than one million. Using American data, he showed that there was no firm evidence that

JANUARI 71 — PL

WHOSE TORONTO?

Restore Democracy in Toronto
Stop Bill 103!

CITIZENS FOR LOCAL DEMOCRACY

Local democracy and a high quality of life are two sides of the same coin. Take away decision-making which can respond well to local demands, and the quality of life in the city declines sharply.

It's easy to forget that most programs and policies urban residents rely on are the result of decisions made by local city councils. Many programs have been carefully tailored to meet different local needs, and vary from municipality to municipality.

If local councils are dismantled, the different approaches they have taken to respond to local wishes will surely soon be dismantled as well. The high quality of life in Toronto neighbourhoods will decline if the province abolishes responsive local councils.

There are many examples of locally developed programs and policies that will disappear if local councils are destroyed by Bill 103, the Megacity Bill. Here are eight:

1. In North York, household garbage is picked up twice a week. In most other Metro municipalities, garbage collection is a once-a-week affair.

2. In the city of Toronto, grants to arts and culture exceed $10 million a year. Other municipalities in Metro leave prime responsibility for arts and culture with Metro council, which spends about half that amount.

The proposed megacity will destroy carefully tailored local programs that make our municipalities good places to live for all kinds of different people.

3. In Toronto, recreation programs operate at no charge to children. In other municipalities, kids are generally required to pay a fee.

4. The City of York has responded to the loss of industries and jobs with innovative, cost efficient, and effective economic development programs. Other municipalities are so impressed they are copying York's programs.

5. The City of Toronto's animal shelter has adopted a unique policy of refusing to comply with provincial legislation requiring that abandoned pets be turned over for research.

6. The City of North York clears snow from sidewalks, as well as roads. Other municipalities leave sidewalk care to abutting owners.

7. The Borough of East York runs an exceptionally open city council process, allowing significant resident participation which other cities would reject out of hand.

8. The City of Toronto has created strong programs — like community safety initiatives and pressuring the provincial government not to abandon rent controls — which are now at risk.

These are the kinds of local programs which make Toronto municipalities good places to live for all kinds of different people. As well, many resident groups have negotiated with staff to ensure that road improvements and traffic regulations meet local needs, that parks are designed to fit well in the neighbourhood, and that city programs are geared to local language preferences.

The province has no right to wipe out the councils which enable these programs.

Local democracy works effectively to improve the quality of life for Toronto residents. When we lose local democracy, the quality of all our lives will decline.

It's easy for the province to criticize councillors — they meet in public session (unlike the provincial Cabinet which meets in secret), and their thoughts are not filtered through the layers of staff available to provincial cabinet ministers. It's not until the power of city councils to make decisions about local matters is threatened that their importance becomes clear.

To protect Toronto's quality of life, local councils must not be put under trusteeship. Local councils must not be replaced with one big megacity.

WHAT YOU CAN DO

1. Join the meetings of Citizens for Local Democracy — every Monday evening at 7.30 pm.. Call our hot line at 977-8736 for the location. At these meetings, strategies are planned and tasks are assigned to willing volunteers. At these meetings you will realize just how many people share your concerns about the loss of local democracy.

2. Ensure you are listed as a speaker at the Legislative Committee which will hold hearings on Bill 103. Please write this letter as soon as possible, to meet whatever deadline the province imposes. To ensure you are on the speakers list, send a letter (or fax 325-3505) to:

Committees Branch, Clerk's Office
Room 1405, Whitney Block,
Queen's Park, Toronto M7A 1A2.

In your letter, indicate that you wish to be listed as a speaker at the committee hearings on Bill 103. Provide your address and phone number.

Also, please send our committee a copy of the letter by faxing it to 348 0438, or bring it to a Monday evening meeting.

3. Please distribute this newsletter to your friends and colleagues (you can copy this on most copying machines) and ask them to write the Clerk as well.

Progressive Conservative Joyce Trimmer (former mayor of Scarborough), the first person asked by Mike Harris to study reforms to the Greater Toronto area, has blasted his government's megacity legislation.

Trimmer called the legislation "appalling" and "dishonest," while also accusing the government of "playing games" that threaten to leave Metro neighbourhoods "whipped to death."

"I have always been a Conservative supporter, but I am questioning it right now," said Trimmer. — from the Toronto Star, December 20, 1996

Figure 10.1 C4LD broadsheet, Bulletin No. 1.
Source: Citizens for Local Democracy, December 1996.

consolidation results in savings. He said that if there were to be savings, it would be a result of better management, not amalgamation.

The city also retained Professor Andrew Sancton of the University of Western Ontario. He suggested that if there were savings, as suggested by KPMG, they would be the result of service cuts, not because of amalgamation. He suggested that amalgamation would actually increase costs, as salaries of the six local governments being forced together would increase to the highest level.

These arguments appealed to those interested in a reasonable approach to the issues, but that did not seem to include anyone in a senior position in the Harris government. The provincial government had decided it would not only destroy local government in Toronto but also that it would entirely reorder a number of significant functions for which it was responsible. This became clear during 'mega week,' which began on Monday, 13 January 1997. That day the government introduced Bill 104, the *Fewer School Boards Act,* which entirely restructured the system of public education in Ontario. In Toronto, the six school boards were to be replaced by one school board with twenty-two trustees, each paid no more than $5,000 a year for what was considered an almost full-time position. The provincial government ruled that local governments would no longer be responsible for funding education – that would be a provincial responsibility, and to provide the needed funds, the province grabbed hold of the municipal property tax system to use for its own purposes. (Bill 34, referred to earlier, had been just a prelude to a wider change.)

On Tuesday, 14 January the province announced major downloading arrangements. Municipalities would be required to pay half of all welfare costs, half of all childcare costs, and half of all hostel beds. Previously, municipalities had paid 20 per cent of these programs. All of the subsidies previously paid for social housing by the province were now to be paid by the municipalities. The costs of public health would be borne entirely by municipalities – previously the province had paid 25 per cent – as well as half the costs of long-term care (previously entirely covered by the province), and the full cost of women's shelters (previously entirely funded by the province). These were enormous sums that the province was unilaterally downloading onto municipalities.

On Wednesday, 15 January, the province announced that it was transferring to municipalities some 8,000 kilometres of roads that it felt served primarily local needs, and municipalities would now be responsible for the costs of keeping these roads in good repair. The province also announced it was ending all subsidies to public transit, and that its subsidy share of $110 million for GO Transit would be downloaded entirely to regional governments in the Greater Toronto Area. Provincial subsidies for municipal libraries were terminated as well as subsidies to municipal policing. The independent complaints process for police was terminated and replaced with a system of police investigating themselves.

On Thursday, 16 January, the province announced that municipalities would be required to use Current Value Assessment (virtually the same as the reviled MVA), and that they would be responsible for all the costs of the property assessment function, costs previously borne entirely by the province. On Friday, 17 January, the province announced it was ceasing all other grants to municipalities, and that the fees paid in lieu of property tax by telephone and telegraph companies would no longer go to municipalities but directly to the province.

City of Toronto staff estimated that the province had downloaded to municipalities about $540 million in annual costs during this week of announcements. The direct impact on the City of Toronto itself was $220 million per year. These changes were embodied in Bills 104, 105, 106, 107, 108, and 109, following Bill 103 that created the Megacity. While this was occurring, consideration was also being given to a report of the Health Services Restructuring Commission. The Ministry of Health proposed to close ten of the thirty-three hospitals within Metro, including the famous Women's College Hospital and the Wellesley Hospital.

These actions constituted an unprecedented attack on the people of Metro Toronto and on other municipalities throughout the province, although the impacts were felt most severely

within Metro Toronto. Those living in the fringes outside
Metro did not feel that they were directly affected. Their local
governments were not affected, nor were their programs upset
to any substantial degree. In Metro Toronto there were more
than 73,000 units of rent-geared-to-income housing requiring
subsidies, whereas in the four outlying regions there were just
21,000 units,[16] so the downloading of housing subsidies wasn't
such a financial threat there. The fringes had little public transit to worry about funding, and expenditures on social programs such as welfare and day care were small, since the
number of low-income households there were few. But in
Metro Toronto, local politicians had prided themselves for four
decades on strong social service infrastructure, including a
great deal of social housing and many innovative programs serving those with lower incomes. The education system in Metro
also played a strong social role, and in the City of Toronto itself
many shared-use programs happened in schools, staffed by personnel from the city's recreation department. Schools had become places where kids could experience not only good
education but also an array of recreation and social programs.
Harris' new rules for schools put an end to this: funding for the
schools was substantially limited and schools were not allowed
to rent out space for community programs except at full cost –
costs so high that most community programs were unable to
meet them, forcing them to close. It was hard not to see the
changes as a direct attack on Metro Toronto and on the people
who lived there.

   C4LD became the group that focused public opposition to
the megacity proposal and these other radical changes. Keeping the opposition organized and focused required a new kind
of central organization. The C4LD steering committee saw itself as a clearing house for information and strategies rather
than as the main agent and actor in the struggle. The steering
committee positioned C4LD as an enabler, that is, helping people to take action themselves. At the Monday meetings people
could learn what was going on and what new actions were being
planned by others. There they could pick up signs and newsletters. The Monday meetings were places where people could get

support, feel a sense of solidarity with others, and be encouraged to take individual action. Under the direction and leadership of Liz Rykert and a group she organized – which started as mostly male and ended up as entirely female and called itself the 'wild web women' – C4LD attained an online presence. Individuals could publish their opinions online, see copies of the latest bulletins and news clippings, and share information on everything that was going on in the city. The site was a repository of accurate information that was instantly made available to everyone.

Kathleen Wynne chaired the C4LD meetings, which now attracted between 1,500 and 2,000 people. A set format quickly developed for the meetings: sharing important new information; speeches by some of the city's leading political opponents; a performance, a reading, or a speech by a cultural leader, including heavyweights Jane Jacobs, Margaret Atwood, Anne Michaels, John Ralston Saul, Michael Ondaatje, and Dennis Lee; music; and a concluding inspirational speech by John Sewell. Tables were available for people to share information about the prolific number of activities throughout the city.

The steering committee decided that there were two ways in which opposition could best be expressed. One was by having individuals writing letters to the legislature requesting the opportunity to speak to the standing committee that would review Bill 103. At each C4LD meeting in December and January, an opportunity was provided for letter writing. They were then collected and sent in batches to the clerk of the legislature. Minister Leach had said that four or five days of hearings would take place on Bill 103, but about 1,200 letters requesting the right to speak were submitted, and this avalanche meant the province had no choice but to extend the hearings. In the end, the hearings lasted six weeks.

The other way of voicing opposition support was in the referendums that all six municipal councils agreed to hold in early March. Organizing for these referendums gave those who opposed the megacity a real sense of purpose. C4LD encouraged people to hold meetings in their own community, and it coordinated speakers and material for distribution. C4LD also pro-

duced a broadsheet published biweekly starting in December
(see fig. 10.1). Copies were available to be picked up at the
weekly Monday meetings. Often the broadsheet was handed
out on subway platforms, where transit riders snatched up copies. C4LD's costs were not large – printing newsletters, paying
for a phone hotline where a daily announcement (with Bronwyn Drainie providing the voice) was available, providing support for the Democracy March in mid-February, and so forth. A
collection was taken at every meeting to cover these expenses.
No individuals were paid for their time – people just threw
themselves into the battle.

Toronto's three daily newspapers each voiced editorial support for amalgamation as the best way to rationalize local government. Many radio and television stations took the same
position. The *Toronto Star* thought that having one big council
in Toronto (rather than six) would boost its suburban sales and
reduce its costs, as was learned later from internal newspaper
memos. Its editorial position spilled over to its journalist responsibilities, and it refused to report on the early large meetings of C4LD. Requests to the *Star* editors to assign people to
cover the C4LD meetings were refused for more than a month.
In late January, the paper finally sent a reporter to a meeting
and ingenuously appeared to have discovered that something
was happening. The *Globe and Mail,* perhaps doubting that the
large Monday meetings reflected substantial opposition, chose
one evening when its reporters would cover every community
meeting that was scheduled in Metro. It chose an evening in
February, when it discovered, to its surprise, that seventeen local meetings had been scheduled with an average attendance at
each gathering of 200 people.

In early February, the standing committee of the legislature
began its hearings on Bill 103. C4LD's website provided ideas
that people could draw on while composing their presentation,
but presenters were urged to use their own words to voice their
own opinions. In all, 590 deputations were made, of which 550
were in opposition to amalgamation. Most of those who spoke
in opposition had never made a public presentation before, but
they spoke from the heart about their knowledge of local gov-

ernment, and their deputations were enormously moving. The proceedings were reported on a daily basis by the media and also broadcast in full by the government television channel as part of legislative proceedings. It was extraordinary television, as ordinary people expressed anger and concern with Bill 103 and about the other changes that the government was making. The hearings meant that the opposition to the megacity was now general news. The anger and upset spread to the city at large.

C4LD agreed to hold a Democracy March in mid-February, re-enacting the march down Yonge Street by William Lyon Mackenzie in 1837, known at that time as the rebellion. A group of individuals organized a performance which would begin once the march reached Queen's Park. It was estimated that close to 9,000 people joined the march.

The referendums were held by the six local governments on 6 March. The question was: 'Are you in favour of eliminating your local municipality and the other existing municipalities in Metro Toronto and amalgamating them into a megacity?' C4LD reserved Massey Hall for the evening since it accommodated 3,500 people, but the meeting was so crowded people were turned away at the door. The referendum results poured in and showed that, in spite of what all the newspapers had tried to get people to believe, most were opposed to amalgamation. Voter turnout in Toronto, East York, and North York was at record high levels, with more voters than in regular municipal elections. Voters in all six municipalities overwhelmingly opposed amalgamation. The highest opposition was in East York, with 81 per cent of voters opposed. The average was 76.8 per cent in opposition.

Had the citizens won? No. Minister Leach remarked the next day, 'From all the information I have seen ... everything indicates to me the majority of people still favour amalgamation.'[17] It was clear that the Ontario government would go ahead with this legislation, no matter what. Premier Harris tried to allay public fears, saying that the Financial Advisory Committee to be established by Bill 103 would not really make decisions, and that 'trustees no longer have the power of veto.'[18] The *Toronto*

Star took the same position, arguing that the Transition Team was just an advisory body. But that was not what the bill said: both bodies had final decision-making powers that could not be appealed or otherwise challenged. The elected council was being displaced by provincially appointed officials. Indeed, section 19 of Bill 103 stated explicitly that when the Transition Team hired a person for the new megacity, 'the new city is bound by the resulting employment contract.'

In April, the government proceeded with third reading of Bill 103. Leach proposed several amendments literally out of the blue – enlarging the megacouncil from forty-five to fifty-seven members, and creating six community councils with very limited powers. Opposition members filibustered, and the debate lasted for ten days and ten nights without interruption. As one sign that this legislation was a serious intrusion on democracy, there were no allegations by the media of game-playing or abuse of process by the opposition. When opposition legislators who had maintained the filibuster finally collapsed in exhaustion, the bill was given third reading and rushed into the Office of the Lieutenant Governor for immediate Royal Assent. The province immediately appointed trustees, who took over decision-making from Metro Toronto and the six local governments in Toronto. Democratically elected local government in Metro Toronto was suspended.

On the other side of the world, a similar kind of change was occurring. The government of China decided to replace the democratically elected government of Hong Kong with its panel of hand-picked advisers. There were cries of protests from many world leaders about the loss of democracy and what it would mean for Hong Kong. Canadian Foreign Affairs Minister Lloyd Axworthy voiced his concern. C4LD wrote Axworthy and pointed out the parallels between what was happening in Hong Kong and in Toronto, and asked him to make a public statement about Toronto similar to the one he had made for Hong Kong. Axworthy did not reply to the request, bearing out the adage that it is easier to find fault with others than with ourselves. Demolish democratic institutions in Canada? It could never happen here.

A group of citizens brought legal action to quash Bill 103, claiming it was beyond the province's power. It was a difficult argument to make. The 1867 *British North America Act* is the basis of the Canadian constitution, and it states in section 92(8) that a provincial legislature may 'exclusively make laws in relation to ... municipal institutions.' The Canadian courts have interpreted this section to mean that municipalities are 'creatures' of provinces, a strange ruling, given that many cities and towns existed before 1867 and the creation of the provinces. The court was asked to rule whether this power also included unilaterally restructuring one of the largest cities in Canada. Lawyers raised concerns under the Charter of Rights and Freedoms, particularly around the lack of consultation. The Divisional Court showed sympathy, but was not convinced by the legal arguments, and the challenge was denied. Judge Stephen Borins released the judgment in early July, stating:

In my view, the applicants' real complaints are that the government did not engage in meaningful consultation with the inhabitants of the six municipalities before it introduced Bill 103, and that it ignored the results of the referenda, which opposed the creation of the megacity, by taking the bill to final reading. These complaints were supported by the evidence. It may be that the government displayed mega chutzpah in proceeding as it did ... However, the question for the court is not the government's political posture, but rather its legal and constitutional authority to proceed as it did. In any event, the *Charter* does not guarantee an individual the right to live his or her life free from government chutzpah or imperiousness ...[19]

As quickly as the legislation was passed, the Harris government appointed its Transition Team. The Transition Team began to retain staff to manage the new city, including the Chief Administrative Officer. The more the government disregarded any opposition, no matter how sizable, the more it was debilitating for activists. C4LD generally lost its momentum. The government continued with its deluge of repressive legislation. Bronwyn Drainie, a C4LD stalwart, summed up the mood in a presentation to a legislative committee in September 1997:

My concern from the beginning of this horrible year, 1997, has more generally been with the process you have employed in attempting to get that legislation passed. You have refused meaningful consultation with the citizens. You have ignored a legitimate referendum that expressed the will of the people. You have changed the rules of debate in the legislature so as to seriously curtail the ability of the opposition parties, the media and the public to understand the substance and impact of your bills.

You have put in place illegitimate appointed authorities such as the Transition Team, the Education Improvement Commission and the Health Services Restructuring Board to ride roughshod over our democratic right to decide how we should be governed through our elected representatives. You have amassed a record of arrogance, deceit and contempt for the public. You'll perhaps remember the one word Judge Stephen Borins used to sum up your attitude when he regretfully ruled that you had the constitutional right to push through the hated legislation known as Bill 103. His word for your government's behaviour was 'mega chutzpah' and none of us could say it better ...[20]

The first municipal election for the megacity was held in November 1997, pitting Mel Lastman of North York, where he had been mayor for two decades, against Toronto Mayor Barbara Hall. Hall's campaign was lacklustre, and the voting showed a split between those in the inner city (the part of the city built before 1950) and the outer city (built after Don Mills in the early 1950s). Lastman, who was from the outer city, carried the day. This seemed to be perfectly fine for the provincial Progressive Conservative Party, since Lastman had loyalties to the party; further, he was seen as a weak administrator with little sense of policy. Lastman was a dealmaker and a buffoon, and these two characteristics marked his six years as the first mayor of the megacity.

The split between the inner and outer cities within the new Toronto City Council immediately made itself known. Lastman appointed his staff from North York to most of the senior positions in the new city, most importantly Paula Dill as the commissioner of Urban Development Services. Senior staff from the former City of Toronto were probably the most experienced and imaginative group of civic staff in the province, but they found themselves frozen out of positions of responsibility, and after a year or two many left in frustration. The inner–outer split within the former Metro had an even more telling effect. Outer city politicians thought that, compared to their experience, the former City of Toronto spent too much money downtown on garbage collection and street cleaning. Scarborough, Etobicoke, and North York politicians cut these expenditures to the levels with which they were familiar. The result was that garbage and litter became very evident in the downtown, and the inner city had the look of generally being unkempt and uncared for. Outer city politicians also did not like the former City of Toronto policy that treated recreation for children and youth as a social program offered at no cost. They saw this as a ridiculous luxury, and began to impose fees for recreational programs that, for a century had been free in the former City of Toronto. Attendance at these programs dropped precipitously, and then the programs themselves were cut. In 1995, for example, at the community centre run out of Hillcrest School in the Bathurst and St Clair area where there were a lot of latchkey kids, children could choose from thirty-eight hours of after-school programs a week. The array of choices meant that a child in any age bracket could find a program fitting his/her needs after school, and attendance was high. In 1999, less than two years after amalgamation, after-school programs at Hillcrest had dropped to a mere six hours a week. The new City Council had simply abandoned most recreation programs for inner-city kids. Few had expected that these divisions between the inner and outer city within the new Toronto would manifest themselves in such powerful ways.

Studies on the effects of amalgamation showed that it substantially increased costs, caused extraordinary bureaucratic confusion, and resulted in a silencing of local voices.[21] One time transition expenses included paying staff exit costs ($75 million), retraining staff ($5 million), creating new business information systems ($83 million), consolidating and modifying work spaces ($82 million), and covering such related costs as consultant studies and collective agreement obligations ($30

million) for a total of $275 million.[22] To pay these costs, the new
city had to strip the reserve fund of $80 million and borrow to
pay for the rest – with annual debt repayment costs of $29 mil-
lion a year for ten years. The provincial estimates of one-time
costs had been extremely optimistic – between $150 and $220
million.

What must be remembered is that a considerable number of
services such as the police, public transit, and social services,
were already being delivered by Metro – they were already
'amalgamated' – and thus were not affected by the megacity
amalgamation. The new city had an operating budget of $5.5
billion in 2000, of which $4 billion was spent on services former-
ly delivered at the regional level. The services being amalgamated had a cost of $1.5 billion a year, and that, apparently, was
where the savings would be found.

Staff found there were no savings resulting from the so-called
efficiencies. The cost of harmonizing services from the six municipalities was $17.8 million per year. The estimated savings
from service consolidation were estimated to be $153 million
per year, but the savings resulted almost entirely from staff lay-
offs and dismissals. Staff reductions resulting from amalgamation totalled 1,935.[23]

These staff reductions created extraordinary confusion, just
as Lorne Cumming had predicted in 1953 when he recommended against amalgamation. The number of departments
was reduced from 52 to 6, and the number of divisions within
these departments was reduced from 206 to 37. Executive management positions were chopped by two-thirds, from 381 to 154
positions. Area manager positions were cut by one-third, from
1,837 to 1,204 positions. The remainder of the cuts were of
front-line staff. This very significant downsizing in managers resulted in very low levels of morale for the first five years of amalgamation, a result of the loss of organizational memory that
followed the loss of senior staff, and the reduction in problem-
solving abilities among staff, particularly since the very good
staff tended to leave and find other jobs more quickly than others. The loss of so many people meant there was general confusion about who should be doing what. Another result of this

confusion has been that since amalgamation, Toronto City Hall
has not been a place where innovative policies can be developed or delivered. It seems as though everything was put on
hold when amalgamation took over centre stage.

   Services that had previously been run at the Metro level were
only marginally affected by these changes, but services formerly
delivered locally (parks and recreation services, for example)
suffered enormously. There is little good analytical data on exactly how these local services changed, but there is a great deal
of anecdotal information. For example, the waiting time for
having the city attend to deal with a damaged tree on city property climbed from one week to five or six months. Part of the
reason for this change was the confusion that amalgamation
caused, but another reason was simply the loss of an adequate
number of staff. As noted, litter-picking and street cleaning
downtown suffered enormously.

   Harmonizing fees – that is, establishing a common rate
across the amalgamated city – usually meant lowering fees in
the outer-city municipalities and increasing them in the centre.
It caused much anger. Thus, user fees were increased for permit parking in downtown neighbourhoods where permit parking on streets was one of the few residential parking options
available. User fees were imposed on many people for recreation services, as already noted, and fees were increased for
commercial garbage removal, planning applications, and building permits. The revenues generated by these user fees was relatively small, but the impact of higher user fees was felt most by
downtown residents, that is, those living in the older part of the
city.

   The Minister of Municipal Affairs had announced amalgamation with the promise that it would be less expensive to run
one fire department than to pay six fire chiefs and their support
staff. He was wrong. Once the six fire departments had finally
been amalgamated, the new operation was found to be about
13 per cent more expensive than the old operations. The ratio-
nalization of fire stations and equipment turned out to be more
expensive than envisaged and didn't save money. But the key
cost was staff: it proved impossible to reduce numbers of fire-

fighters (in fact, City Council decided to increase staff), and the salaries were changed to the highest level paid in each job category.

More than five years after amalgamation, Toronto City Council had still not found a way to harmonize job categories or levels of pay for staff. Staff worked side by side doing the same work under the different job descriptions and rates of pay that survived the original seven municipalities once amalgamated. City Council decided it would be too expensive to raise the salaries of everyone doing the same job to the level of the person highest paid for that job or to simplify the number of job categories, particularly since the former Toronto and Metro Councils had implemented a plan of pay equity, which finally paid women the same as men for similar work. No one was able to propose a reasonable alternative that could attract the necessary union support.

The extent of the financial problems was reflected in the city's inability to balance its operating budget during each of the two years following amalgamation. The *Municipal Act* required municipalities to have a balanced budget, but in contravention of that law, the city's operating shortfall was covered by loans of several hundred million dollars provided by the provincial government. If a lawsuit had been brought, it's hard to see how any councillor supporting the operating budget could escape personal liability for these loans and the city's deficit.

Many problems resulted from the enormous size of the new city government. The physical area covered by the government was so large that many council members were not familiar with addresses and streets referred to in some items requiring council decision. Many local government decisions are location-specific, but when decision-makers aren't able to visualize a locale it is hard for them to make a good decision, and since they don't feel fully informed, they often do not engage in debate. There was much ward-heeling rather than shared city-building. The community councils established in Leach's surprise and last-minute amendment to Bill 103 did not prove to be an effective response to this problem. Community councils did not have full and final decision-making powers – that rested only with City Council – and they were not authorized to deal with staffing issues or budgets, keys areas of governance that rested with the full City Council.

The amount of business dealt with by City Council at each meeting was overwhelming. The agenda for a single council meeting often amounted to more than 3,000 pages, and few council members had the time or energy to read all of this material and digest it. Handing off more decisions to staff was not popular, since so many decisions involved an exercise in discretion.

Even once the council was reduced in size from fifty-seven to forty-five members (that occurred two years later), the council was too big to permit full discussions of important issues. Councillors were restricted to a speaking time of a meagre five minutes, far too brief a time to address a significant issue, and given the large size of council, the speakers' list was so long that what was said early on in the debate might be lost at the end. Most municipal councils in Canada have less than twenty members, which means that all members of council can have reasonable personal relationships with one another and fully address important issues. The megacity council was far too big.

The megacity contained different and competing urban cultures, which demanded different policies to meet their particular needs. With a one-size-fits-all megacouncil, that proved almost impossible to deliver. As well, the body of staff necessary to serve the big city – more than 60,000 individuals – was so large that City Council had no effective control over it. Even senior managers seemed unable to control what line managers and others removed by one or two levels of management from City Council actually did. Staff problems in the first five years of amalgamation made this painfully clear.

The evidence was overwhelming. The megacity was disastrous on all accounts for Toronto residents. It imposed higher costs, less efficiency, less local input, and the problems were all aggravated by the downloading of costs that the new city was unable to pay. Amalgamation generally disabled council members and created a body of staff who were out of touch with local needs and aspirations. One could only conclude that the imposition of amalgamation had rendered local government in Toronto dysfunctional. There are many who believe the purpose and intention of amalgamation was to accomplish that goal, so that Toronto City Council would not be an open critic of Mike Harris' proposals to reshape the public sector in Ontario, and in that respect the Harris government succeeded enormously well. It destroyed effective local and regional government in Toronto. For the next five or six years, the city was so disabled politically and financially that it had difficulty providing a reasonable standard of governance and was unable to participate meaningfully in regional issues that were important to it.

11

Re-establishing
a Regional
Agenda

The Common Sense interregnum lasted for eight years, and ended with the election of a Liberal Party government under Dalton McGuinty in September 2003. The amount of low-density suburban housing built in the Toronto fringes during this eight-year period exceeded all expectations. In the early 1990s, some 25,000 new housing units a year were built in the Toronto area, of which about 25 per cent happened within Metro. After the Harris government was elected and the controls were loosened, that number increased to almost 35,000 new units in 1999 (of which 27,000 new units were in the fringes), increasing to 45,475 units by 2003. The number then declined slightly to 42,115 in 2004, and to 37,000 in 2006.[1]

In the fringes, the growth was generally at the edge of the urban area as it pushed outwards, often onto prime agricultural land.[2] Gross residential densities were generally in the range of fifteen to twenty units per hectare (uph), and that figure included higher-density developments that occasionally were built in older parts of the settlement or close to a shopping plaza. These densities were slightly higher than in 1990, when they were about 10 uph.[3] These were significantly lower than some of the communities closer to the centre of the city, communities known for their houses such as Riverdale (30 uph), Leaside (20 uph), or the Beaches (27 uph).[4] Densities just beyond the edge of the fringe were lower still at seven uph and less, as these areas were thought to be rural, not urban, even though they were being developed as subdivisions.[5]

The new government showed considerable interest in addressing questions of low-density development. In December 2003, it introduced Bill 26 to amend the *Planning Act* to require that planning decisions 'be consistent with' provincial policies. This was the standard enacted by the Rae government, but then abandoned by the Conservatives who said municipal decisions simply had 'to have regard for' provincial policies, and this change provided the sense that reasonable order was returning to Ontario. The McGuinty government also proposed a comprehensive set of planning policy statements that bore many similarities to the policies adopted by the Rae government as a result of the New Planning for Ontario initiative more than a decade earlier. The new policies stated that planning decisions were required to promote efficient development and to minimize land consumption and servicing costs. Intensification became a serious goal, with appropriate densities required to make efficient use of infrastructure and public services. As with any thirty-seven page policy statement, there were more loopholes than one would wish, but the objective was clearly to contain rather than promote sprawl, and that signalled a substantial change. After considerable public discussion, the statements were adopted in 2005.

More spectacularly, the McGuinty government committed itself to a regional plan for the Toronto area. This would be the first such plan since the Toronto-Centred Region Plan was announced in 1970 and then quickly abandoned, and unlike the TCR Plan, which drew heavily on Metro's 1959 plan, this one had no clear antecedent. It was the province's fresh start, and the province claimed that work had begun as far back as 2001, presumably a reference to the Smart Growth panels. A discussion paper was released in 2004 entitled 'Places to Grow.' It proposed a plan for an area slightly larger than the Greater Toronto Area, calling it the Greater Golden Horseshoe. The intention of this plan was to stop sprawl by encouraging intensification, containing growth, and directing it to locations that would not adversely impact good agricultural land or the natural environment. It proposed to show leadership in public investment by shaping urban form and promoting public transit use. The maps in the document were precise about areas where further development would be permitted and not permitted. A considerable amount of the new development would be required to take place not on green fields (which generally was quality agricultural land) but on land that was already developed and part of an existing settlement. When the enabling legislation was passed in 2005, the plan in its final form specified that 'a minimum of 40 per cent of all residential development occurring annually' would be required to be within built-up areas (see fig. 11.1).[6]

It was a remarkable initiative. In December 2006, the American Planning Association awarded the province the prestigious

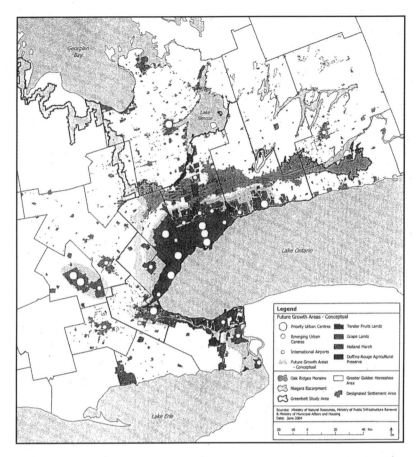

Figure 11.1 Map of development and growth opportunities as set out in
Places to Grow.
Source: Province of Ontario, Ministry of Public Infrastructure Renewal, *Places
to Grow: Proposed Growth Plan for the Greater Golden Horseshoe,* November 2005, 4.

2007 Daniel Burnham Award for a Comprehensive Plan. Burnham had developed the 1909 Chicago plan. Carol Rhea, chair
of the awards committee, said the plan 'provides a strategic, innovative and coordinated approach to sustainable growth and
development for 110 different municipalities,' noting that it integrated land-use planning with infrastructure investment. The
minister responsible for the plan, David Caplan, enthused,

'Five years ago stakeholders were divided about how to respond to growth. Today, an unprecedented consensus has emerged behind the idea that our region will be more successful and prosperous by following a set of smart planning principles.'[7]

Also remarkable was that the plan was introduced at a time when the market for new homes was booming, and opposition could be expected from the many developers and municipal politicians who did not wish to see a provincial government interfering with their ideas of progress. Apart from those who generally opposed plans as being a heavy-handed intrusion by government, there was only limited objection to the plan, perhaps because the detail deflated many of the good intentions. For example, while the plan called for low-density development to be halted, that would not happen for many years, long after existing land assemblies had been developed and the owners had retreated into retirement. The draft contained this explanatory sentence: 'Most municipalities have sufficient land designated to accommodate urban growth in the Greater Golden Horseshoe for the next 15 to 25 years, even without implementing compact urban form measures as proposed in this discussion paper.'[8]

As the plan was being finalized, the Minister of Municipal Affairs, John Gerretsen, stated that there were 200,000 hectares of land set aside in *Places to Grow* for future development.[9] He thought that was enough land to accommodate all development during the next quarter century. Allowing low-density suburban development to continue for another two or three decades, as it had for the previous five decades, proved a useful way of blunting opposition. A close look at the areas where development was permitted showed that it included many hectares of farmland and of other land well outside existing settlement areas.[10] These sections of the plan allowed and perhaps even encouraged low-density sprawl to continue, and basically delayed action until the next generation of voters arrived.

Places to Grow also required existing settlement areas to be redeveloped. Section 2.2.3.1 required that 40 per cent of new development occur within built-up areas already urbanized. It sounded like an impressive objective, and for some cities it probably was, but not for the Toronto area. Study by one foundation concerned with regional growth concluded that during the years 1991 to 2001 within the inner ring of the Horseshoe – that is, Toronto and the Regions of Durham, York, Peel, and Halton, the area commonly called the GTA – 43 per cent of all development had occurred on land that was already urbanized.[11] In this area, where there still remained considerable stretches of agricultural land and other undeveloped land, the plan's intensification goal was actually lower than what had been achieved without a plan. In the whole of the Greater Golden Horseshoe, 36 per cent of the intensification that had occurred was in already urbanized areas, which mean that the 40 per cent requirement would shift relatively little development activity away from green fields to built-up areas. It would not be unfair to conclude that the provincial goal was unambitious.

'Places to Grow' was a lost opportunity to tackle the sprawling behemoth. Low-density development would continue for the time being.

A related proposal by the McGuinty government was the introduction of the Greenbelt Plan. This Plan, put in place in 2005, designated some 760,000 hectares in the Greater Golden Horseshoe as a greenbelt so that the land affected could not be used for suburban development, thus protecting working farms and natural features. This was generally seen as a positive step, but again it was a question of detail that limited the plan's effectiveness. A great deal of land vulnerable to development pressure was not within the greenbelt designation, and accordingly not protected from development. In fact, three-quarters of the region's prime farmland[12] and two-thirds of its green lands fell into this unprotected category. Further, the outer boundary of the greenbelt proved to be too limited, as developments jumped beyond it.

The development industry was not standing still as the province introduced and passed these plans. It continued to acquire land and make suburban subdivision applications for land that, while well within reasonable commuting distance of Toronto, was not constrained by either plan. The most spectacular examples of such proposals were north of Toronto in the Bond

Head/Bradford area, where a community of more than 100,000 was proposed on a greenfields site, and near Alliston where a new community of about 50,000 people was proposed to complement the Honda automobile plant which, with the encouragement of the province, had located there in the mid-1980s.[13] These were extraordinary examples of new suburban leap-frog development, indicating how single-use, automobile dependent, low-density development proposals continued to set the agenda in the Toronto area. The behemoth lumbered along almost at will within the commutershed of the big city.

The third related initiative of the McGuinty government has been its strategy for infrastructure investment revealed in the document *ReNew Ontario, 2005–2010*, much of which is directed at the Greater Golden Horseshoe. The strategy notes, 'Growth is positive, but for the past two decades development has been allowed to happen in a haphazard way. The resulting urban sprawl and gridlock are strangling our economy and diminishing our quality of life.'[14] These words are very similar to those accompanying the Toronto-Centred Region Plan in 1970. This time the strategy document cites the cost of gridlock and congestion in the GTA and concludes that commute times and vehicle emissions will increase unless there is a substantial investment in transit. It states:

Delays caused by gridlock and congestion in the Greater Toronto Area cost the economy about $2 billion per year in lost time and lost productivity. According to the Toronto Board of Trade, the cost of congestion in the Greater Toronto Area, if left unchecked, will exceed $3 billion per year by 2021 ... If current development patterns continue and rates of investment in public transit do not increase, commute times may increase by as much as 45 per cent in southern Ontario; emissions from vehicle may increase by 42 per cent.[15]

These were the fears that led to the initiatives for both transit and road transportation. The transit initiatives in the GTA committed the government to extending the Spadina Subway to the north and west of York University; with other government providing $1 billion to GO Transit and a similar amount to the

TTC; and $150 million for York Region rapid (bus) transit.[16]
The federal government committed to the construction of the
York University extension in the Spring of 2007, with a contri-
bution of close to $750 million.

Some have questioned the wisdom of some parts of this strategy. One journalist has noted that the York University subway
line is projected to have very low ridership – less than 50,000 a
day in 2021, seven years after it opens, or less than a minor bus
route in the inner city.[17] As well, the subway will terminate in a
shopping mall next to a Wal-Mart, with a massive parking lot for
suburban riders.

The strategy also proposed to re-establish the Greater Toronto Transportation Authority, which was done in late 2006. It has
been charged with devising a transit plan for the region under
the rubric Metrolinks. Some fear the result will be a financial attack on the Toronto Transit Commission given that the TTC's
service is many, many times larger than any surrounding transit
property, as already noted in chapter 5. These strategies and
structures continue to assume that Toronto's transit system
should be reshaped from a weakened but still popular local service into a money-losing long-distance commuter service that
does not serve the needs of downtown transit riders.

Another part of the infrastructure strategy concerns road improvements in the Greater Golden Horseshoe and the GTA. It
notes, 'Planning is underway for new corridors including the
Niagara-GTA corridor, the completion of Highway 407 east,
and [northerly] extensions of Highways 404 and 427.'[18] These
projects had also been proposed by the Harris government, and
they were the same kind of superhighways the provincial government had been building for half a century, roads that would
open more land to development pressures because of easy access to the superhighway system, as well as creating problems of
congestion, poor air quality, loss of farmland, and sprawl. The
superhighway strategy also calls for high occupancy lanes – that
is, lanes reserved for cars carrying two or more people – to be
added to Highways 403 and 404 and the Queen Elizabeth Way.
These lanes are to be created by widening highways and thus
increasing their capacity for more vehicles (see fig. 11.2). This

is a continuation of the strategy the provincial government has pursued for more than fifty years – build more highway capacity with the intention of relieving traffic congestion, and when more sprawl happens and the congestion becomes more severe, complain about those results, commit the government to take effective action, then build more highways. The McGuinty government has apparently learned little from the evident failures to control sprawl during the previous fifty years.

The infrastructure strategy also contains proposals regarding water and sewage services, but it is not clear how the GTA will be affected by these investments. It seems likely that the province has already constructed all of the water and sewage services needed by municipalities in the GTA, and that its focus will now fall elsewhere.

Regarding the new megacity structure in which the former Metro Toronto and its local municipalities find themselves, the McGuinty government has made it clear that there will be no rethinking and no change. In 2006, a new *City of Toronto Act* was introduced into the legislature and quickly given three readings. The Act confirmed the megacity structure, although recognizing this does not work well, it stripped City Council of several important powers and lodged them in the office of the mayor. Councillors had no interest in rethinking the megacity and none have pushed the province for change. The city seems trapped in a structure designed to make it dysfunctional.

The language of the McGuinty government seems appropriate to change – plans and strategies to curb sprawl and its impacts, and to make the fringe areas more like the inner city – but the actions go hand in glove with yet more low-density development in the fringes. Toronto's fine history as a place where regional thinking and planning had found a secure foothold since the 1940s seemed no longer to inform decisions. The centre of the urban area – the former city of Toronto, East York, and York – continued to intensify – developers have found there was a strong market for moderate- and higher-density housing in the downtown core, and some parts of North York, Etobicoke, and Scarborough saw intensification. These parts of the city were attractive to both residents, tourists, and

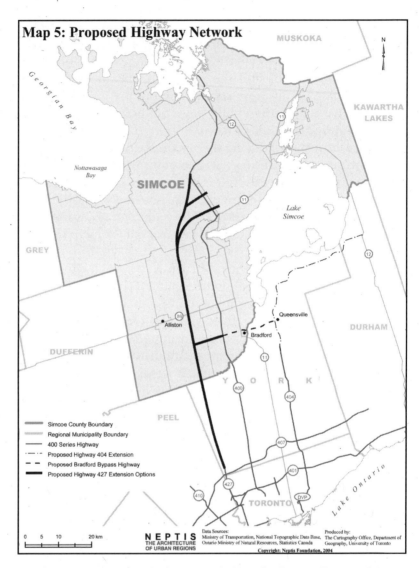

Figure 11.2 Proposed new highways north from the Greater Toronto Area,
extending the superhighway grid into large swaths of rural land.
Source: Leah Birnbaum, Lorenzo Nicolet, and Zack Taylor, *Simcoe County:
The New Growth Frontier*, map 5. Used with permission of the Neptis Foundation.

investors, and they made Toronto recognizably different from other North American cities. But with Toronto city politics still lodged in a dysfunctional structure, city leaders were unable to speak strongly or imaginatively about regional planning issues.

As a result, Toronto's urban area continued to be more dense than most other large American cities. As Robert Bruegmann shows, from 1950 to 1990 densities had generally fallen by half, depending on the city, to about 3,000 residents per square mile (4.6 persons per acres) while Toronto remained closer to 7,000 residents per square mile (11 persons per acre).[19] Thus Toronto was a special case, undoubtedly because of the planning initiatives in 1943 and 1959, and the creation of the Metro Federation in 1953. There was no reason why Toronto had to fall into the kind of city thought 'normal' by a critic such as William Bogart, with a density of 3,000 per square mile.[20] More critical is the fact that Toronto did not take full advantage of these extraordinary initiatives to shape an efficient and compact urban area when it had the opportunities to do so as described in this book. One can only sadly conclude that the culture of sprawl has established the upper hand and is now the unquestioned dominant force in the Greater Toronto Area. The battle to maintain the urban values that had found expression in the older city and protection in the Metro structure have been apparently lost.

Notes

1: Introduction

1 Province of Ontario, Department of Planning and Development, *Don Valley Conservation Report* (Toronto: King's Printer, 1950).

2 James Lemon, *Toronto Since 1918* (Toronto: James Lorimer, 1985), 113.

3 Vincent Pietropaolo, *Not Paved with Gold* (Toronto: Between The Lines, 2006), 1, quoting Tony Coleman from Richard Gambino, *Blood of My Blood*, 2nd ed. (Toronto: Guernica Editions, 2002).

4 See, for example, Howard Kunstler, *The Geography of Nowhere* (New York: Simon and Schuster, 1993).

5 See, for instance, Robert Bruegmann, *Sprawl: A Compact History* (Chicago: University of Chicago Press, 2005), William T. Bogart, *Don't Call It Sprawl: Metropolitan Structure in the Twentieth Century* (New York: Cambridge University Press, 2006), and Joel Kotkim, *The New Suburbanism: A Realist's Guide to the American Future* (Costa Mesa, CA: The Planning Center, 2005).

6 Joe Berridge, 'Suburbia Forever,' *Literary Review of Canada* 15, no. 7 (September 2007), 24–6. Toronto's suburban density is about twice that of American suburbs. See Pamela Blais, *Inching towards Sustainability: The Evolving Urban Structures of the GTA* (Toronto: Neptis Foundation, 2000).

2: Toronto in Mid-Century

1 Jacob Spelt, *Toronto* (Toronto: Collier Macmillan Canada, 1973), 85.

2 Gore & Storrie, *Water Supply and Sewage Disposal for the City of Toronto and Related Areas*, Report to the Toronto and York Planning Board (Toronto: Gore & Storrie, 1949).

3 For a history of the TTC prior to 1921, see 'TTC History,' www.transit.toronto.on.ca/spare/0012.shtml.

4 See John F. Bromley and Jack May, *Fifty Years of Progressive Transit* (Toronto: Electric Railroaders' Association, 1973); 75.

5 Ibid., 61.

6 Ibid., 76.

7 See Ontario Committee on Taxation, *Report*, vol. 2 (Toronto: Queen's Printer, 1967), 411–15. This is a complicated area. The report seems to argue that the incidence of actual grants to cities on average were less in the early 1960s for construction and maintenance of roads (about 35.5 per cent) than to counties (55.5 per cent), townships (58.8 per cent), and Metro (50 per cent.) The Annual Report of the Commissioner of Finance for Toronto, 1948 (series 185, City of Toronto Archives), states the grant for roads was either 50 per cent of the cost or 1 mill of taxation, whichever was less, and in Toronto's case, the 1 mill was less (see pp. 12–13 of the report). That annual report also states that municipalities had the statutory authority to levy income tax until 1936 when the province enacted an *Income Tax Act* – and reimbursed the city by paying it $1,210,000 (23). When in 1944 municipalities lost the authority to levy corporate taxes, Toronto received a payment from the province of $150,000. One can only imagine what might have happened if municipalities still had those two taxation powers.

8 *Daily Star*, 13 July 1948, City of Toronto Archives, RG32, box 6, series 721, file 44.

9 City of Toronto Archives, RG 32, box 6, series 721, file 43.

10 Letter from Norman A. Wilson to Tracy leMay, 19 June 1939, City of Toronto Archives, series 721, file 26.

11 Spelt, *Toronto*, 85.

12 Gore & Storrie, *Water Supply and Sewage Disposal for the City of Toronto and Related Areas*, 14.

13 Ibid., 16.

14 It was not the first time the term 'Metro' had been used. In 1924, George S. Henry, a member of the provincial cabinet, proposed the creation of a metropolitan district for Toronto, but he was unable to convince his Toronto colleagues on the idea and it was not proceeded with. See Frances Frisken, *The Public Metropolis: The Political Dynamics of Urban Expansion in the Toronto Region, 1924–2003* (Toronto: Canadian Scholars' Press, 2007), 55– 6.

15 Gore & Storrie, *Water Supply and Sewage Disposal for the City of Toronto and Related Areas*, 7.

16 Richard White, *Urban Infrastructure and Urban Growth in the Toronto Region, 1950s to the 1990s* (Toronto: Neptis Foundation, 2003).

17 Timothy J. Colton, *Big Daddy: Frederick G. Gardiner and the Building of Metropolitan Toronto* (Toronto: University of Toronto Press, 1980), 64. Also see Lemon, *Toronto Since 1918*, 108–11, for a brief recounting of the creation of Metro.

18 Ontario Municipal Board decision, 20 January 1953, 28. Available at the Urban Affairs Library (352.0713 053).

19 Ibid., 29.
20 Ibid., 44.
21 Ibid., 90.
22 Ibid., 46.
23 F. Scott Fitzgerald, 'The Crack-Up,' in *The Crack-Up*, ed. Edmund Wilson (1931; reprint, New York: New Directions, 1945), 69.
24 The idea embodied in Metro that two concepts which are complementary are necessarily paired for each to flower is best set out in the remarkable book by J.A. Scott Kelso and David Engstrøm, *The Complementary Nature* (Cambridge, MA: Bradford Books, 2006). For a powerful Canadian interpretation, see John Ralston Saul, *A Fair Country: Telling Truths about Canada* (Toronto: Viking Canada, 2008), esp. 80.
25 Region of York, *Insights: Local and Regional Government in York Region* (Newmarket, ON: Regional Municipality of York, 1981), 16.
26 Ontario Municipal Board decision, 66.
27 Frisken recounts the story of the creation of Metro, with some different emphasis, in *The Public Metropolis*, 66–75.
28 Ontario Municipal Board decision, 72.
29 Metropolitan Toronto Commission of Inquiry, First Report, 1958, Chair, Lorne Cumming. Available at Urban Affairs Library (352.0713 0561).
30 For a full history of Don Mills, see John Sewell, *The Shape of the City: Toronto Struggles with Modern Planning* (Toronto: University of Toronto Press, 1993), chap. 3.
31 M.W. Frankena, *Urban Transportation Financing: Theory and Policy in Ontario* (Toronto: Economic Council, 1982), 106; table 9 on 106–7 summarizes the funding sources of subways in Toronto until the late 1970s.
32 Bromley and May, *Fifty Years of Progressive Transit*, 94.
33 See James Bow, 'A History of Subways on Bloor and Queen Streets,' available online at www.transit.toronto.on.ca/subway/5104.shtml.
34 Frankena, *Urban Transportation Financing*, 106–7.
35 Bromley, *Fifty Years of Progressive Transit*, 107, 117.
36 Frankena, *Urban Transportation Financing*, 114, table 15.
37 Bromley, *Fifty Years of Progressive Transit*, 107, 117.
38 Spelt, *Toronto*, 85.
39 Ibid., 88.

3: Planning for the Future

1 James Lemon, 'Tracey Deavin leMay: Toronto's First Planning Commissioner, 1930–1954,' *City Planning* (Winter 1984), 4, see also 7.
2 Toronto Planning Board, The Master Plan for the City of Toronto and Environs (1943). The booklet can be found at the Urban Affairs Library,

Toronto Public Library. The quotes from the booklet are not referenced by page as it unpaginated.

3 John Bousfield, interview with author, Toronto, ON, 23 March 2006. Bousfield was told this story by Faludi himself.

4 A history of planning thinking in Canada in the first half of the twentieth century can be found in Sewell, *The Shape of the City*, chaps. 2 and 3.

5 Spelt, *Toronto*, 92.

6 Toronto City Council approved a formal city plan in 1949, but it covered only the area within the city's jurisdiction, not within the surrounding areas. As well, it consisted almost entirely with public works, which leMay costed out as part of the plan.

7 Robert Fishman, *The American Planning Tradition: Culture and Policy* (Washington, DC: Woodrow Wilson Center Press, 2000), 13.

8 Ibid., 15.

9 Ibid., 16.

10 *Urban America: Documenting the Planners*, an exhibition, curated by Elaine D. Engst and H. Thomas Hickerson, at the John M. Olin Library, Cornell University, Ithaca, New York, 21 October–31 December 1985.

11 Richard Harris, *Creeping Conformity: How Canada Became Suburban 1900–1960* (Toronto: University of Toronto Press, 2004), 168.

12 Len Gertler, *Radical Rumblings: Confessions of a Peripatetic Planner* (Waterloo, ON: Department of Geography, University of Waterloo, 2005), 54.

13 Hans Blumenfeld, *Life Begins at 65* (Montreal: Harvest House, 1987), 249.

14 Metropolitan Toronto Planning Board, Official Plan for the Metro Toronto Planning Area (1959), 19. Hereafter Official Plan.

15 Ibid., 10.

16 Ibid., 11.

17 Ibid.

18 Ibid., S8.

19 Ibid., 123.

20 Ibid., 40, table 8.

21 Ibid., 123.

22 Ibid., 97, tables 30, 31.

23 Ibid., 48, table 12.

24 That is Lemon's opinion, *Toronto since 1918*, 140.

25 Blumenfeld, *Life Begins at 65*, 245.

26 Ibid., 247.

27 Official Plan, 182.

28 Ibid., 185.

29 Ibid., 189.

30 Quotes from Colton, *Big Daddy*, 156.

31 Frisken has a good discussion about the reasons for reluctance in the United States to use regional approaches. See *The Public Metropolis*, 19–26, 32–45.

32 See John R. James, 'Regional Planning in Britain,' in *Planning for a Nation of Cities*, ed. Sam B. Warner Jr. (Cambridge, MA: MIT Press, 1966), 193–200.

33 James T. Lemon, *Liberal Dreams and Nature's Limits: Great Cities in North America since 1600* (Toronto: Oxford University Press, 1996), 43.

34 Province of Ontario, Department of Municipal Affairs, Metro Toronto and Region Transportation Study, *Choices for a Growing Region* (Toronto: Queen's Printer, 1967). Available at Robarts Library, University of Toronto.

35 Ibid., 65.

36 For a fuller description of the origins of the TCR Plan, see Sewell, *The Shape of the City*, 208–24, and the references provided there.

37 Province of Ontario, *Design for Development, the Toronto-Centred Region Plan* (Toronto: Queen's Printer, 1970), 2. Hereafter the Toronto-Centred Region Plan.

38 Ibid., 3.

39 Ibid., 18.

40 Ibid., 13.

41 Ibid., 12.

42 Graham Fraser, Jay Richardson, David Wood, and Dennis Wood, *The Tail of the Elephant: A Guide to the Regional Planning and Development in Southern Ontario* (Toronto: Pollution Probe, 1974), 6.

43 Sewell, *The Shape of the City*, 212–14.

44 Metro adopted an Official Plan in 1980, and another one in 1994, but in both cases the plans did not touch on regional issues, but instead dealt with the replanning of Metro itself as it became fully built-up. See Frisken, *The Public Metropolis*, 161, 210.

4: Building a Superhighway System

1 Province of Ontario, Department of Highways Report, Annual Report for the year ending 31 March 1935, 97. Available at the Legislative Library.

2 See John C. van Nostrand, 'The Queen Elizabeth Way: Public Utility versus Private Space,' *Urban History Review* 12, no. 2 (October 1983), 1.

3 Kenneth J. Jackson, *Crabgrass Frontier: The Suburbanization of the United States* (New York: Oxford University Press, 1987), 166.

4 John C. Best, *Thomas Baker McQuesten: Public Works, Politics, and Imagination* (Hamilton: Corinth Press, 1991), 113.

5 Ibid., 114.

6 Province of Ontario, Department of Highways, Annual Report for the year ending 31 March 1937, 12.

7 Province of Ontario, Department of Highways, Annual Report for the year ending 31 March 1938, 8.

8 Ibid., 12.

9 See E.C. Guillet, *The Story of Canadian Roads* (Toronto: University of Toronto Press, 1966).

10 See van Nostrand, 'The Queen Elizabeth Way,' 9.

11 Province of Ontario, Department of Highways, Annual Report for the year ending 31 March 1939, 10.

12 Ibid., 19.

13 Ronald E. Richardson, George H. McNevin, and Walter G. Rooke, *Building for People* (Toronto: Ryerson Press, 1970), 8.

14 Best, *Thomas Baker McQuesten*, 199–200.

15 Richardson, McNevin, and Rooke, *Building for People*, 20. See also Province of Ontario, Department of Highways, *A Plan for Ontario Highways* (Toronto: Queen's Printer, 1956). Available at Robarts Library, University of Toronto.

16 *Daily Star*, 13 July 1948, City of Toronto Archives, RG32, box 6, series 741, file 43.

17 See *The History of Ontario's Kings Highways*, 'The History of Ontario's Highways, King's Highway 401,' at www.thekingshighway.ca/Highway401.htm.

18 William Kaszynski, *The American Highway: The History and Culture of Roads in the United States* (Jefferson, NC: McFarland and Company, 2000), 130.

19 Kenny Ausubel, *Nature's Operating Instructions* (San Francisco: Sierra Club Books, 2004), 178.

20 See City Planning Board, Third Annual Report, 30 December 1944, plate 27. City of Toronto Archives, SC 41, box 1, file 35.

21 City of Toronto Archives, series 721, file 21.

22 See *Annual Reports* of the Department of Highways, Province of Ontario. Available at the Legislative Library, Queen's Park.

23 Annual Reports of the Department of Highways.

24 Annual Reports of the Department of Highways, 1946, 16.

25 Ibid., 22.

26 See Minutes, Toronto and Suburban Planning Board, 1 April 1947, City of Toronto Archives, box 047156.

27 See note 17 above.

28 Annual Report of the Department of Highways, 1953.

29 Ontario Select Committee on Toll roads, *Report* (Toronto: Queen's Printer, 1957), 13. Available at the Robarts Library, University of Toronto.

30 See Department of Highways, *A Plan for Ontario Highways*, 9.

31 Richardson, McNevin, and Rooke, *Building for People*, 12, 20.
32 W. Darcy McKeough, 'The Regional Municipality of York' (speech presented at Toronto, Ontario, May 1970). Available at the City of Toronto Urban Affairs Library.
33 See papers of Norman D. Wilson, City of Toronto Archives, file 39, box 1.
34 See Sewell, *The Shape of the City*, 177–81. Davis' quote was apparently created by the brilliant strategist and wordsmith Dalton Camp.
35 William Davis, 'An Urban Transportation Policy for Ontario' (speech presented at the Ontario Science Centre, Toronto, Ontario, 22 November 1972). Available at the Urban Affairs Library (388.40971 N266).
36 Chandian Mylvaganam and Sandford Borins, '*If You Build It...*' : *Business, Government and Ontario's Electronic Toll Highway* (Toronto: University of Toronto Centre for Public Management, 2004), 7.
37 Ibid.
38 Ibid., footnote 36.
39 York Region, 'State of the Region Report,' August 1995. Available at the Urban Affairs Library (352.0713547 S74).
40 IBI Group and Hemson Consulting, *Funding Transportation in the GTA and Hamilton-Wentworth* (Toronto: IBI Group and Hemson Consulting, 1999).

5: Transit and Commuting Alternatives

1 See the papers of Norman D. Wilson, City of Toronto Archives, file 39, box 1.
2 Don Stevenson conversation with author, 12 January 2006.
3 Frisken thinks the suggestion of using existing rail lines first came from planners with Metro. See Frisken, *The Public Metropolis*, 139.
4 Province of Ontario, Department of Highways, *GO Transit: A New Approach to Urban Transportation* (Toronto: Queen's Printer, ca. 1968), 3.
5 Ibid.
6 See Frisken, *The Public Metropolis*, 186.
7 Annual Reports of Toronto Area Transportation Operating Authority, 1969, 1976, 1985. Available at Robarts Library, University of Toronto (CA2 ON DT 160 A56).
8 Department of Municipal Affairs, *Choices for a Growing Region*, 14.
9 Richard M. Soberman, *Understanding GO Transit*, Report to Greater Toronto Services Board, November 1998. Available at the Urban Affairs Library (385.50971 S57).
10 GO Transit, Annual Report 1965.
11 The comparison of different transit modes in the GTA in 2003, showing riders and per-passenger subsidies, is as follows: TTC, 415 million rides at

a cost of $0.47 per rider; GO Transit, 44 million rides at a cost of $4.71 per rider; York Region Transit, 10 million rides at a cost of $2.44 per rider. See 'Transit Facts' at www.torontoenvironment.org/campaigns/transit/facts.

12 Bromley and May, *Fifty Years of Progressive Transit*, 107, 117.

13 Frankena, *Urban Transportation Financing*, 120.

14 Frisken, *The Public Metropolis*. Frisken uses metric measurements; 6,287 per square kilometer in 1951, 5,903 in 1971.

15 In metric, 2,544 per square kilometers.

16 Toronto and Suburban Planning Board, Minutes, 23 September 1947, City of Toronto Archives, box 047156.

17 City of Toronto Archives, RG32, box 6, series 721, file 44.

18 Frankena, *Urban Transportation Financing*, 122.

19 Lawrence Solomon argues that the central city was required to transfer enormous financial resources for the TTC to serve the suburbs even within Metro. See *Toronto Sprawls*, 61 and chap. 1.

20 For a more complete history of this line, see the SLRT study at www.stevemunro.ca/wp-content/uploads/2006/04/SLRTstudyEXT.pdf.

21 Steve Wickens, 'Rapid Transit? Not on Spadina,' *Globe and Mail*, 7 May 2005, M2.

22 Richard Soberman, *Choice for the Future: Metropolitan Toronto Transportation Plan Review Summary Report, No. 64* (1975; reprint, Toronto: University of Toronto/York University, 1979).

23 Analysis provided by Steve Munro, 24 March 2004, letter to TTC in response to the TTC Ridership Growth Strategy. See 'Transit's Lost Decade' at www.torontoenvironment.org/newsroom/reports/transit/lostdecade.

24 Ridership Growth Strategy, Toronto Transit Commission, March 2003, available online at www.toronto.ca/ttc/pdf/ridership_growth_strategy.pdf.

25 See (Streetcar) Ridership 1976 to 2005 at http://stevemunro.ca/wp-content/uploads/2007/12/streetcars19762005.pdf.

6: Pipe Dreams

1 James F. MacLaren Associates, 'Report on Water Supply in Metropolitan Toronto' (Toronto, 1957).

2 Ibid., 10. Also see Richard White, *Urban Infrastructure and Urban Growth in the Toronto Region, 1950s to the 1990s* (Toronto: Neptis Foundation, 2003), 44.

3 Ibid., 11.

4 Ronald Bordessa and James M. Cameron, 'Servicing Growth in the Metro Toronto Region during the Early Years of the Ontario Water Resources Commission, 1956–68,' *Canadian Water Resources Journal* 5, no. 1 (1980), 17.

5 See Metropolitan Toronto Planning Board, Official Plan of the Metropolitan Toronto Planning Area, 28f. Hereafter Official Plan.

6 Richmond Hill Historical Records, 'Ontario Water Resource Commission,' file A24. Town of Richmond Hill Archives.

7 Ibid., 1, for early history of Ontario Water Resources Commission.

8 Ibid., 2.

9 See Bordessa and Cameron, 'Servicing Growth in the Metro Toronto Region,' 22.

10 Official Plan, 58.

11 White, *Urban Infrastructure and Urban Growth*, 33.

12 See Ontario Water Resources Commission, Annual Report, 1957. Available at Robarts Library, University of Toronto (CA2 ON WR A56).

13 See *The Peel Water Story: A Local History of Water* (Brampton, ON: Region of Peel, Department of Public Works, 2006), 70.

14 Ibid., 73–4.

15 White, *Urban Infrastructure and Urban Growth*, 33.

16 See Roger E. Riendeau, *Mississauga: An Illustrated History* (Windsor, ON: Windsor Publications, 1985), 97.

17 John Bousfield, interview with author, Toronto, ON, 20 February 2006.

18 Sewell, *The Shape of the City*, 203–4.

19 Ibid., 202.

20 See Bramalea Developments, Region of Peel Archives, file 2002–046 SP 72.

21 White, *Urban Infrastructure and Urban Growth*, 35–6.

22 Ibid., 11–12.

23 Ibid., 38–9.

24 John Sewell, *Houses and Homes: Housing for Canadians* (Toronto: James Lorimer, 1994), 85.

25 T.H.B. Symons, *A History of Peel County, 1867–1967* (Brampton: Corporation of the County of Peel, 1967), 276.

26 Quotes taken from Ronald Bordessa and James M. Cameron, 'The Investigative Gene: Problems and Prospects,' *Professional Geographer* 32 (1980), 164, see also 166, 169.

27 White, *Urban Infrastructure and Urban Growth*, 38–9.

28 Honourable William Davis, interview with author, Toronto, ON, 25 March 2006.

29 Bordessa and Cameron, 'The Investigative Gene,' 16.

30 Carl H. Goldenberg, *Report of the Royal Commission on Metropolitan Toronto* (Toronto: Queen's Printer, 1965), 77. Available at the Urban Affairs Library (392.97155 0565).
31 Ibid., 168.
32 OWRC Report, 17 February 1966, Region of Peel Archives, Public Works Files, 1937–71, 1993 O20.
33 Mayor Hazel McCallion, interview with author, Mississauga, ON, 8 February 2006.
34 Contract, South Peel Project, 1993, Region of Peel Archives, 020 AR, Public Works Files, 1931–71.
35 Davis interview, 25 March 2006.
36 Minutes of the South Peel Advisory Committee, 29 October 1971, Region of Peel Archives.
37 Riendeau, *Mississauga*, 108.
38 Bousfield interview, 22 March 2006.
39 Don Mills Development Ltd., 'Erin Mills – New Town' (April 1969), section 2.11. Available at the City of Toronto Urban Affairs Library.
40 Sewell, *The Shape of the City*, 94–5. Regarding the planning of Erin Mills, see 200ff.
41 Bousfield interview, 4 February 2006.
42 Province of Ontario, Ministry of Treasury, Economics, and Intergovernmental Affairs, *Design for Development Status Report* (Toronto: Queen's Printer, 1970). Hereafter *Design for Development.*
43 Official Plan, 58.
44 Ibid., 11.
45 Ibid., 58.
46 Ibid., S8–S9.
47 Ron Bordessa and James M. Cameron, 'Growth Management Conflicts in the Toronto-Centred Region,' in *Conflicts, Politics and the Urban Scene*, ed. Kevin R. Cox and R.J. Johnston (New York: Longman, 1982), 19.
48 Ibid., 20–1.
49 See letter from Mayor Broadhurst, 4 May 1964, in Richmond Hill Historical File 'Metro Toronto Official Plan.'
50 OWRC Report, Richmond Hill Historical Records, file A24.
51 Ibid.
52 See White, *Urban Infrastructure and Urban Growth*, 47.
53 *Design for Development*, 12.
54 For a brief history of the Ontario Water Resources, see 'Watertight: The Case for Change in Ontario's Water and Waste Water Sector,' 13–15, available online at www.waterpanel.ontario.ca.
55 Province of Ontario, Ministry of the Environment, *York-Durham Water and Sewage Service Systems* (Toronto: Queen's Printer, 1974), 6.

56 James F. MacLaren Associates, 'Central York/Pickering Water and Sewage Works,' Report to the Ministry of Environment (Toronto: N.p., 1973). Also see White, *Urban Infrastructure and Urban Growth*, 49.
57 Bordessa and Cameron, 'Growth Management Conflicts in the Toronto-Centred Region,' 127. Also see, *Design for Development Status Report*, 12.
58 See White, *Infrastructure and Urban Growth*, 50–1.
59 See Lawrence Solomon, *Toronto Sprawls: A History* (Toronto: University of Toronto Press, 2007), 70.
60 Bousfield interview, 4 February 2006.
61 Michael McMahon, 'Moving *Beyond Sprawl* in the Toronto Bioregion,' October 2000, section 5.2, is a self-published report documenting this issue. Available at the Urban Affairs Library.
62 Region of York, Official Plan (1994), 70.
63 Region of York and Consumers Utilities, *York Region Long-Term Water Project* (Newmarket, ON: Regional Municipality of York, 1997).
64 Anonymous interview with the author, Toronto, ON, May 2003.
65 Sewell, *The Shape of the City*, 76–8.
66 See Official Plan, 58.
67 Sewell, *The Shape of the City*, 94–5.
68 For a brief history of development charges in Ontario, see David Amborski, 'The Incidence of Development Charges: Theory and Early Evidence' (Toronto: N.p., 1988), and Enid Slack, 'An Economic Analysis of Development Charges in British Columbia and Ontario' (Vancouver: Laurier Institute, 1990).
69 Frisken, *The Public Metropolis*, 310.

7: Reshaping Governance

1 Ontario Legislative Assembly, Report of the Select Committee on the Municipal Act and Related Acts, 1963–5, Chair, Hollis E. Beckett, 169. Available at the Urban Affairs Library (352.0713 05605).
2 Ibid., 169.
3 Ibid., 173.
4 Goldenberg, *Report of the Royal Commission on Metropolitan Toronto*, 170.
5 Ibid., 158–9.
6 Ontario Committee on Taxation, *Report*, vol. 2, 497.
7 Ibid., 499.
8 Ibid., 501–2.
9 Ibid., 550.
10 Ontario Department of Municipal Affairs, Annual Report 1970, 90. Available at the Urban Affairs Library (352.0713 0557.2).

11 Ibid., 42.

12 John Gillies, 'Toronto Twp Rejects City Plan,' *Globe and Mail*, 20 December 1963, n.p.

13 Goldenberg, *Report of the Royal Commission on Metropolitan Toronto*, 158.

14 Ibid., 77.

15 See 'Proposed Amalgamation,' Region of Peel Archives, file 2002.046 SP 108, box 7 and file 2002.046 SP 126.

16 Thomas J. Plunkett, *Peel-Halton Local Government Review: A Report* (Toronto: Department of Municipal Affairs, 1966), 49.

17 Ibid., 57.

18 Ibid.

19 Symons, *A History of Peel County, 1867–1967*, 134–5.

20 Tom Urbaniak, *Farewell, Town of Streetsville* (Belleville: Epic Press, 2002), 72.

21 McCallion interview, 8 February 2006.

22 Davis interview, 25 March 2006.

23 Material regarding these internal struggles can be found in Regional Government Review Committee, Region of Peel Archives, file 1992.092 AR, box 34, and Town Status, file 2002.046 SP126.

24 See Urbaniak, *Farewell ...*, 75–6, for a history of Streetsville's opposition.

25 See Regional Government Review Committee and Town Status in note 23.

26 Undated brief by Hamilton Branch, Canadian Institute of Management, in Regional Government Review Committee, Region of Peel Archives, file 1992.092 AR, box 34.

27 Ministry of Treasury, Economics, and Intergovernmental Affairs, 'Proposal for Local Government Reform in an Area East of Metro,' Toronto, December 1972, 5 and 7.

28 Ibid.

29 Debates, Legislature of Ontario, Office of the Speaker, Parliament Buildings, Toronto, 20 May 1973, 2311.

30 Goldenberg, *Report of the Royal Commission on Metropolitan Toronto*, 160.

31 See letter from Richmond Hill Mayor T. Broadhurst to the OWRC, 19 May 1966, in Ontario Water Resources Commission, Richmond Hill Archives, file A24.

32 See York County Planning Office, 'York County – A Responsible Unit of Regional Government,' 12 March 1970, Report A703–11, 4. Available at York Region Archives.

33 'General Report on the County of York,' part 3: 'The Political County.' York County Planning Office (1969), City of Toronto Archives, series 10, item 447, box 45303.

34 McKeough, 'The Regional Municipality of York.'

35 Ibid.

36 Darcy McKeough, interview with author, Toronto, ON, 2 February 2006.

37 Ibid.

38 Richmond Hill Council Minutes, 10 May 1970. Available at the Richmond Hill Central Library.

39 York County Council Minutes, 29 December 1970. Available at York Region Archives.

40 Province of Ontario, Ministry of Treasury, Economics, and Intergovernmental Affairs, *Proposals for Local Government Reform in the Area West of Metropolitan Toronto* (Toronto: Queen's Printer, 1973), 3.

41 Ibid., 4.

42 See Municipality of Metropolitan Toronto, 'A Policy to Implement the Toronto-Centred Region Development Concept,' November 1971. Available at the Robarts Library, University of Toronto (HT 395 C23 T665 257). This compiles the reports before Metro Council on 16 November 1971.

43 The history of restructuring proposals for the areas east of Metro Toronto is recounted in Ministry of Treasury, Economics, and Intergovernmental Affairs, *Proposals for Local Government Reform in an Area East of Metro Toronto* (Toronto: Queen's Printer, 1972).

44 Nigel Richardson, 'Insubstantial Pagent: The Rise and Fall of Regional Planning in Ontario,' *Journal of Canadian Public Administration* 24, no. 4. (1981), 574.

45 See John G. Chipman, *A Law Unto Itself: How the Ontario Municipal Board Has Developed and Applied Land-Use Planning Policy*, IPAC Series in Public Management and Governance (Toronto: University of Toronto Press, 2002).

46 Frisken, *The Public Metropolis*, 147–50. The quotes are referenced by Frisken.

8: The Challenge of Unbridled Suburban Growth

1 Official Plan, 28.

2 James F. McLaren Associates, 'Central York/Pickering Water and Sewage Reports,' table 2.1.

3 'GTA Urban Structures Concept Study,' prepared for GTA Coordinating Committee, June 1990, by IBI Group, Exhibit 1. Available at the Urban Affairs Library.

4 Richard Gilbert, 'Integrity of Land-Use and Transportation Planning in

the Greater Toronto Area,' in *The Integrity Gap: Canada's Environmental Policy and Institutions*, ed. Eugene Lee and Anthony Perl (Vancouver: UBC Press, 2003), 201.

5 Greater Toronto Coordinating Committee, 'An Enviable Quality of Life, Phase 1, Statistical Indicators' (October 1995), 16. Available at the Urban Affairs Library (307.76097 R245). Expressed in metric units, residential density in the former City of Toronto in the 1990s was 2,787 units per square kilometer; in the rest of Metro, 3,300 units; in the fringes, 1,800 units.

6 Gilbert, 'Integrity of Land-Use and Transportation Planning in the Greater Toronto Area.' Frisken has comparable figures in *The Public Metropolis*, 310. Expressed in metric units, there were 8,500 residents per square kilometer in the former City of Toronto; 2,900 in the rest of Metro; and 2,300 in the developed portion of the fringes.

7 See Pamela Blais, 'The Economics of Urban Form,' prepared for the GTA Task Force, January 1996, 2. Expressed metrically in the former City of Toronto, there were 126 residents and jobs per hectare; in Metro, 57; in Mississauga, 35; in Vaughan, 24.

8 See James Lorimer, *The Developer* (Toronto: James Lorimer, 1978).

9 See John Sewell, *Houses and Homes: Housing for Canadians* (Toronto: James Lorimer, 1994), chap. 6, which provides a full discussion of this issue. Also see Sewell, *The Shape of the City*, 214–15.

10 For 1953–81, see Sewell, 'The Suburbs Then and Now,' in *The Changing Canadian Metropolis*, ed. Frances Frisken (Berkeley, CA: University of California, Institute of Governmental Studies, and Toronto: Canadian Urban Institute, 1994), 341–53. For 1990 and 2000, see Urban Development Services Department, 'Profile Toronto: September 2004' (Toronto: City of Toronto, 2004); for 2005, see the MLS website at www.toronto-mls.info.

11 From a 1995 study by the IBI group for CMHC, cited in Pamela Blais, *The Growth Opportunity* (Toronto: Neptis Foundation, 2005), 11.

12 Ibid.

13 Gilbert, 'Integrity of Land-Use and Transportation Planning ...,' 8.

14 Toronto Transit Commission, *Ridership Growth Strategy*, A4, table C2.

15 See Eric Miller, *Travel and Housing Costs in the Greater Toronto Area, 1986–1996* (Toronto: Neptis Foundation, 2004).

16 York Region, 'State of the Region Report,' August 1995, 3. Available at the Urban Affairs Library (352.0713547 S74).

17 Mylvaganam and Borins, '*If You Build It ...*,' 7.

18 Government of Ontario, *ReNew Ontario, 2005–2010: Strategic Highlights* (Toronto: Queen's Printer for Ontario, 2005), 9.

19 See David Gurin, *Understanding Sprawl: A Citizen's Guide* (Vancouver: The

David Suzuki Foundation, 2003), 11–16, available online at www.
davidsuzuki.org/files/Climate/Ontario/Understanding_Sprawl.pdf.
Estimates of deaths in Toronto resulting from smog are made by Toronto
Environmental Alliance. See 'Transit Facts' at www.torontoenvironment.
org/campaign/transit/facts.

20 Suburban problems have been documented by many. For a good summary in the first few years of the twenty-first century, see Gurin, *Understanding Sprawl.*

21 Blais, *The Growth Opportunity*, 2.

22 The best summary of the policy guidelines and statements and their impact can be found in Commission on Planning and Development Reform in Ontario, *New Planning for Ontario, Final Report* (Toronto: Queen's Printer, 1993), 12, 13.

23 Jack Ferguson and Dawn King, 'Behind the Boom: The Story of York Region,' *Globe and Mail*, 26 October 1988 to 3 November 1988.

24 Frisken, *The Public Metropolis*, 207.

25 See Sewell, *The Shape of the City*, 220–2.

26 Traffic Integration Task Force, *Coordinating Public Transit in the Toronto Area, Final Report* (Toronto: Ministry of Transportation Ontario, 1994).

27 City of Mississauga, *Running the GTA 'Like a Business,'* August 1995. Available at the Urban Affairs Library (352.07135 M39).

28 See City of Mississauga, Background Paper No. 2, 'Urban Form and Infrastructure' (1995), 3–4.

29 Greater Toronto Area Task Force, *Greater Toronto (Golden Report)* (Toronto: Queen's Printer, 1996).

30 Ibid., 112.

31 Ibid., 115, 116.

9: A Triumph for Suburban Values

1 Alice Coleman, *Utopia on Trial: Vision and Reality in Planned Housing* (London: Hilary Shipman, 1990).

2 Oscar Newman, *Defensible Space* (New York: Macmillan, 1972).

3 And different incomes, too. Family incomes in the fringes are generally 20 to 40 per cent higher than in Metro. See Frisken, *The Public Metropolis*, 213.

4 Edmund P. Fowler, *City's Culture and Granite* (Toronto: Guernica Books, 2004), 37.

5 See Frisken, *The Public Metropolis*, 170–2.

6 See City of Mississauga, Background Paper No. 3, *Running the GTA 'Like a Business.'*

7 See Mark Winfield, 'Smart Growth in Ontario: The Promise vs. the Provincial Performance' (Toronto: Pembina Institute, 2003), 10, available online at http://communities.pembina.org/pub/149.

8 See Royal Commission on the Future of the Toronto Waterfront, *Watershed: Second Interim Report* (Toronto: Queen's Printer, 1990), 22–4. The commissioner was David Crombie.

9 The provincial government of David Peterson had already begun to address the issue of the Moraine by appointing Ron Kanter who in 1990 recommended a Greenlands Strategy to protect the Oak Ridges Moraine and other greenlands. See Frisken, *The Public Metropolis*, 208.

10: Death of Metro

1 Municipality of Metropolitan Toronto, 'Metro's Plan for Reform,' Chief Administrators Office, 18 August 1995. Available at the Urban Affairs Library (UAL).

2 Greater Toronto Mayors and Regional Chairs, *Leading by Example*, 11 September 1995. Available at UAL.

3 Greater Toronto Co-ordinating Committee, *Documenting the Fiscal Facts*, January 1996. This report also summarizes the findings of *Rethinking the Fundamentals*, the earlier report by the GTCC. Available at UAL.

4 Mayors Hazel McCallion, Barbara Hall, Nancy Diamond, and Mel Lastman, *Moving Forward Together* (January 1996), 9. Available at UAL (352.07135 M595).

5 Robert A. Richards, 'Speech to the CUI [Canadian Urban Institute] Conference on the Greater Toronto Area Task Force,' 14 February 1996, 1. Available at UAL.

6 Toronto Mayor's Office, 'Mayor Hall Teams Up with Board of Trade to Oppose Provincial Plan to Take Toronto Taxes,' News Release, 10 April 1996. Available at UAL.

7 David Crombie's Panel 'Who Does What,' 'GTA-Wide Service Board essential, Crombie Panel Says,' News Release, 6 December 1996, 1. Available at UAL.

8 See Frisken, *The Public Metropolis*, 249, for further detail on reactions.

9 Alan Tonks, 'More Thoughts on a Unified City,' letter to the Honourable Al Leach, 28 November 1996, 2. Available at UAL.

10 *Fergus-Elora News Express*, 28 September 1994, 1, quoting from Mike Harris in Elora, Ontario, on 19 September 1994.

11 Mayors of local governments in Metro (Mayor Frank Faubert, City of Scarborough; Mayor Doug Holyday, City of Etobicoke; Mayor Frances Nunziata, City of York; Mayor Barbara Hall, City of Toronto; Mayor Mel

Lastman, City of North York; and Mayor Michael Prue, Borough of East York), *Changing for the Better: A Vision for the Future of Our Communities*, 29 November 1996. Available at UAL.

12 For a favourable recounting of the megacity story, see John Ibbitson, *Promised Land: Inside the Mike Harris Revolution* (Toronto: Prentice Hall, 1997), chap. 11. Frisken takes a more neutral stance, *The Public Metropolis*, 245–57.

13 James Rusk, 'Metro to Become One Big City,' *Globe and Mail*, 17 December 1996, A1.

14 Complete material relating to the history of C4LD (including minutes of meeting, bulletins, and photographs) can be found in City of Toronto Archives, fonds 121, Citizens for Local Democracy (C4LD).

15 The steering committee in the first few months consisted of the following: Doris Bradley, a strong organizer and activist from a downtown community who made sure C4LD ran smoothly; John Cartwright, a union organizer with the construction trade; Doug Hum, school board employee with deep roots in the Chinese community; Peggy Karfilis, a resident in the Annex with exceptional communication and media skills; Barry Lipton, involved with the labour movement and a resident on Toronto Islands, a community which has always played a formidable role in city politics; Arthur Lofsky, resident of North York who knew its politics well; Jane Marsland, administrator with a theatre company in Toronto with good roots in the arts community; Janet May, heavily involved in the environmental community; Clyde McNeil, broadcaster and activist in the black community; Helen Melbourne, resident of Scarborough with roots in the Quaker community; Liz Rykert, social worker who was exceptionally skilled with computers and knowledgeable about how the Internet could be an organizing tool (the Internet was a device still in its infancy in the mid-1990s); John Sewell, a former mayor of Toronto, a columnist on urban affairs with *NOW Weekly*, and a person who had been active in organizing around different kinds of city interests; Jan Sugarman, involved in education politics in Toronto; Carlos Torchia of the Spanish community, involved in education politics; Chris Wilson, resident of the Toronto Islands; and Kathleen Wynne, who ran a community mediation service and who with John Sewell had helped to organize the Together Group in 1995 to look at larger city issues.

The steering committee bore a very heavy load since it met weekly and tried to give some direction to the growing movement, and its membership changed over time. Others who became part of it included Janice Etter, resident of Etobicoke; Doreen Lalor, from Scarborough and a child care worker; Amanda Oakley, then a university student; and Bryan Grimes who was knowledgeable about provincial politics.

16 Frisken, *The Public Metropolis*, 219.
17 John Barber, 'Nothing Funny about Tory Wooden-Heads,' *Globe and Mail*, 5 March 1997, A2.
18 James Rusk, 'Harris Sticks to Metro Merger,' *Globe and Mail*, 5 March 1997, A1.
19 The decisions of the Ontario Divisional Court may be found in C4LD files, City of Toronto Archives, fonds 121, series 642. This particular quote is reproduced in C4LD Bulletin No. 15, July 1997.
20 Bronwyn Drainie, presentation to the Standing Committee on General Government, Ontario Legislature, 18 September 1997, reproduced in C4LD Bulletin No. 19, September 1997.
21 Chief Administrator's Office, City of Toronto, 'Building the NEW City of Toronto: Final Three Year Status Report on Amalgamation' (Toronto, May 2001).
22 Ibid., 22.
23 Ibid., 28.

11: Re-establishing a Regional Agenda

1 For raw data, see 'Canada Housing Survey, Residential Building Activity 2006,' on the website for Canada Mortgage and Housing Corporation, www.cmhc-schl.gc.ca. For interpretation of and comment on the data, see Blais, *Inching towards Sustainability*.
2 Blais, *Inching towards Sustainability*, fig. 31.
3 Ibid., fig. 3.9.
4 Ibid., fig. 3.11.
5 Ibid., 12.
6 Province of Ontario, Ministry of Public Infrastructural Renewal, *Places to Grow: A Guide to the Proposed Growth Plan for the Greater Golden Horseshoe* (Toronto: Queen's Printer, 2005), 12.
7 See '2007 Awards,' American Planning Association website, www.planning .org.
8 Government of Ontario, 'Places to Grow: Better Choices, Brighter Future. A Growth Plan for the Greater Golden Horseshoe,' Discussion Paper (Toronto: Queen's Printer, 2004), 18.
9 *Globe and Mail*, 28 February 2006, n.p.
10 Neptis Foundation, 'Commentary on Draft Greenbelt Plan' (Toronto: Neptis Foundation, 2005), 9; also see 'Commentary on the Ontario Government's Proposed Growth Plan for the Greater Golden Horseshoe,' rev. ed. (Toronto: Neptis Foundation, 2006).

11 Neptis Foundation, 'Commentary on the Ontario Government's Proposed Growth Plan for the Greater Golden Horseshoe,' 8.
12 Neptis Foundation, 'Commentary on the Draft Greenbelt Plan,' 6, 7.
13 Leah Birnbaum, Lorenzo Nicolet, and Zack Taylor, *Simcoe County: The New Growth Frontier* (Toronto: Neptis Foundation, 2004).
14 Government of Ontario, *ReNew Ontario, 2005–2010*, 15.
15 Ibid., 9.
16 Ibid., 10.
17 John Barber, 'All Aboard the Wal-Mart Express,' *Globe and Mail*, 10 March 2007, M2.
18 Government of Ontario, *ReNew Ontario*, 10.
19 See Bruegmann, *Sprawl*, 62–3, where charts compare densities for twenty-eight American urban areas. In metric, general urban densities in American cities fell to about 1,200 residents per square kilometre by 1990 (13 persons per hectare). Toronto's density in 1990 was closer to 3,000 residents per square kilometer (30 persons per hectare).
20 See Bogart, *Don't Call It Sprawl*, 8.

Bibliography

Amborski, David. *The Incidence of Development Charges: Theory and Early Evidence.* Toronto: N.p., 1988.

Ausubel, Kenny, ed. *Nature's Operating Instructions.* San Francisco: Sierra Club Books, 2004.

Barber, John. 'All Aboard the Wal-Mart Express.' *Globe and Mail,* 10 March 2007: M2.

Best, John C. *Thomas Baker McQuesten: Public Works, Politics, and Imagination.* Hamilton: Corinth Press, 1991.

Birnbaum, Leah, Lorenzo Nicolet, and Zack Taylor. *Simcoe County: The New Growth Frontier.* Toronto: Neptis Foundation, 2004.

Blais, Pamela. 'The Economics of Urban Form.' Prepared for the Greater Toronto Area Task Force. Toronto: N.p., 1996.

– *Inching towards Sustainability: The Evolving Urban Structures of the GTA.* Toronto: Neptis Foundation, 2000.

– *The Growth Opportunity.* Toronto: Neptis Foundation, 2005.

Blumenfeld, Hans. *Life Begins at 65.* Montreal: Harvest House, 1987.

Bogart, William T. *Don't Call It Sprawl: Metropolitan Structure in the Twentieth Century.* New York: Cambridge University Press, 2006.

Bordessa, Ronald, and James M. Cameron. 'The Investigative Gene: Problems and Prospects.' *Professional Geographer* 32 (1980): 164–72.

– 'Servicing Growth in the Metro Toronto Region during the Early Years of the Ontario Water Resources Commission, 1956–68.' *Canadian Water Resources Journal* 5, no. 1 (1980): 1–29.

– 'Growth Management Conflicts in the Toronto-Centred Region.' In *Conflicts, Politics and the Urban Scene,* edited by Kevin R. Cox and R.J. Johnston (New York: Longman, 1982).

Bromley, John F., and Jack May. *Fifty Years of Progressive Transit: A History of the Toronto Transit Commission.* Toronto: Electric Railroaders' Association, 1973.

Bruegmann, Robert. *Sprawl: A Compact History.* Chicago: University of Chicago Press, 2005.

Chief Administrator's Office, City of Toronto. 'Building the NEW City of
    Toronto: Final Three Year Status Report on Amalgamation, January 1998 –
    December 2000.' Toronto: City of Toronto.
Chipman, John G. *A Law Unto Itself: How the Ontario Municipal Board Has Devel-
    oped and Applied Land-Use Planning Policy.* IPAC Series in Public Manage-
    ment and Governance. Toronto: University of Toronto Press, 2002.
City of Mississauga. *Running the GTA 'Like a Business.'* Mississauga: City of Mis-
    sissauga, 1995.
City of Toronto Planning Board. Master Plan. Toronto, 1943.
Coleman, Alice. *Utopia on Trial: Vision and Reality in Planned Housing.* London:
    Hilary Shipman, 1990.
Colton, Timothy J. *Big Daddy: Frederick G. Gardiner and the Building of Metropol-
    itan Toronto.* Toronto: University of Toronto Press, 1980.
Commission on Planning and Development Reform in Ontario. *New
    Planning for Ontario, Final Report.* Toronto: Queen's Printer for Ontario,
    1993.
Crombie, David. *Report of Who Does What Panel.* Toronto: Queen's Printer,
    1996.
Don Mills Development Ltd. 'Erin Mills – New Town.' Toronto: N.p., 1969.
Faubert, Frank, Doug Holyday, Frances Nunziata, Barbara Hall, Mel Lastman,
    and Michael Prue. *Changing for the Better: A Vision for the Future of Our Com-
    munities.* Toronto, 1996.
Ferguson, Jock, and Dawn King. 'Behind the Boom: The Story of York
    Region.' Eight-part series. *Globe and Mail,* 26 October 1988 to 3 November
    1988.
Fishman, Robert. *The American Planning Tradition: Culture and Policy.* Washing-
    ton, DC: Woodrow Wilson Center Press, 2000.
Fowler, Edmund P. *Cities, Culture and Granite.* Toronto: Guernica Books, 2004.
Frankena, M.W. *Urban Transportation Financing: theory and policy in Ontario.*
    Toronto: Ontario Economic Council, 1982.
Fraser, Graham, Jay Richardson, David Wood, and Dennis Wood. *The Tail of
    the Elephant: A Guide to the Regional Planning and Development in Southern
    Ontario.* Toronto: Pollution Probe, 1974.
Frisken, Frances. *The Public Metropolis: The Political Dynamics of Urban Expansion
    in the Toronto Region, 1924–2003.* Toronto: Canadian Scholars' Press, 2007.
Gambino, Richard. *Blood of My Blood.* 2nd ed. Toronto: Guernica Editions,
    2002.
Gertler, Len. *Radical Rumblings: Confessions of a Peripatetic Planner.* Waterloo:
    Department of Geography, University of Waterloo, 2005.
Gilbert, Richard. 'Integrity of Land-Use and Transportation Planning in the
    Greater Toronto Area.' In *The Integrity Gap: Canada's Environmental Policy*

and Institutions, edited by Eugene Lee and Anthony Perl. Vancouver: UBC
    Press, 2003.

Goldenberg, Carl. H. *Report of the Royal Commission on Metropolitan Toronto.*
    Toronto: Queen's Printer, 1965.

Gore & Storrie. *Water Supply and Sewage Disposal for the City of Toronto and
    Related Areas.* Report to the Toronto and York Planning Board. Toronto:
    Gore & Storrie, 1949.

Government of Ontario. 'Places to Grow: Better Choices, Brighter Future. A
    Growth Plan for the Greater Golden Horseshoe,' Discussion Paper. Tor-
    onto: Queen's Printer, 2004.

– *ReNew Ontario, 2005–2010: Strategic Highlights.* Toronto: Queen's Printer for
    Ontario, 2005.

Greater Toronto Area Task Force. *Greater Toronto (Golden Report).* Toronto:
    Queen's Printer, 1996.

Greater Toronto Coordinating Committee. 'An Enviable Quality of Life.'
    Toronto: N.p., 1995.

Guillet, E.C. *The Story of Canadian Roads.* Toronto: University of Toronto
    Press, 1966.

Gurin, David. *Understanding Sprawl: A Citizen's Guide.* Vancouver: The David
    Suzuki Foundation, 2003. Available online at www.davidsuzuki.org/files/
    Climate/Ontario/Understanding_Sprawl.pdf.

Harris, Richard. *Creeping Conformity: How Canada Became Suburban 1900–1960.*
    Toronto: University of Toronto Press, 2004.

Ibbitson, John. *Promised Land: Inside the Mike Harris Revolution.* Toronto:
    Prentice-Hall, 1997.

IBI Group et al. *Greater Toronto Area Urban Structure Concepts Study.* Prepared
    for Greater Toronto Co-ordinating Committee. Toronto: N.p., 1990.

IBI Group and Hemson Consulting. *Funding Transportation in the GTA and
    Hamilton-Wentworth.* Toronto: IBI Group and Hemson Consulting, 1999.

Jackson, Kenneth J. *Crabgrass Frontier: The Suburbanization of the United States.*
    New York: Oxford University Press, 1987.

James, John R. 'Regional Planning in Britain.' In *Planning for a Nation of Cities,*
    edited by Sam B. Warner Jr. Cambridge, MA: MIT Press, 1966.

James F. MacLaren Associates. 'Report on Water Supply in Metropolitan
    Toronto.' Toronto: N.p., 1957.

– 'Central York/Pickering Water and Sewage Works.' Report to the Ministry
    of Environment, Toronto: N.p., 1973.

Kaszynski, William. *The American Highway: The History and Culture of Roads in the
    United States.* Jefferson, NC: McFarland and Company, 2000.

Kelso, J.A. Scott, and David Engstrøm. *The Complementary Nature.* Cambridge,
    MA: Bradford Books, 2006.

Kunstler, Howard. *The Geography of Nowhere*. New York: Simon and Schuster,
    1993.
Lemon, James. 'Tracey Deavin LeMay: Toronto's First Planning Commis-
    sioner, 1930–1954.' *City Planning* (Winter 1984): 4–7, 36.
– *Toronto Since 1918*. Toronto: James Lorimer, 1985.
– *Liberal Dreams and Nature's Limits: Great Cities in North American since 1600*.
    Toronto: Oxford University Press, 1996.
Lorimer, James. *The Developers*. Toronto: James Lorimer, 1978.
McMahon, Michael. 'Moving *Beyond Sprawl* in the Toronto Bioregion,' Octo-
    ber 2000. Available at the Urban Affairs Library.
Metropolitan Toronto Planning Board. Official Plan for the Metro Toronto
    Planning Area. Toronto: Municipality of Metropolitan Toronto, 1959.
Miller, Eric. *Travel and Housing Costs in the Greater Toronto Area, 1986–1996*.
    Toronto: Neptis Foundation, 2004.
Mylvaganam, Chandran, and Sandford Borins. *'If You Build It ... ': Business,
    Government and Ontario's Electronic Toll Highway*. Toronto: University of
    Toronto Centre for Public Management, 2004.
Neptis Foundation. 'Commentary on Draft Greenbelt Plan.' Toronto: Neptis
    Foundation, 2005.
– 'Commentary on the Ontario Government's Proposed Growth Plan for the
    Greater Golden Horseshoe.' Revised edition. Toronto: Neptis Foundation,
    2006.
Newman, Oscar. *Defensible Space*. New York: MacMillan, 1972.
Ontario Committee on Taxation. *Report*. Vol. 2. Toronto: Queen's Printer,
    1967.
Ontario Legislative Assembly, Select Committee on the Municipal Act and
    Related Acts. Reports 1961, 1963–5.
Pietropaolo, Vincent. *Not Paved with Gold* . Toronto: Between the Lines, 2006.
Plunkett, Thomas J. *Peel-Halton Local Government Review*. Toronto: Queen's
    Printer, 1966.
Province of Ontario. *Design for Development: The Toronto-Centred Region Plan*.
    Toronto: Queen's Printer, 1970.
Province of Ontario, Department of Highways. *A Plan for Ontario Highways*.
    Toronto: Queen's Printer, 1956.
Province of Ontario, Department of Planning and Development. 'Don Valley
    Conservation Report.' Toronto: King's Printer, 1950.
Province of Ontario, Department of Municipal Affairs. *Choices for a Growing
    Region*. Metro Toronto and Region Transportation Study. Toronto:
    Queen's Printer, 1967.
– *GO Transit: A New Approach to Urban Transportation*. Toronto: Queen's
    Printer, ca. 1968.

Province of Ontario, Ministry of Treasury, Economics, and Intergovernmental Affairs. *Design for Development Status Report.* Toronto: Queen's Printer, 1971.
– *Proposal for Local Government Reform in an Area East of Metro Toronto.* Toronto: Queen's Printer, 1972.
– *Proposals for Local Government Reform in the Area West of Metropolitan Toronto.* Toronto: Queen's Printer, 1973.
Province of Ontario, Ministry of the Environment. *York-Durham Water and Sewage Service Systems.* Toronto: Queen's Printer, 1974.
Province of Ontario, Ministry of Public Infrastructure Renewal. *Places to Grow: Proposed Growth Plan for the Greater Golden Horseshoe.* Toronto: Queen's Printer, 2005.
Region of Peel, Department of Public Works. *The Peel Water Story: A Local History of Water.* Brampton, ON: Region of Peel, Department of Public Works, 2006.
Region of York. *Insights: Local and Regional Government in York Region.* Newmarket, ON: Regional Municipality of York, 1981.
– Official Plan. Newmarket, ON: Regional Municipality of York, 1994.
Region of York and Consumers Utilities. *York Region Long-Term Water Project.* Newmarket, ON: Regional Municipality of York, 1997.
Richardson, Nigel. 'Insubstantial Pageant: The Rise and Fall of Regional Planning in Ontario.' *Journal of Canadian Public Administration,* no. 4 (1981): 563–86.
Richardson, Ronald E., George H. McNevin, and Walter G. Rooke. *Building for People.* Toronto: Ryerson Press, 1970.
Riendeau, Roger E. *Mississauga: An Illustrated History.* Windsor, ON: Windsor Publications, 1985.
Royal Commission on the Future of the Toronto Waterfront. *Watershed: Second Interim Report.* Toronto: Queen's Printer, 1990.
Saul, John Ralston. *A Fair Country: Telling Truths about Canada.* Toronto: Viking Canada, 2008.
Sewell, John. *The Shape of the City: Toronto Struggles with Modern Planning.* Toronto: University of Toronto Press, 1993.
– *Houses and Homes: Housing for Canadians.* Toronto: James Lorimer, 1994.
– 'The Suburbs Then and Now.' In *The Changing Canadian Metropolis,* edited by Frances Fisken. Berkeley, CA: University of California, Institute of Governmental Studies, and Toronto: Canadian Urban Institute, 1994.
Slack, Enid. *An Economic Analysis of Development Charges in British Columbia and Ontario.* Vancouver: Laurier Institute, 1990.
Soberman, Richard. *Choices for the Future: Metropolitan Toronto Transportation*

Plan Review Summary Report, No. 64 (1975; reprint, Toronto: University of Toronto/York University, 1979).

– *Understanding GO Transit.* Prepared for Go Transit, 1998.

Solomon, Lawrence. *Toronto Sprawls: A History.* Toronto: University of Toronto Press, 2007.

Spelt, Jacob. *Toronto.* Toronto: Collier Macmillan Canada, 1973.

Symons, T.H.B. *A History of Peel County, 1867–1967.* Brampton: Corporation of the County of Peel, 1967.

Toronto Transit Commission. 'Ridership Growth Strategy,' March 2003. Available online at www.toronto.ca/ttc/pdf/ridership_growth_strategy.pdf.

Toronto Urban Development Services. *Profile Toronto, September 2004* . City of Toronto.

Traffic Integration Task Force. *Coordinating Public Transit in the Toronto Area, Final Report.* Toronto: Ministry of Transportation, 1994.

Urbaniak, Thomas. *Farewell, Town of Streetsville.* Belleville: Epic Press, 2002.

van Nostrand, John C. 'The Queen Elizabeth Way: Public Utility versus Private Space.' *Urban History Review* 12, no. 2 (October 1983): 1–23.

White, Richard. *Urban Infrastructure and Urban Growth in the Toronto Region, 1950s to the 1990s.* Toronto: Neptis Foundation, 2003.

– *The Growth Plan for the Greater Golden Horseshoe in Historical Perspective.* Toronto: Neptis Foundation, 2007.

Winfield, Mark. 'Smart Growth in Ontario: The Promise vs the Provincial Performance.' Toronto: Pembina Institute, 2003. Available online at http://communities.pemsina.org/pub/149.

Index